Illegitimate Practices

LINGUISTIC DIVERSITY AND LANGUAGE RIGHTS
Series Editor: Dr Tove Skutnabb-Kangas, *Roskilde University, Denmark*

Consulting Advisory Board:
François Grin, *Université de Genève, Switzerland*
Kathleen Heugh, *University of South Australia, Adelaide*
Miklós Kontra, *Linguistics Institute, Hungarian Academy of Sciences, Budapest*
Robert Phillipson, *Copenhagen Business School, Denmark*

The series seeks to promote multilingualism as a resource, the maintenance of linguistic diversity, and development of and respect for linguistic human rights worldwide through the dissemination of theoretical and empirical research. The series encourages interdisciplinary approaches to language policy, drawing on sociolinguistics, education, sociology, economics, human rights law, political science, as well as anthropology, psychology, and applied language studies.

Full details of all the books in this series and of all our other publications can be found on http://www.multilingual-matters.com, or by writing to Multilingual Matters, St Nicholas House, 31-34 High Street, Bristol BS1 2AW, UK.

LINGUISTIC DIVERSITY AND LANGUAGE RIGHTS
Series Editor: Dr Tove Skutnabb-Kangas, *Roskilde University,*
Denmark

Illegitimate Practices
Global English Language Education

Jacqueline Widin

MULTILINGUAL MATTERS
Bristol • Buffalo • Toronto

Library of Congress Cataloging in Publication Data
Widin, Jacqueline.
Illegitimate practices : Global English Language Education / Jacqueline Widin.
Includes bibliographical references and index.
1. English language—Australia.   2. English language—Study and teaching.
3. English language—Influence on foreign languages.
4. Languages in contact—Australia.   5. Sociolinguistics—Australia.   I. Title.
P130.52.A8W53 2010
428.00710994-dc22 2010025434

British Library Cataloguing in Publication Data
A catalogue entry for this book is available from the British Library.

ISBN-13: 978-1-84769-307-5 (hbk)
ISBN-13: 978-1-84769-306-8 (pbk)

Multilingual Matters
UK: St Nicholas House, 31-34 High Street, Bristol BS1 2AW, UK.
USA: UTP, 2250 Military Road, Tonawanda, NY 14150, USA.
Canada: UTP, 5201 Dufferin Street, North York, Ontario M3H 5T8, Canada.

The policy of Multilingual Matters/Channel View Publications is to use papers that are natural, renewable and recyclable products, made from wood grown in sustainable forests. In the manufacturing process of our books, and to further support our policy, preference is given to printers that have FSC and PEFC Chain of Custody certification. The FSC and/or PEFC logos will appear on those books where full certification has been granted to the printer concerned.

Typeset by Integra Software Services Pvt. Ltd, Pondicherry, India.
Printed and bound in Great Britain by Short Run Press Ltd.

Contents

List of Figures and Table

Figures

Table

Acknowledgements

Firstly I wish to convey my sense of gratitude to the teachers, teacher educators and government officials in Laos, Japan and Australia for sharing their stories. Their experiences, insights and analyses are the critical components of this book.

My debt to those who provided the theoretical inspiration and thinking of this book is inestimable. There are many who contributed greatly but in particular, Professor Robert Phillipson and Dr Tove Skutnabb-Kangas offered me the frameworks within which to analyse the implications of my academic work.

I am also indebted to Dr Paul Black he was immensely important in the initial development of my work in this area, his patience, perseverance and input helped me to undertake this study. My close colleague and friend, Sheilagh Kelly enabled the whole project to be completed. Lastly but most importantly my family and friends were the people that gave me the day to day support and encouragement to keep going.

Acknowledgements

Chapter 1

Setting the Scene: The International Context of English Language Education

This is a story about the internationalisation of education. In particular, it is a story about the struggles within international English language education projects (IELEPs) and the increasing commodification and corporatisation of English. The story is set in South East Asia, East Asia and Australia and the actors include students, teachers, university and aid organisation staff and government officials. A central theme is the exportation of English language education by so-called English-speaking countries such as Australia to countries, often poor, which are linguistically and culturally diverse, with few English first language speakers. Specifically I am concerned with offshore English language education projects, the role of Australian universities in the export of English language education and the seeming necessity for 'global inequality in the commercial market in international education' (Marginson, 2004: 23). In my exploration of these concerns I am driven to ask: who benefits from the international spread of English language education? Will the economic success of English language teaching (ELT) continue to grow? Will English continue to hold the position of power and domination?

In my thinking about this book my motivation was to problematise the position of the 'beneficiary'. I began by working within the binary framework between the donor/provider and the beneficiary. I was concerned with how the particular interests of the beneficiary could be more effectively negotiated and represented. However, during one of my first interviews with a key stakeholder, Murray, in a fee-for-service project in Japan my thinking was completely turned around. In his interview, he spoke candidly about the many different interests and different beneficiaries in the project and how at different times in a project's life particular interests may be paramount. In the extract below he succinctly outlined Australia's 'grand interests':

> The purpose of this particular project is not to deliver great, you know, English language teaching methodology into this country's teaching system. Actually by doing that we put many Australians out of a job . . . I mean . . . in fifteen years time if great English is being taught here then we're, you know, Australians out of business.
>
> But . . . it is to demonstrate Australia's ability to operate in an area that this country is not accustomed to and not expecting in higher education. It is to enhance our reputation as a provider of education and training . . . the Agency is after enhancing Australia's interest in Australia's and this country's relationship. So I couldn't care less whether this country wants it, or needs it, or likes it, at the end of the day it's not the judgement of the teachers, it is a decision we've made against the background of what would enhance Australia's interest. (Murray P1AM1)

Looking back now this is axiomatic of the dynamics of the international English language education project (hereafter referred to as IELEP) field, but in that initial period of my exploration my assumptions were still fairly naively based in the binary relations in the ELT project field.

The notion of 'interest' is pivotal in any discussion about international English language teaching projects. So I must declare my interest in writing about IELEPs in the way I do. I work with an Australian university and I have been involved in a number of IELEPs in a variety of roles. It was through my involvement in projects as teacher, project adviser, project proposal writer and project implementer that I became aware, quite belatedly I suppose, that all was not as it seemed. I felt a growing unease that we were not all working to the same goals. While I and other colleagues ostensibly took on the onerous work of the project objectives or tasks, others did not seem to be working towards what I assumed were the principal aims of the project. At the same time I came across the growing body of literature, of articles, books and conference discussions addressing 'the problem of international education projects'. What the literature suggests is that international education projects fail, and not only do they fail, they cause damage and destruction to the areas they are located in, not just in the provision of services, or lack of, but to the individuals (or at least some) working in the projects. A number of researchers describe the project staff as the 'scrapnel' left in the wake of the ravages of the international language education project (Abdul-Raheem, 2000; Griffin, 1991;

Magrath, 2001; Morris, 1991; Murphy, 1999; Pottier, 1993; Swales, 1980). Swales (1980: 62) describes a scenario which reflects current dilemmas of project work.

> Expatriate staff of projects often ignore the real needs of the beneficiaries and appear in the 'busy work' mode to pursue their own interests and produce materials satisfactory to their own standards – independent of local interests. They then achieve a validity which was internal to the expatriate world of the project; but they failed to achieve external validity, in the terms of the host institution.

Such criticisms may seem harsh but experience in the field of IELEP projects at least in part supports them and has provided me with the opportunities to investigate the struggles and power lines that delineate the field. Initially, the struggles were ones that as an academic I easily recognised; they were 'naturally' over what are considered the valuable resources in the field. A most obvious one is the struggle for Australian universities to win bids for aid projects. Another critical one is to attract international students. A third one is over language, firstly 'which language?'. In the case of ELT projects it is English. Related questions are how Australia keeps ownership of English and wins the struggle to keep the 'so-called' native speaker of English dominant.

Struggles emerged that contested and challenged embedded notions of the 'normality' of work practices and social life held by the academy. 'Culture' emerged as a most complicated concept. With respect to struggles around work practices questions emerged such as who occupies the dominant position? Which language dominates in the workplace? How are the language rights of the host-country participants recognised or not recognised? How are these struggle carried out? What forms of symbolic violence and abuse are taking place?

The question of who benefits contests the conventional assumption of recipients as beneficiaries. One of my main interests in the problematising of the beneficiary took the form of examining the position given to the first language (L1) in English language teacher training projects located in non-English-speaking countries. Although project stakeholders represented both the recipient countries and the donor countries, all meetings were conducted in English, all project documentation was in English and general communication was in English. This situation, which potentially disenfranchises recipient stakeholders from the project process, prompted me to look more deeply into the impact of language education projects in terms of the relationships they set up between the language/s of the recipient and that of the donor and/or the provider. The notion of the beneficiary became more problematic as I became aware that there were differing views about who would, or rather should, benefit from the project.

My growing awareness of the complications in the project field is not reflected in the specific ELT project literature analysing and describing this field. The beneficiary is usually depicted as an easily identified singular group or community (AusAID, 2001; Davis, 1991; Marsden & Oakley, 1990; World Bank, 1998), yet this literature identifies the multitude of problems integral to the running of international language education projects and the apparent failure of many projects to meet their objectives. Why such consistent and systematic failure? As the struggles in the project field became more pronounced and the notion of the beneficiary became more problematic, I turned to examine the overall picture of the planning and implementation of university-led IELEPs both in the aid and in the fee-for-service context.

I owe much to Pierre Bourdieu in the telling of this story. In order to understand the dynamics of the international language education field I used Bourdieu's conceptual framework and his explanatory devices of field, capital and habitus. These allowed for a multi-layered investigation into both the field of the IELEPs and the broader social context, the field of power (Bourdieu, 1984, 1989, 1990a, 1990b, 1998, 1999). Any analysis of the international field of education must account for two distinctive elements (Marginson, 2008). One element is cross-border flows of people, ideas, knowledge, technologies and economic resources. This element is relatively visible. The other less tangible and one most relevant to this study is the flow of differences and delineations. These include differences in languages, pedagogies, work practices, inclusion and exclusion. Bourdieu provides the tools to investigate the unequal distribution of resources and power. The field of power in this instance is represented by the powerful institutions at national and international levels. Institutions such as Australian aid agencies, Australian foreign relations organisations, international aid and finance organisations, Australian universities and universities in the countries other than Australia are located in the field of power. Although Bourdieu's research was carried out previous to the intense and volatile globalisation of the late 20th and early 21st centuries and in some eyes is nation-bound (Marginson, 2008), it offers much to my study of domination and subjugation in the international field. Bourdieu's framework allowed me to examine the relationships between the different agents, the positions they occupied in the field, the capital (the stakes or resources: linguistic, economic, cultural and social) which they accumulated and the dispositions (habitus: life experiences, expectations, education, knowledge, skills, age, gender and tastes) they brought to the field. The ways in which the agents carried out their practice of project implementation is what Bourdieu refers to as a 'feel for the game'. An agent or actor's habitus is not deterministic but can influence how well one 'plays the game'. Bourdieu speaks eloquently about habitus below:

> social reality exists, so to speak, twice, in things and in minds, in fields and in habitus, outside and inside agents and when habitus encounters a social world of which it is the product, it finds itself 'as a fish in water', it does not feel the weight of the water, and takes the world and itself for granted. (Bourdieu in Wacquant, 1989: 43)

Bourdieu's (1988, 1998) work encouraged me to make visible the invisible relations of power, to unearth those 'naturally' occurring regularities that become known as 'the norm'. And so my declared interests in this story are to uncover the invisible webs of power which cause the practices to be carried out in a certain way. Given that the field of international language education projects is wrought with difficulties and stories of 'failure', I want to understand how such a wide-ranging and repetitive venture is overlaid with this burden of failure. This means that an analysis of the field will have to make apparent and unravel those taken-for-granted understandings of, in particular, power relations. It will have to identify the resources or stakes (capital) that are sought after by the agents in the field and the strategies employed by agents in the field; these are informed by their position, capital and habitus.

The remainder of this chapter familiarises the reader with the specific project sites and the agents (or actors) involved in the projects. It also gives a brief overview of issues such as: the internationalisation of English, the position of the first language in each site and the concept of the project and culture. The chapter concludes with an outline of the book chapters. The countries central to this story are named but I have changed the details of the participants to protect their identity.

The Sites

The stories in this book are drawn from the experiences of participants in two projects. Project 1 is an aid-funded English language teacher training project located in Laos, a small land-locked country in South East Asia. This project was tendered for and won through a collaboration between an Australian project management company and a large metropolitan Australian tertiary institution. The relationship with the host-country

Ministry of Education (MOE) and other relevant government representatives was formed according to the rhetoric of 'bilateral aid projects' within the Australian Government aid programme. Project 2 is a university fee-for-service project developed by a consortium of Australian universities – the consortium's goal is to provide for the multi-level professional development of English language (EL) teachers in Japan. The project was developed under the auspice of an Australian Government Agency (AGA) located in the host country. The government organisation liaised with the host-country MOE and other key language teaching organisations. The consortium of universities was to present a national image of Australian higher education.

There are similarities and differences between the projects: they were both purporting to introduce a new ELT approach for use with secondary school students and both had a component of English language development for the teacher participants. However, there are key differences, some of which include the role of English in the two countries, the conditions under which the Australian team members participated in the projects and the time frames of the projects. One significant difference is the way in which each project was conceived. Project 1 (P1) was funded by Australia's international aid programme and was jointly managed by a university and a private project management company. Project 2 (P2) was more explicitly an entrepreneurial venture developed under the auspice of an AGA which provided some seeding funding. In spite of these essential differences the goals of the projects were very similar, the main one being to enhance the teaching and provision of English language education in the host countries.

The projects were located in two countries distinguished from each other by their historical, social and material conditions. Laos had emerged from a long history of colonial and quasi-colonial relations with a number of different international powers (Arnst, 1997). In Laos the teaching of foreign languages has been driven by the particular colonial power of the time. Project 2, located in Japan, an industrialised economy, is marked by very different struggles around the role of foreign languages. The post-Second World War focus on ELT was driven by a number of complex international relations.

The ELT goals of Project 1 as expressed in the project documents were based on the notion of 'capacity building'. They assumed that the 'building up' of the ELT sector would lead to improved social and economic growth. The documents go on further to illuminate the way that improved teaching and learning of English will strengthen the country's capacity to develop and sustain the type of English language provision initiated by the project. The proposal document for Project 2 differs in that the goal was not to enhance social or economic development as the host country was already one of the most industrially developed countries in the world. Rather, the inference was that the English language teaching and learning approaches in this host country were deficient and that improvement in these areas would enhance the country's involvement in the international arena.

This story clearly draws on the experiences of participants within two IELEPs; while the particularity of these experiences is important, the analysis and findings can be applied to a broader context. Throughout this book I refer to and weave in stories from education projects around the world; projects based in East Timor, Cambodia, Vietnam, Hungary and countries in Africa are all echoes of the story I am about to tell you.

Australian Universities and the Project Field

Australian universities have a principal role in this story. They are key players in the international English language field in the Asia-Pacific region. The international role of these institutions has changed dramatically over the last three decades. In 1988 the Australian Government phased out international education programmes premised on foreign aid objectives (e.g. the Colombo Plan); it then confirmed the full-fee market as the dominant framework for cross-border education (Marginson, 2004; Meiras, 2004). This major change in focus began in the mid-1980s when Australia shifted its orientation towards the Asia-Pacific region from its previous ties with countries in the British Commonwealth. During the late 1980s and 1990s the Asia-Pacific region became a lucrative market for recruiting fee-paying students. International students were no longer regarded as an 'elite group'; instead they were recognised as a mass market. The recruitment of these students became an export industry and was based upon an analysis of cost-benefit ratio and profit margins.

Because of Australian Government policy changes in the 1990s, Australian universities were driven to generate an increasing amount of their own funding and the market in international education promised to ease the funding crisis for universities. The notion of 'the internationalisation of education' featured in the critical development themes of Australian universities (Marginson, 1995, 1997b, 2004; Meiras, 2004). Between 1990 and 2002, the number of international students enrolled in Australian universities increased from 24,998 to 185,058 (Marginson, 2004). The Organisation for Economic Co-Operation and Development (OECD) (2005) report, *Education at a Glance*, estimated that international students comprised 19% of Australia's tertiary student body in 2003. This was the largest percentage recorded in any OECD country. Internationalisation is an uneven global activity. While the number of students studying outside of their country of origin is increasing at an exponential rate, a relatively small number (five) of OECD countries are the majority exporters of education. In 2003, 2.12 million tertiary students enrolled in universities outside of their country of origin (OECD, 2005) and 93% of these students studied in an OECD country. This was an 11.2% increase since 2002.

A statistic which makes this increase even more significant is that since 1998 there has been a 50% rise in the absolute numbers of international students enrolled in tertiary institutions in the OECD countries. As mentioned in the above paragraph, in 2003, the vast majority of these students (70%) were enrolled in only five OECD countries (USA 28%, UK 12%, Germany 11%, France 10% and Australia 9% [OECD, 2005]). These statistics do not necessarily reflect the absolute increase in student numbers in all countries. For example, the USA has experienced a 1% decrease since 2002 and also the data do not distinguish between resident and non-resident international students in countries such as Germany. New Zealand, while not in the largest group of exporting countries, has experienced enormous growth in the numbers of international students since 1998, now 13% of their total tertiary student body.

The latest figures from the OECD (2005) reveal a massive demand for foreign education (from the UK, the USA, Australia and New Zealand) in the Asia-Pacific. In 2003, 46% of all international students were from countries in Asia (OECD, 2005). Four of the five major importing nations are China (12.8%, this was 9.6% in 2002), Korea (4.2%), India (5%) and Japan (3%). Malaysia (1.9%), Indonesia (1.7%), Hong Kong (1.6%), Singapore and Thailand (together 2.3%) are also in the top 20 importing nations.

International education was Australia's third largest service export in 2003 (OECD, 2005). Australian universities earned over $1.5 billion from student fees, approximately 15% of their revenue. This at first does not seem excessive. However, Australia earned more than $5 billion in total from international students spending on fees, food, transport, accommodation, living costs and entertainment, on and offshore (Marginson, 2004). In its recently released policy on aid funding (Australian Government, 2006), the Australian Government has doubled the number of higher education scholarships it will offer in the Asia-Pacific region over the next five years (from 9500 to 19,000) (Australian Government, 2006). Unlike previous years the in-country demand for ELT will be met in the main by an increased number of volunteers and integrated development projects with an English language component. The Government itself is claiming to revive the Colombo Plan which essentially carried out colonial objectives with scholarships as the core of its programme (Marginson, 2002a, 2004; Rhoades 2002).

Sammels (2006), in his critique of the Australian aid policy, states that the overarching objective for the aid programme has been re-formulated from:

> Advancing the national interest by helping developing countries reduce poverty and achieve sustainable development

to:

> To assist developing countries to reduce poverty and achieve sustainable development, in line with Australia's national interest. (Sammels, 2006: 1)

The re-formulation of Australia's aid objectives does not change the dominant and subordinate relations in the aid field. Australia is still the major beneficiary and has a top-down approach to its aid programme. University activity in the education field is framed by several pivotal concepts including internationalisation, globalisation and cross-cultural/intercultural relations. These terms are particularly pertinent to Australian university activity in the international field. They are used widely in the literature and in many cases have assumed a 'common sense' meaning (Way, 2002). For example, in most current Australian university strategic plans the term 'internationalisation' is a mandatory goal and is an assumed university activity in the 'global education context' (Poole, 2001). However, the term does not necessarily give a clear direction for educational activities. In Marginson's (2000: 24) research on university practices, internationalisation describes the growth of relations between nations and between national cultures. In that sense internationalisation has a long history.

Australian university internationalisation activities take many forms. One lucrative form is the tendering for government-funded aid projects (Accounting for Development, 2000). This, however, is not the only international activity undertaken by universities. Internationalisation of education encompasses:

- aid and/or humanitarian programmes delivered offshore;
- aid-funded overseas students studying in Australia;
- fee-paying students from countries outside of Australia studying in Australia;
- the internationalisation of the curriculum and award or non-award programmes delivered offshore. These may be as part of a larger project or as individual programmes.

Internationalisation is viewed differently from different national positions and from different sections within a nation; for example, education sectors within non-English-speaking countries most often see 'internationalisation' as increasing the provision of teaching English and upgrading the English language skills of priority areas of the society/economy (Hashimoto, 2000). Those in the education sector within Australia most often describe 'internationalisation' as a process of increasing the export market of Australian education (Devos, 2003; Marginson, 1995, 2002a, 2002c, 2004), either by attracting larger numbers of international students to Australian institutions or by providing in-country courses. Habu (2000) describes this process as one of the ironies of globalisation in her account of Japanese women studying in the UK. Her research showed an uneven passage in this international trade and that global educational experiences were often reduced to narrow economic views of the students as a source of funding for British universities.

A negative aspect of internationalisation is its role in exacerbating global inequalities. Education in the 'developed' world is always afforded more value than that from the 'developing' world. One very rarely hears of students from wealthy countries seeking higher education in poorer countries or countries where there is a colonial past and English is the dominant language in education and the government. Internationalisation of education has had detrimental effects on linguistic and cultural diversity, an issue raised later in this chapter. Australia's main area for trade in education, the regions of East Asia and South Asia, contains some of the languages with the largest numbers of speakers (as a first language) in the world. *Ethnologue* (15th edition) estimates the numbers of speakers of the two main languages from the Asia-Pacific region, for example, Putonghua (Mandarin), 1000 million, Hindi and Urdu, 900 million. These figures far outnumber the first language speakers of English. In other parts of the world, Spanish and Arabic are challenging English for the numbers of first language speakers. Graddol (2006) comments that English could soon be placed fourth (rather than second as it is now) in the list of language size according to numbers of first language speakers. Any of the languages discussed above could become a lingua franca but because of its accumulation of linguistic capital, English maintains it hegemonic position in the global higher education market. Marginson (2004: 24) makes an astute observation about this situation: 'the bedrock assumption of English-language universities is that native English speakers have little to learn in other languages.'

Another aspect of this scenario is the future economic and social status of the monolingual English speaker. Monolingual English speakers in countries such as England, the USA, Australia or New Zealand, according to Graddol (2006), will no longer hold the linguistic capital. Graddol predicts that there will be less economic opportunities for the English-speaking monolingual and, along with Skutnabb-Kangas (2000: 244–246), debunks the myth that 'monolingualism is sufficient.'

The situation in the Asia-Pacific region mirrors the developments in the European arena. The internationalisation of education provision (the Bologna Process, see page 12) is hand in hand with the commodification of education and deepening global inequalities (Phillipson, 2006). The notion of education as a 'public good' is no longer a current value; rather education is an item to be traded under the defenders of centralised wealth, the World Trade Organisation (WTO) and General Agreement on Trade in Service (GATS) (Naidoo, 2003; Phillipson, 2006). English has a hegemonic position in higher education field in Europe and the native speaker has 'unfair market advantages' (Grin, 2006; Phillipson, 2006).

It appears that Australian universities are now placed in a contradictory position with regard to internationalisation as it is commonly practised. On the one hand, they may want to contribute to the development of poorer countries by helping students through scholarships and aid-funded projects. On the other hand, the universities are on a more explicit path of attracting fee-paying international students to raise income for themselves. These two goals may not seem at first contradictory and could be mutually beneficial as funds raised through the fee-paying activity could be used to support work in developing countries. However, on closer examination the aid programmes that universities often engage in pretend to benefit those other countries, but in fact they are designed to be as much or more beneficial to the Australian institution itself and the Australian economy in general. This was the case with the aid project under discussion in this book. Phelan and Hill's (1998) analysis of Australian Government education aid in Papua New Guinea (PNG) shows that Australia accumulates economic and political benefits through the aid subsidising Australia's under-funded tertiary education sector and in other non-economic ways:

> ...on the assumptions that Papua New Guineans educated in Australia will return to PNG and undertake leadership roles, the next generation of prominent PNG leaders will have an appreciation of things Australian, especially Australian academic, administrative and business methods. Thus the education aid program also operates as a form of diplomacy. (Phelan & Hill, 1998: 12)

The statistics highlighted in this section further underscore the dimensions of the internationalisation critiqued in this book. The increasing corporatisation and commodification of education maintain internationalisation as a one-way process, that is, the students and money continue to flow into the dominant wealthy countries.

Clearly the internationalisation of education is of great concern to those who advocate for human rights, language rights, a more equal distribution of wealth in the world and the sustainability of linguistic and cultural diversity. The experiences of the participants in this story give credence to those concerns. The book presents a multi-layered story of encounters, domination, subordination and strategic action in the international education arena.

The Internationalisation of English

The internationalisation of education and internationalisation of English are clearly intertwined and language is a critical factor in the selection of place of study. Overwhelmingly, English dominates as the language of instruction in either preferred exporting country of study or course. Many countries which take large numbers of international students but are not English speaking (e.g. France, Germany and Switzerland) offer a wide range of study in English. The internationalisation of education in Europe, which in 1999 became known as the 'Bologna process', aims to promote and encourage European universities as serious players in meeting commercial and strategic internationalisation goals. Within this seemingly unified vision of higher education internationalisation appears to mean English-medium education (Phillipson, 2006).

English and its critical role in the international education marketplace is a leading player in this story about the struggles in the IELEP field. The international power of English is a recurrent theme in the ELT literature and is of central concern in the analysis of EL teacher education for nonnative speakers of English (Braine, 1999; Ellis & Kelly, 1997; Phan Le Ha, 2008; Holliday, 2005; Medgyes, 1996, 1999; Nunan, 2002; Oda, 1999, 2000; Phillipson, 1992a, 1992b, 1994, 2000). It is imperative to bring to the surface the ways in which English is involved in the internationalisation process. The spread of English across national borders is critiqued from many different perspectives: the notion of linguistic imperialism (Phillipson, 1992b) and language rights and linguistic diversity (Skutnabb-Kangas, 1996, 1999, 2000); the poststructuralist view that locates English and English teaching in discourses of colonialism in the past and their continuity into the present (Canagarajah, 1999, 2005; Kubota, 1999; Pennycook, 1998;

Ramanathan, 2005); and the socio-cultural views of Coleman (1995, 2002), Holliday (1992, 1994, 1995, 2005) and Kenny and Savage (1997) which reflect a critical view of the dynamics in the language marketplace. A main issue to draw from this diversity of construct is that ELT practices are never neutral or apolitical (Kubota, 1998).

Many of these authors have offered a rigorous critique of the role of English in the international arena and as part of their work advocate for more critical approaches to the teaching of English. They critique the role and practice of English teaching (as a foreign or international language) in a range of sites and in line with my central view depict the sites, be it a project, institution or classroom, as a place of struggle. Kubota (1998) below illuminates the struggles embedded in the notion of critical language teaching:

> Critical pedagogy, in essence, aims for creating racial, ethnic, gender, class, cultural and linguistic equality in our society based on morality and ethics. In this philosophy, language culture, and education are viewed as a political site of struggle where particular meanings and practices are constructed and erased in power relations. (1998: 303)

Commentators on the 'global' spread of English put forward different values and beliefs about its impact (see Bruthiaux, 2002; Crystal, 1997; Graddol, 1997, 2006; Hashimoto, 2000; Kachru, 1986; Kubota, 1998; Medgyes, 1994; Pennycook, 1994, 1998, 2000; Phillipson, 1992a, 1992b, 1998, 1999, 2005, 2006). For instance, David Crystal's (1997) *English as a Global Language* paints a blissful, trouble-free picture of the expansion of English and its continued supremacy. He takes as given the world language status of English. In his historical trajectory of its ascension he claims that the success of English is through 'being in the right place at the right time' (p. 110). However, in answering the question about what makes a world language, he does acknowledge that English did engage in some struggle to gain its dominant position. He asserts that the main reason for the success of a 'global' language is 'the power of its people – especially their political power' (p. 7).

Graddol (1997) gives a slightly different slant on the 'worldly power' of English. His work, commissioned by the British Council, seems to map out a way forward for organisations in the ELT field. Unlike Crystal he does problematise the role of English and questions any pre-set notions about the natural position of English. He is not so convinced that English will maintain its dominant position in the language teaching field and recommends that providers, such as the British Council, take a less dominant and more collaborative approach in their negotiations with potential 'outside' customers. Graddol's (2006) latest publication, *English Next*, also commissioned by the British Council, maps out a changed role of English: while it is still in high demand and the target learner group is getting younger, English is no longer in the control of the so-called native speakers. He predicts that this latter group will experience a marked decline in numbers post 2010, and he takes a serious stance in alerting the ELT industry to the demise of English as a foreign language (EFL) as it is currently known.

Crystal's (1997) view of the 'naturalness' of English as a world language is predicated on the fact that there are more speakers of EFL than there are native English speakers. As evidence of this he states that many regional organisations such as the Association of Southeast Asian Nations (ASEAN) and Asia-Pacific Economic Cooperation (APEC) and international organisations such as the International Monetary Fund (IMF), WTO and the United Nations (UN) (the latter is not officially monolingual) conduct their business in English. However, this view does not take account of what power relations may be operating and the ways in which linguistic 'choices' are imposed. Bruthiaux (2002) is particularly concerned with the way that commentators from 'on high' predict the growth and spread of English without revealing their particular audience and base group from which these predictions are drawn. He depicts the consumers of English language study as 'relatively well-off' (p. 290) and believes that 'perceptions of the impact of the worldwide spread of English may well reflect the relatively fortunate circumstances of its beneficiaries, including the English language teaching profession itself' (p. 290). His view is informed by his research into global economic inequality and his findings indicate that to the very poor people in the world the so-called 'global spread of English is a sideshow compared with the issue of basic economic development and poverty reduction' (p. 290). Mohanty (2000), in his research about the very poor in India, also prioritises strategies that will lead to sustainable development and real poverty reduction; these strategies do not include ELT.

As mentioned above, the spread of English is not necessarily benign. In the work of Skutnabb-Kangas (1999, 2000) and Phillipson and Skutnabb-Kangas (1996) English can be 'additive' (where English is added to the person's repertoire of languages) or 'subtractive' (where the person's first language is dominated or replaced by English). There is vigorous debate in the terms of language rights and how the proliferation of EFL is responsible for the 'death' of 'minority' languages (Phillipson, 1992a, 1998, 1999; Phillipson & Skutnabb-Kangas, 1996; Skutnabb-Kangas, 2000). The debate on language rights, as evident in these authors, has mainly focused on the world's poorer countries. Kubota (1998) is keen to diversify this debate. In her article 'Ideologies of English in Japan', she is critical of the lack of discussion on 'ideology' of teaching English in an economically and academically successful country like Japan. She cites commentators like Santos (cited in Kubota, 1998) who feel that discussions of ideology in situations where students are successful in economic and academic terms are unnecessary, since these students do not have an issue about language rights. These are said to be unlike students in countries where their linguistic heritage is vulnerable to a dominant language. However, Kubota claims that there *is* concern about the dominant role of English in Japanese society. This is particularly so in explicit domination by multinational commercial enterprises who choose to advertise in English. She also refers to the debates about what type of English is deemed appropriate for the international context. In Japan these discussions focus on Western conceptualisations of English. The dominant reference is to British or North American forms of English. Non-western forms (e.g. as spoken in India) are relegated to irrelevance.

The conduit for the spread of English is through the various settings and organisations of ELT and the accompanying textbooks and teaching materials. Studies of the spread of English (Kubota, 1998; Pennycook, 1994, 1995, 1998) have addressed the issue of the possible impacts of the construction of the subject of English and the learners in the teaching resources. Though it is difficult to assess the impact of English on the way that, for example, Japanese perceive themselves as constructed by the west in the ELT textbooks that have dominated the markets in Japan, critics such as Nakama (cited in Kubota, 1998) suggest that Japanese views of inferiority of non-westerners originate from exposure to western views of the 'other'. Oda's (2000) account of Japanese students' experiences of racism and linguicism in England bears out the claims by Kubota and others (e.g. Pennycook, 1998) about the ethnocentric ideology of Teaching English to Speakers of Other Languages (TESOL). While Kubota (1998) agrees that the ideological aspects of ELT are far-reaching, she challenges the notion of simply seeing a binary relationship of the 'west' dominating the 'non-west' as she claims that historically Japan has depicted itself as superior to Korea and other Asian countries.

Another enduring critique of the impact of ELT in an ideological sense is the trivial content and way it depicts interactions in communicative language teaching material (Kubota, 1998; Pennycook 1994, 1998, 1999). Textbooks often depict dominant western societies as problem free, and this leads to notions of idealised societies where students can think there are no injustices, discrimination and social disharmony. These texts also assume as true background knowledge that the west has ownership of critical thinking and that non-western countries are underdeveloped in their logic, critical and analytical skills. Appleby (2002) addresses the issue of teaching texts in her work and suggests that this supposed 'content free, uncontroversial approach' is required by donors of aid projects, as she experienced in an ELT project in Timor. She also believes a language programme relevant to students' cultures and needs involves engagement with the 'social, historical, political and economic concerns that constitute their daily reality'.

The above views about the 'worldly positions' of English are historically linked to two seminal models developed by Kachru (1986) and Phillipson (1992b) which seek to represent the spread of English.

Kachru's (1986) diagrammatic representation of English in the world is widely used (and critiqued) in discussions of the spread of English. He views English as operating on three levels:

- Inner circle – the USA, Britain, Australia, New Zealand, Canada and Ireland.
- Outer circle – are those countries that have usually had a colonial history, for example, India, Singapore, Philippines and Ghana. The result at this level of the circle is different varieties of English.
- Expanding circles – this is where English is taught as a compulsory language in the school system and is used in fields such as finance and science and in international communication, for example, Japan, China, Russia and Poland.

Underlying his analysis of English in the world, Kachru (1986) essentially sees the spread of English as a positive development, as a tool that will aid in the development of an international community.

Phillipson (1992b) proposes a model to describe and analyse the spread of English that at first glance may seem to resemble Kachru's. Phillipson divides that world into two:

Core – which consists of those so-called English-speaking countries: the USA, Britain, Australia, New Zealand, Canada and Ireland (most of these countries have many living and viable indigenous languages and large numbers of speakers of languages such as Spanish in the USA)

and

Periphery – there are three types of relationships to English in English-periphery countries:

(a) where there has been a colonial past, for example, India and Nigeria;
(b) where English is used as an 'international link', for example, Japan and Scandinavia;
(c) where English is not the dominant or official language but where it is used widely as the language of education and business, for example, Singapore and Malaysia.

However, unlike Kachru, Phillipson does not view the spread of English as always a benign or positive process; rather he focuses on the unequal distribution of benefits from this spread of English. He addresses the negative aspects as the 'subtractive' role of English in its wide-reaching spread (Phillipson & Skutnabb-Kangas, 1996). He borrowed the terms 'core' and 'periphery' from the development field and chooses them as appropriate dividers to discuss notions of control and power. Phillipson (1992b) establishes a framework which is an explicit critique of imperialism; from his point of view the spread of English is never neutral. Phillipson's grouping of both former British colonies and those other parts of the world where English is taught as a foreign language as peripheral communities, at least in the context of ELT, is supported by a number of other critical commentators on the spread of English (Canagarajah, 1993, 1999, 2006; Hall & Eggington, 2000; Kubota, 1998; Kumaravadivelu, 1994, 2001, 2008; Mitsikopoulou, 2002; Oda, 1999, 2000).

Phillipson (2002, 2003, 2005, 2006) adds further depth to the discussion on the spread of English and examines how it is bound up with many international, cultural, economic and political forces. He writes at length about the world dominance of the US media (in English), the role of international corporations, the spread of particular forms of culture and knowledge and the development of a very particular 'world order' and how these factors are reflected in and also force the spread of English. From this point of view, the native English speakers are in a dominant position in the international arena; their skills in English language allow more access to information on global systems (e.g. technological, financial and scientific). Continuing in this vein then the learning of English in the current international language market is predicated upon the inequalities in the field, specifically the inequalities between the learner and the native English-speaking communities.

It is worth mentioning briefly in this examination of internationalisation of English Bourdieu's (1989) analytical work in the area of language and power. Bourdieu's notion of the legitimate speaker is helpful in understanding the way English dominates in international arenas. This notion allows me to ask questions such as: Who is a legitimate speaker within the field of ELT projects? How is one recognised? In my study the projects' goals were to improve English language teaching and learning skills but did a commensurate improvement in these skills make for a legitimate speaker? These questions are well illustrated in the interview extract below (Bolitho & Medgyes, 2000). Peter Medgyes, involved with a British Council English language project in his Hungarian university, is asked by Rod Bolitho (from the British Council) about the difficulty of operating in a 'new professional register' in terms of working out shared understandings of the approaches to language teaching. Bolitho was referring to the communicative approach advocated by the British Council team working in the university. He assumed that the 'new' teaching methodology would pose the greatest problem in carrying out the project. Medgyes did not identify this area of professional practice as the one that posed the problems:

Peter: I had much more difficulty with project jargon.
Rod: What do you mean?
Peter: We just didn't understand terms such as implementation, costing, sustainability, accountability etc. As a matter of fact, nonnatives are linguistically handicapped in every sense of the word. Obviously, there's no way we can use the English language as fluently and efficiently as you can. And native-speaker colleagues have often used this to their advantage in professional debate.
Rod: So the playing field isn't level.
Peter: There you are. Level playing field. I've never come across this term, for example . . . Seriously though, at CETT we had a mixed staff. Hungarians, Brits and Americans. The working language was English. We would often argue over various professional matters, and let me tell you, beyond a certain point in the argument the natives invariably got the upper hand, and not because they were always right.
Rod: But because they spoke better English?
Peter: That's right . . . People tend to believe that native speakers speak better English, therefore they're better teachers too.
(Bolitho & Medgyes, 2000: 382)

This short extract is instructive of how the struggles and power lines delineate the field in IELEPs. Project rhetoric and the opportunities that are offered through projects, counterpart positions, university courses or scholarships are put forward as ways that the country and individuals will 'get ahead' but in effect the 'benefits' are unequally distributed in non-transparent ways and are often impossible to access. The rhetoric may be very powerful but absolutely inaccessible for much of the population, and in this way those who cannot find access to English see themselves as 'disadvantaged' or unfortunate (Bruthiaux, 2002). The supposed benefits of English are not always realised.

Bruthiaux's (2002) study of microlending and poverty alleviation concluded that the language priorities for most of the world's population are to become proficient and literate in their native languages and that English language education is an expensive luxury that is beyond the reach of most of the population in poor countries (Bruthiaux, 2002). Garcia's 1995 study (cited in Tollefson, 2000) revealed that with Spanish-speaking communities in the USA other factors such as age, sex and discrimination against the minority language among other things influenced whether a person benefited economically from learning English. This leads to broader questions about whether all students really benefit from the time, effort and expense of learning English and which of them benefit most. If the benefits of English are not so clear then why does it continue to spread?

These questions may seem simplistic in the sense that 'English as an international language' has embedded itself in terms of international political communication and in disciplines such as business, science and technology. Nevertheless, I contend that there is a need to problematise the notion of 'English as an international language'. The spread of English manifests itself differently in different places according to the particular interests of the aid donors and other international and national organisations. If looked at closely in different contexts the spread of English is closely linked to the political decisions that benefit some groups at the expense of others (Tollefson, 1995). This view underpins the stories in this book. The case studies reveal the way the competition in the international language education marketplace is uneven and exposes the ways in which use of English allows some players dominate the market.

The First Language: Endangered in the Project

As the above pages have attempted to explain, in this story English is not a neutral tool of communication, especially so within the context of IELEPs. Numerous issues emerge from this position. The teaching of English in the colonial context has often been at the expense of the first language development (Bruthiaux, 2002; Ellis & Kelly, 1997; Joseph & Ramani, 1998; Phillipson, 1992a, 1992b; Phillipson & Skutnabb-Kangas,

1996; Skutnabb-Kangas, 2000). In a recent Australian aid-funded project in a South East Asian country, the project produced ELT textbooks in a situation where there is a dearth of first language teaching material and low first language literacy levels (Forman, 1999). This type of aid project funding is clearly in the interests of the donors. Among other arguments it upholds Gunning-Stevenson's (2001) claims that the aid supports consultants in the gaining of lucrative overseas projects.

Another crucial issue is the position of the non-native-speaker teacher of English. Medgyes' (1994) work in this area revealed the complexities of the power relations operating in the teaching of EFL, in particular the struggles of the bilingual teacher to be recognised as a legitimate teacher of English. Medgyes challenges dominant perceptions of who is a good teacher of English. His work calls to mind Phillipson's (1992b) 'myths of English language teaching' including, 'the native speaker fallacy', where he demonstrated that a primary belief in the ELT field is that the native-speaker teacher is the best. The work of Bourdieu (1991), Braine (1999), Ellis and Kelly (1997), Holliday (1994, 1996, 2005, 2006), Kubota (1999, 2001a), Kumaravadivelu (2001), Nayar (1997), Norton (1997), Pennycook (1994, 1998, 2000), Phillipson (1992a, 1992b), Rajagopalan (1999), Rampton (1990), Skutnabb-Kangas (2000, 2001) and Tollefson (2000) critically discuss the positioning(s) of the bilingual/non-native speaking teacher of English and the native speaking teacher. A question which emerges from this body of work is, 'Who is the native speaker of English?'. How are teachers from Kachru's (1986) outer circle or Phillipson's periphery (1992b) positioned? The aforementioned authors critique the way that the ELT profession assumes that the native speaking teacher invariably means a person from 'inner circle' (Kachru, 1986) or 'core' (Phillipson, 1992b) countries.

Related to the above issue is the approach the projects take towards the teaching and learning of the learner's first language. If the teachers, and later the students, are to learn English better, they are to become bilingual. Even if the projects concentrate on ELT, learning a foreign language is both directly and indirectly related to the competence in and development of the first languages of the learners. Countless studies demonstrate this correlation. Therefore, neglecting them completely makes for bad pedagogy.

The goal of the international education projects is to teach English and conduct teacher education programmes based on current NABA (North American, British and Australian) language teaching methodologies. In carrying out their work the projects largely relied on English as the language of instruction. This then begs further questions:

- What is the role of the first language of the host-country project participants?
- If it is not accounted for, why is it neglected?
- Should it be and should there be goals in regard to the first language(s)?

It is crucial to examine why the projects are framed and run in English and correspondingly what understandings of English, its role and theories of both language and language learning a project requires a team member to have. The teaching of English is a link, at least superficially, between the stakeholders in the projects discussed in this book.

There is, however, an additional and necessary way to view the role of English, particularly in the aid context. Inside the projects English is deeply implicated in structuring social, economic and political inequality. Appleby (2002), in her work on an ELT project in East Timor, critically assessed the so-called neutrality of the project and concluded that 'Discourses of language in development create the abnormality of the person who does not speak English' (Appleby, 2002: 336). The case studies in this book allow us to look at different ways English was used for purposes to carry out project work at a local level and/or for international communication and the learning and teaching practices of the projects in relation to these different needs and contexts. They also allow us to reflect on how and why the mother tongues of the non-English speakers are made invisible and how the two languages are hierarchised.

The participants' stories are rich in detail about the issues or struggles and perceived inequalities of language rights, pedagogy, teaching and learning and the projects' stated priorities. The book critiques the way the donor countries' language policies are replicated in offshore projects and offers views about how more equitable and rewarding goals may be realised in language education projects.

Projectisation of ELT

The concept of the 'project' underlies much of the discussion of IELEPs in this story. Briefly here, the project model of aid funding has been (willy-nilly) embraced by the education sector (Sharp, 1998). The diverse accounts of the design, implementation and impact of international education projects have predominantly focused on project implementation in the aid and development context, and up until the early 1990s this research was primarily based on agricultural and health projects (Kenny & Savage, 1997, Pottier, 1993). Since the early 1990s there has been a significant increase in focus on English language education and teacher training projects (Coleman, 1992, 1995; Crooks & Crewes, 1995; Holliday, 1992, 1994, 1995, 2005; Kachru, 1992; Kenny & Savage, 1997; Language in Development Conference papers, 1997, 1999, 2001, 2003, 2005; Lo Bianco, 2002a; McGovern, 1995; Pennycook, 1994, 1996; Phillipson, 1992a, 1992b, 1994; Prabu, 1990). However, a significant gap in this research is on the analysis and development of an approach to project implementation that engages with the complexity and unpredictability of English language education projects. A related area similarly neglected is the emergence of the Australian university as a player in the international project field.

As noted early in this chapter, critics argue that both international aid-funded and fee-based (ELT and other) projects fail (London, 1993). Project planning is a highly contextualised and contested area of work and there is seemingly a significant investment in finding the 'right' model. A question here is: do the 'problems with projects' rest in a problem with the model?

According to commentators such as Little and Mirrlees (1974), Iredale (1990) and Pottier (1993), the project approach promised 'successful' delivery of the aid services. However, in spite of the attempted measures to ensure success, in both temporal and spatial terms, project results were often disappointing. During the 1960s and 1970s the Pan African Institute of Development (PAID) conducted broad-ranging assessments of the then current internationally funded projects (predominantly in agriculture) and generally found that (1)objectives were rarely achieved; and (2) project performance was regularly hampered by the absence of detailed analyses of initial conditions, for instance, of agro-ecological, economic and sociological relations (PAID, 1981: 14).

The perceived poor performance of the projects was seen more as a feature of the times rather than as anything inherent in the way that the delivery of aid was organised. In the 1960s and 1970s the pre-Second World War colonial systems had been dismantled but still there were remnants of the system, which meant that seeking assistance required learning the rules of the game and accepting the imposition or continuation of economic ties. The projects were perceived to be given to those governments which were more likely to cooperate with the donors' views on development and trading relations (PAID, 1981).

More recent literature analysing the impact of projects in the education sector draws similar conclusions. Murphy (1999: 217), in his study of ELT projects, is damning about the impact of such projects: 'Projects in education tend to produce problems of disruption and failure, and as part of education, ELT follows this pattern.' I take up such criticisms in this book and discuss ways in which projects are assessed and in whose terms projects are considered to be successes or failures. Integral to the success or otherwise of a project are questions about the ways in which education projects are complex, contested and unpredictable (Coleman, 1995) and how these characteristics may or may not guarantee how well the project product meets the needs of the recipients. International government and institutional literature on project development is large, yet it is also diffuse and generally lacking in a strong research tradition. Critiques of this literature (Crehan & Von Oppen, 1988; Crewe & Harrison, 1998; Crooks & Crewes, 1995; Kenny & Savage, 1997; Language in Development, 1997; Lo Bianco, 2002b; Pottier, 1993; Shaw, 1997) point to the superficial explorations of project practices. Through the stories in this book I offer a new understanding of how project implementation and development are represented and therefore accessible to evaluation beyond budgetary issues and objectives stated in the project documents.

I characterise international education projects in Bourdieu's terms as a dynamic field with shifting boundaries. While individual staff and/or management members will change, the characteristics of hierarchy and advantage are consistent in the field. It is this consistency that is significant in project life and allows for analysis of the dominant interests in the project field. The supposed lack of knowledge about the implementation of international education projects, I contend, is not accidental. Rather it is an intentional strategy on the part of the donor or provider. The regularity with which projects are said to have failed to meet their educational objectives evidences that other interests are being met. It is my intention to reveal the ways in which ELT project work pursues particular interests. In the light of the conundrum surrounding project implementation and the disaffected views in this area, it is imperative to rethink project implementation, to pull apart the pre-set notions used to represent it and to articulate the varied interests of the stakeholders and the power relations in the field. The participants in the case studies critique common sense understandings and make visible the power relations in the project field which inevitably hijack the stated goals.

Practices in the Field

Practices in project work are not separate entities but dimensions of the particular field. My analysis shows how a Bourdieuian approach to the study of practices in IELEP work can open up new ways of understanding activities such as project management, distribution of project tasks, relationships between stakeholders and work practices such as collaboration and consultation. Both projects were purported to be bilateral, to involve a partnership between all participants and to employ current Australian academic practices. Yvonne, an Australian teacher trainer with the project in South East Asia, discusses a training programme that was originally intended as being jointly developed by host-country and Australian trainers:

> But in the end you see . . . it was not a collaborative effort in the end, really, it was all done by the Australian side. There was lot of painful effort, you know, the translators, but that wasn't the creating of it. So, you know, we could yet be left with a white elephant. Because, I mean, I'm thinking this now for the first time . . . You know, it could be a white elephant because it wasn't jointly constructed. (Yvonne P1AU1)

Clearly here, project practices are determined by the dominant actor in the IELEP field.

The interviewees reveal the different ways in which project work is legitimised, in Bourdieu's terms, how the game is played and the ways in which some agents are better players than others and how for some players everything about project work is 'natural'. Within this aspect of my analysis I demonstrate how the organisation of work serves some interests better than others. The interviewees speak about work practices that are deemed either dominant or subordinate, legitimate or illegitimate. Some of the interviewees view the Australian university's role in educational projects as illegitimate. That is, the Australian institutions did not undertake the necessary preparatory work or gain the necessary knowledge of the project's context to undertake such endeavours. Yet the universities have the cultural capital to judge whether particular participants are legitimate in their work practices.

In the book the participants tell their stories about teaching (and learning) and other work in the project. The case studies allow insights into how the dynamics in the project field produce certain type of practices and how the dominant players viewed these practices as 'normal', 'regular' or otherwise.

Cultural Practices

In familiarising the reader with the context of my story, the notion of culture requires specific comment. The interviewees' stories offer multi-layered concepts of culture in the context of IELEPs. In general, IELEP goals are rarely explicit about the project's view of culture and the assumed cultural values inherent in its language education practice. I explore the competing notions of culture (as represented by the interviewees) embedded in the projects and ask how the diversity of the constructions of culture and the relationship of language and culture impact on the work of the projects. I view culture as a dynamic, contested notion constructed by external forces of history and social conditions as well as from the internal actions of members of the particular cultures.

I have worked with Bourdieu's notion of habitus (see definition, page 4) to analyse what has often been termed as 'culture'. The explanatory tool of habitus has brought to light a dimension of the field that is not recognised by the literature on intercultural or cross-cultural relations in ELT practice. With this concept Bourdieu seeks through his social research to illuminate empirically why people act as they do and what potential space exists for transformation. The resulting action of the relationship between field, habitus and capital, the practice of project work, is investigated to reveal the diverse constructions of culture and their relationship to language. I expose an 'invisible side' (see page 5) of the projects; they are not what they present themselves as. Even if a project product is put up as a real 'commodity', the dominant stakeholders do not necessarily take project goals seriously.

The interviewees spoke of their practice in ways that exemplified habitus. Habitus focuses on our ways of behaving, thinking and feeling. It captures how we carry our history within us, how we make choices to act in certain ways but not others. We are engaged in a continuous process of making; how we are in life at any one moment is the result of numberless events in the past which have shaped our path (Maton, 2008). Interviewee stories encapsulated the ways in which a person's dispositions are partly individually subjective but also influenced by the objective positions and social, material and historical traditions in which that person lives.

Throughout this story I critique the notion of the international language education project as a small site of culture (Holliday, 1994, 2005) which is different from the culture outside of the project and different from the culture of the expatriate staff. I contend that the projects are not unique entities of culturally appropriate practice; rather they embody symbolic violence (see Chapter 2, p. 39 for definition) in their constructions of cultural and national characteristics (Morris, 1991; Murphy, 1999; Swales, 1980). The issues of culture and language are paramount in the work of international language education projects but as I reveal there are many dynamics at work in the 'complex and unpredictable' (Coleman, 1995) life of projects.

I concur with Raymond Williams (1983) in *Keywords* that the word 'culture' is one of the two or three most complicated words in the English language. The data yielded rich material about the differing ways that culture is referred to and the many meanings it carried in the broad field of project work and the social relations within the project. Notions of 'culture' were revealed in both the ways in which the projects were constructed through project documentation and the official institutions of both the donor/provider country and the host countries. I do caution the reader however that the stories about culture and habitus in project life are necessarily partial. The interviews speak of the individual's experience and views and can only offer glimpses into the way that the constructions of meanings of these concepts shaped the practices of the IELEPs.

Summary of the Book

The book is based on my own experiences; it is an investigation of practices in which I have been involved. I argue that international language education projects are messy and volatile and the boundaries of their practices are permeable to the social life outside of the project. The investigation of such projects must account for this and not view the project as a discrete and separate social and cultural entity. I present myself in this story as an 'insider', a 'participant observer' and, in the spirit of Bourdieu, present a reflexive account of the projects' practices. A reflexive, insider account represents both a position taken in the field and a personal construction of the relative positions of others within the same field (Grenfell & Hardy, 2003: 24). My interviews, document analysis, personal correspondence and conversations with project participants offer insider accounts which reveal the different accumulations of capital, the relations and practices in the field and in doing so reveal the many layered answers to: who benefits and in whose interests are such projects conceived and executed.

Chapter 2 provides a more detailed description of the countries of both projects, explains the research tools used, maps the IELEP field in relation to other fields and internally and centrally locates the concept of 'interest' in project work, firstly describing the stakeholders and then exploring the data to show how all stakeholders display their particular interests in participating in project work. Chapter 3 names some key struggles which constitute this story and examines the concepts of success and failure in project work. It shows that notions of success and failure cannot be understood simply in terms of meeting set goals or outcomes, but rather are related to often competing and conflicting interests of the stakeholders.

Chapter 4 explores the EL teaching and learning practices in the project and reveals the ways in which project work is carried out. The core work of the projects is the training of EL teachers and English language education. This is a complicated area of work that involves the debates around the native speaking teacher versus the non-native speaking teacher, use of first and second language in the English language class as well as the transference of a particular approach to ELT. There is conflict over the teaching practices in the projects. The goal of the Australian projects is to replace host-country teaching practices with an Australian product. The projects are located in countries where English is not the native language and Australia is positioned as the expert in English language. Australia is a linguistically diverse country and its experience with decades of TESOL has given credibility to all Australian language teaching institutions. The struggle over expertise is a major struggle in the field as the host-country teachers are the experts in their own context, and they are already trained teachers. This chapter will report experiences in teacher education and school classrooms.

I use Bourdieu's metaphor of 'a game' to critique the way project work is carried out. Using this metaphor I expose how the game is played and the ways in which some players are better than others and how for some players everything about project work is 'natural' (from the perspective of those who transport these work practices). I also employ valuable critiques from other critical language education and language rights theorists to give voice to the assumptions and strategies that underpin the actions of the dominant agents in the field.

The project field, in Bourdieu's terms, is a place of struggle over scarce resources. It is possible to problematise the notions of success and failure in relation to the various interests in the field. These notions are relative to one's own and others' standpoint in the field. The different ways in which success, failure or even project completion might be viewed are responsible for difficulties and complications and ultimately struggles that arise in project work. These difficulties expose the structure of the project field, the apparent incongruity of the agents' interests and the subsequent outcomes that reflect the dominant interests in the field.

In Chapter 5 (and Chapter 6) I explore the validity of the challenges and analysis outlined in previous chapters. Language is the key to many of the issues which confront all the agents in the ELT project field. The teaching of it is the central task of the projects, it is the means of communication and the linguistic field is dominated by one particular language, English. This chapter examines the way host-country languages are positioned, how linguistic capital is distributed and accumulated and the resulting power relations in the field. I show that the distribution of power is uneven in this language learning and teaching field. Even though the goal of both projects is to teach English, the host country's project staff/participants' development of expertise in English does not bestow legitimacy in the project.

Chapter 6 contests the assumptions about culture made in the design, implementation and work practices in ELT projects. I present a critique of what is often presented as a 'common sense' understanding of culture which informs the actions of donors and project-implementers. This understanding of culture, which defines culture as an essential quality related to one's national identify, is repeatedly drawn on to give explanations how people behave and think. I show how the view of culture as a dynamic, contested notion constructed by external forces of history and social conditions as well as from the internal actions of those members of the particular cultures is much more appropriate for discussing this aspect of the project field.

In the final chapter (Chapter 7), the commodification and projectisation of ELT are questioned and politicised further. I present different possible future scenarios for project design and implementation. This chapter takes risks in that it does not propose a model but, following the book's theme of critical education strategies, suggests processes that more fully engage project participants in more collaborative relationships. I take on board the issues raised in related research and policy work which problematise the role of English and seek to promote language rights and strengthen linguistic diversity.

Chapter 2

Naming the Game: Positions and Interest in the IELEP Field

The introductory chapter briefly sketched the intent and shape of each project. This chapter examines the context in more detail; it defines the ELT project field and describes the power relations operating in it. Here I map out the positions, interests and the dimensions of the project field: the recipients, host-country staff, the donors, contributors and the project workers. What positions are made available to whom and who makes these decisions? Whose interests are served by these decisions? In general, the IELEP fields contain certain regularities: stakeholder positions and interests, valued capital, positions of dominance and subordination. These features are recognisable in projects around the globe.

This chapter is also an attempt to understand the complexity of the stakeholder interests. What are the interests of the many stakeholders already identified in this story and how are their interests represented in project negotiations and what are the processes by which some stakeholders have their interests negotiated and represented and others do not? Here the notion of the beneficiary is problematised in relation to the different types of capital stakeholders are able to deploy.

I approach this section with caution, heeding Dilley's (1999) words on the problems of specifying context as the construction of the sites that has the capacity to produce only partial pictures. I recognise that I have chosen to describe some things about the projects and ignore others. What I have sought to do is draw a picture of the projects that locates the reader in the particular project situation as given in the data. In some sense this is a traditional notion of context in that it describes the material and social characteristics of the site with the expectation that this description gives the reader the ability to understand the phenomena arising from the data. This is a limited view of context as I cannot describe a 'true' objective picture of each project. In the process of presenting the data and analysis here I have endeavoured to make visible a range of views to illustrate that what actually constitutes each project depends on one's perspective.

Understanding that I cannot present the whole picture, I use the information I have collected about each context to make connections between the agents' practices in the field. By making connections, I mean the ways that project work connects or disconnects to other practices within the project field and in the fields which intersect with the IELEPs, for example, how the academic practices the Australian staff bring with them interact and effect the teaching and learning practices within the project.

A complication is that while there is homology of the two project fields, they are differentiated by their particularities, for example, the different countries, the different ELT histories, the different economic situations of the teachers and the different education traditions.

Project 1: Laos

Project 1, hereafter referred to as P1, is located in Laos, often described as 'one of the ten poorest countries in the world'. It shares a similar ruptured history of many other countries in its region, South East Asia, and those other countries which have experienced colonial rule. In recent decades Laos has suffered from foreign assaults and occupation, civil war and the loss of many skilled and educated people as refugees from the 1970s onward (Evans, 2002). In general, Laos' context is framed by inequitable access to resources for economic, industrial and technological development (ADB, 2000; Kenny & Savage, 1997). Following the collapse of the Soviet Union and withdrawal of its aid programme, and supported by the nation's government's moves to open up the country to foreign investment and free market enterprises, there has been increased activity by aid agencies and interest by investors since 1986. A striking characteristic of the aid and investment directions and priorities is that they are decided in the corridors and boardrooms of the aid and donor government agencies and are most often in reference to the economic needs of the donor countries (Morris, 1996).

The Lao education sector and, in particular, the paucity of funding and resources available to that sector have recently been the subject of much research and interest (Keolivay, 2005; King & Bessell-Brown, 1993; Sithirajavongsa, 2003). The history of the provision of school education and the development of the tertiary sector are thematised by disruption and interference from colonial administrations. The country's education system has had little input, financial or otherwise, since 1975. Prior to that, it was run on the French model with French language as the medium of instruction in secondary schools. During the French colonial rule, the Lao languages were not taught or recognised as official languages. In the

1980s, many secondary and technical graduates received training in the former Soviet Union and Russian was instituted as the country's second language. The struggle for language rights in Laos has a long history (Vongvichit, 1967, cited in Sithirajvongsa, 2003).

In the early 1990s the government began the long process of restructuring the education system at all levels. The Lao interviewees are particularly descriptive about the way that they saw the transition to English as the main foreign language to be taught in schools and the tertiary system and to be positioned as the official second language. The interviewees drawn on in this section discuss the contradictory position of teachers and education; although education is highly prized and valued and teachers are respected, educational institutions' facilities, resources and training capacities are minimal. As is often the situation in countries of this region, teachers' salaries remain below subsistence level and most teachers need to take on additional private English language teaching or other work. At the time of this research there was an increasing demand for English language (EL) teachers in all areas of society; for example, a government decree in the mid-1990s set out a plan for English language training for all government officials in all provinces of the country. The project's (P1) goals were based on the continuing dominance of English in international relations and the seeming necessity to engage in the type of relations which positioned the host country as less powerful.

Project 2: The Fee-Based Project in Japan

Project 2, hereafter referred to as P2, was situated in Japan. English language was a compulsory subject in the Japanese school curriculum and university entrance exams. During the late 1990s the Japanese Ministry of Education (Monbusho – as it was then named) held discussions with the Australian Government Agency (AGA) in Japan about ELT teacher professional development opportunities. P2's main goal was to develop a professional development pathway for Japanese EL teachers in secondary schools. In particular, components of P2 included: (1) the development of appropriate English language training for EL teachers and (2) an articulated post-graduate programme. The project proposal described how the programmes would be tailored specifically for Japanese EL teachers.

The Positions of English

Despite the vastly different social and economic contexts of the two projects, English was positioned in surprisingly similar ways. In both contexts, bilingual teachers taught English in schools and tertiary institutions but the projects presented the monolingual 'native' speaker teacher as the model, as the ideal teacher educator and in the teacher training and teaching materials (Achren, 2007; Ellis & Kelly, 1997; Phan Le Ha, 2008; Matsuda, 2002). The positioning of English as a desired commodity and owned by 'so-called' English-speaking countries is remarkably durable; little changes under the shifting colonial, quasi-colonial or neo-colonial relations (Kumaravadivelu, 2006; Pennycook, 2007).

The discourses of colonialism, as realised in the position and role of English in international relations and described by Pennycook (1998, 2007), help to explain the way that English maintains a particular power and position in Japan, the host country of P2. Pennycook's (1998) analysis of the position of English in China and the subsequent portrayals of Chinese teachers and learners illustrate how the playing out of colonial relations are not necessarily linked to the material conditions of colonialism. He shows how discourses of English in China present similar types of relations as those that emerged from countries that were at the 'coal-face of colonialism' (Pennycook, 1998: 168). The teachers and learners of the host country of P2 are portrayed by the Australian manager as not being of equal academic standing, as 'so-called' native English speaker teachers and academics. This enduring view of the 'other' has been named and critiqued by influential socio-cultural/political theorists such as Escobar (1985), Goulet (1995) and Said (1978). Oda (2008) critiques a prevailing discourse that ELT is not effective in Japan and that this is somehow the fault of the learners and the teachers; this discourse helps position Japanese teachers in a subordinate role in the EL field and bolster the position of the usually monolingual 'native' English speaking teacher.

Bourdieu's Explanatory Tools

As mentioned briefly in Chapter 1, I draw on Bourdieu's 'thinking tools' to analyse the way IELEPs work. Bourdieu's conceptual framework is eminently suitable as it allows for a many-sided investigation into both the immediate area of study, the field of the IELEPs, and the broader social context, the field of power. As already mentioned, the field of power in this instance is represented by the powerful institutions at national and international levels, institutions such as Australian aid agencies, Australian foreign relations organisations, international aid and finance organisations, Australian universities and universities in countries other than Australia. The framework allows me to examine the relationships between the different agents, the positions they occupy in the field and the capital which they accumulated. The ways in which the agents carried out their practice of project work is what Bourdieu refers to as a 'feel for the game'.

Bourdieu's work is of particular interest in examining the tertiary context because much of his research has looked at his own academic culture as part of a wider intellectual field (e.g. Bourdieu, 1989). Bourdieu expresses the necessity for sociologists to undertake a study of their own social space. I work at a university and spent many years teaching with various international projects and I welcome this opportunity afforded by Bourdieu to scrutinise my area of work.

This story engages with concepts that have a history in sociological research: power, research, internationalisation, culture, beneficiary, success, failure and education among others. Bourdieu (1991) advises researchers to view the language that they use with suspicion. Without caution, researchers may engage in a process of misrecognition; for example, they may not recognise the way the processes and structures in the IELEP field delineate the field and create hierarchies of power and advantage. They may rely on the 'common sense' understandings of everyday terms (Grenfell & James, 1998: 21–25). The problem is then that the researcher may only operate on the understandings they have developed through their own academic trajectory and interests in the field rather than explain and understand it in its own terms (Grenfell & James, 1998: 58). Bourdieu's warning was evident in my own use of the term 'beneficiary'. My 'every day' understanding of this term in a project sense has been challenged by the differing understandings expressed by stakeholders. In the initial stages of my investigations in this field I misrecognised the term 'beneficiary' and described the field as a binary relationship between the 'donor and beneficiary'; my subsequent recognition of the different understandings is given in the following chapters.

Educational research in terms of Bourdieu's theory of practice offers insights and understandings not readily visible in other approaches (Bourdieu, 1983; Grenfell & James, 1998). In my research into project implementation in the international context, I am clearly talking about relations of power and how the interests of the stakeholders, stated or not stated, are allowed to play themselves out in the field. The key tools relevant to mapping the projects are described below.

The notion of interest

Bourdieu's notion of interest (also referred to as *illusio*) underpins this whole book. Bourdieu looked deeply into what agents do in a field, what activities they are involved in, where they are positioned and how well they carry out what they do. Pivotal to this examination is the question about what interests the agent may have in doing what they do (Bourdieu, 1998: 75). For Bourdieu, interest is to 'be there', to participate, to admit that the game is worth playing and that the stakes created in and through the fact of playing are worth pursuing; it is to recognise the game and to recognise its stakes (Swartz, 1997: 77). The metaphor of the 'game' is a way Bourdieu spoke about the dynamics and relationships in a field and 'having a feel for the game is having the game under one's skin; it is to master in a practical way the future of the game; it is to have a sense of the history of the game' (Swartz, 1997: 80).

Why is it important to ask the question about what interest an agent has in doing what they do? On the one hand, an agent's interest may seem obvious and not worth probing into, yet on the other hand, a deeper investigation of the practices or actions of the agent may reveal that 'everything is not as it seems.' What is important is the fact that what happens in the 'game' matters to those who are engaged in it, who are in the game. There may be multiple 'interests' at stake and it is also the case that some 'interests' dominate others.

Bourdieu puts forward the idea of a 'disavowal of interest'. He gives examples of one, in the art field, where there is a powerful notion of 'art for art's sake' and this notion (born in the 19th century) cuts a divide between commercial art and pure art. The 'true' artist then is one who pursues 'pure' art and has no (a disavowal of) interest in commercial endeavours. The other example Bourdieu gives is of the public service field, where agents act with a disavowal of interest; they act only for the public good. This powerful rhetoric of a 'disavowal of interest' is prevalent in the aid and development field and was present in the formative years of Australian university activity in international education work. The 'disavowal of interest' in public service masks the interests, the embodied 'feel for the game' that agents have in their carrying out of the work in the field of international language education projects.

Bourdieu allows us to see that in these fields that are for the 'public good', for those situated agents:

> it is necessary to be 'disinterested' in order to succeed, they can undertake, in a spontaneously disinterested manner, actions in accordance with their interests. There are quite paradoxical situations that a philosophy of consciousness precludes us from understanding. (Bourdieu, 1998: 83)

Later in this chapter I examine practices within the project through the lens of the concept of interest and seek to arrive at an understanding for how relations in the field shape and are shaped by 'interest'.

Field

Field describes the social space which refers to the overall conception of the social world where actors engage in relationships according to capital and habitus (Harker *et al.*, 1990: 91). Fields are crisscrossed by power lines; examples include such fields as the financial system, the public sector or education. Fields are competitive arenas characterised by a struggle for scarce resources. Fields are homologous, that is, characteristics of power, hierarchy and advantage are shared by different fields. Each field has its dominant and dominated, its struggles for gaining power or exclusion, the way it reproduces itself or is transformed. But each of the attributes has its own distinctive, specific form in each field. A field is also defined by its relationship to the field of power, which in Bourdieu's terms is the meta-field.

Much of Bourdieu's research has been in the education field, most often focusing on issues of equity, access and the process by which ideas or language are legitimated (Bourdieu, 1990b). Field is an area of struggle for legitimation. For example, Bourdieu's field analysis of the position of teachers is one where differences in ideas are viewed as strategies in a struggle for intellectual recognition. In his terms, legitimation of ideas or position comes about through:

(a) understanding the rules of game (embodiment of the dispositions);
(b) accumulating the relevant types of capital.

In the case of the university field, the ideas held by those in dominant positions usually become legitimated by the field and struggles ensue around the maintenance or change in these ideas. Participation in a field requires buying into its legitimacy, embodying the stakes of the field, at some level.

As noted in Chapter 1 the field of university-led international education projects is a relatively recent development within the field of higher education. At the time of writing this book higher education is a particularly volatile field: Australian Government funding and education policies have changed dramatically in the last decade, student demographics are changing in line with the general trend of an ageing population in industrialised societies and the role of the university as the prime supplier of tertiary education is contested by training providers in the private sector.

Similar trends are occurring across the OECD countries (as mentioned in Chapter 1) and universities are constantly competing against each other in their search for new markets (Marginson, 2008; Phillipson, 2008). As universities are driven to engage more competitively in income generation, the success of international education projects is paramount. The international education field adds another level of complexity in that it crosses national boundaries and Australian project planners and implementers must take account of how strongly overseas students and their employers wish to accumulate cultural capital in the form of Australian university qualifications.

Capital

Capital determines the social relations of power (Swartz, 1997: 73); capital comprises the resources one accumulates to be positioned in the game. When the forms of capital (as valued resources) become objects of struggle, they are the stakes in the game. In the IELEP field the stakes in the game are numerous: language, money in the form of project funding and also in the form of profit from investment, educational qualifications, knowledge, professional standing, job promotions, national recognition, prestige and honour, to mention some. The field is delineated by the struggles over the most valued forms of capital and in this particular field it would seem that the cultural capital gained through the accumulation of academic qualifications operates to position individuals and subsequently institutions in the field.

This complex IELEP field is governed by its powerful institutions; the various Australian Government organisations (ministries, aid agencies) and educational institutions (faculties of universities, colleges and secondary schools) occupy dominant, and sometimes subordinate, positions in relation to other similar organisations or faculties, nationally and internationally. A particular government department or faculty will also have a 'standing' in relation to other component parts of the institution. Within the department or faculty individuals and groups will also have relationships which may be objectified to some extent by describing their holdings of various forms of capital (James, 1998). In the field of the IELEP the forms of capital could be summarised as economic (money); linguistic (language); cultural (qualifications, ways of work and knowledge); and social (connections, networks).

Symbolic capital and symbolic power are central concerns of Bourdieu's work and are pivotal elements in the relations of power. Symbolic capital is formed when capital is viewed and recognised as legitimate by the group to whom it is relevant. It is then converted to power through the process of legitimation. In a sense all capital is symbolic as it can only be recognised as significant from within a particular field although clearly its forms operate in different ways. Thus, for example, economic capital is symbolically powerful to hold in that it implies purchasing power in a direct, immediate and explicit sense, whereas cultural and social capital have to operate through legitimated valuing systems. Because all capital is symbolic, its action within any particular field is dependant on the participants' understanding of the social, economic and cultural parameters of that field (based on work by Grenfell & Hardy, 2003: 23).

The field of IELEPs 'happens' because the stakeholders/participants believe in the value of the capital in the field. The participants' stories reveal that value of the capital (either linguistic, cultural, social or economic) is differently determined and acted upon by different stakeholders. Some seek to change the practice, some seek to maintain the orthodoxy of the field; however, one thing that underlies the practice of the individuals who participate in the struggle of the field is that they believe in the game and the value of the stakes. Participation in the field buys into its legitimacy to some degree. For example, even those participants who are merely 'doing a job' in the sense that their only goal is to continue to receive a salary take on the 'doxa', that is, the dominant beliefs and values of the field; in Bourdieu's (1998: 57) words, this is 'a particular point of view, the point of view of the dominant'. The stakes, even though unequally distributed, are significantly high enough for all participants to comply with the regularities of the field. Kumaravadivelu (2003a, 2006) offers another way to think about this dynamic of the field with his use of the terms 'the process of marginalization' and the 'practice of self-marginalisation'. These are used by Kumaravadivelu to identify and understand how the colonial concept of method continues to hold hegemonic control over ELT pedagogic practices even after the 'end' of colonialism (2003a: 546). The cooperation of host-country participants in the game of the IELEP, their practice of self-marginalisation, is a strategy which legitimates the field. Through self-marginalisation the host-country teachers take on the language and teaching practices of the donor/project implementers at the expense of their own expertise. Further on in this chapter I discuss the various interests of the participants and look at ways the participants self-marginalise or seek to maintain the orthodoxy of the field to keep hold of their stakes in the game.

I use the concept of capital to understand how the agents in the field invest in particular practices rather than others and to see how different forms of behaviour have different values in different places. The capital that an agent possesses positions her/him in the field.

In Bourdieu's terms, certain types of capital attract the same type of capital, and allegiances form between agents who possess the similar types of capital. In a field, power is distributed according to the amount of symbolic capital an agent possesses. This capital has to be recognised as valuable by other participants in the field. We do not necessarily know that we possess capital until we enter a field where it is recognised as valued (Grenfell & James, 1998: 21–25). This may well describe a view of the 'native speaker teacher of English' as it is represented in the data. The teacher may start work with an IELEP and not be fully cognisant of the recognised 'value' of this particular form of capital and upon engaging with the field then is made aware of the value of this attribute.

However, one of the contradictions of a field is that as more of a certain type of capital is broadly accumulated, the value of that capital decreases. For example, Marginson (1997b) makes this point about educational qualifications as cultural capital. He discusses how as more and more students graduate with a certain qualification, for example, a Master's degree, this degree loses its value in the market place. Therefore, in our current climate, universities must strive to demonstrate the uniqueness of their particular qualifications and strive to gain competitive advantage by developing a 'cutting edge' qualification or by 'discovering' a new international (or national) market. The valued resources of a field are not fixed or sacrosanct. The struggles that occur within a field affect the stakes and values held by the dominant agents. For example, a key struggle in the Australian ELT field is around teaching methodology. Different methodologies dominate at different times. Advocates of new approaches to ELT (i.e. newcomers to the field) challenge dominant approaches and a struggle ensues.

My interest in this book is to understand the practical consequences of Bourdieu's conceptual 'tool', capital, in identifying sites of struggle, distribution of power and, ultimately, in providing insight/further answers to the questions of who benefits, in whose interests are such projects conducted and on whose terms do they succeed or fail.

Habitus

Habitus is a way of discussing the deep embodied tacit understandings of the agent in a particular field. Bourdieu describes habitus as more an acquired sense of when and how to use cultural knowledge in a profitable manner rather than as a set of propositions, beliefs or adherence to rules.

He writes that '...practice is the product of the habitus which is itself the product of the embodiment of the immanent regularities and tendencies of the world...' (1992: 184). In applying this notion and examining the dialectical relationship between habitus and the objective structures of the IELEPs, I have tried to understand how certain habitus in the form of linguistic, cultural, economic and social capital are valued within those objective structures. In *Pascalian Meditations*, Bourdieu (2000) emphasises that the habitus is a result of social practice and that it adapts to social practice. The work of the IELEPs is described here as a practice, just as a game is a practice. The members of the relevant community, the players, constitute a social field. Knowledge characteristics of the appropriate institutions to do with the teaching, learning and running of the projects no doubt assert their influence in the project 'game'; they shape the practice of IELEPs just as a piece of sports equipment shapes an athletic game (Krais, 1996). And, as in other social practices, 'the ways to go about doing what you do' are inculcated in the habitus of the 'players'. The application, theoretically and methodologically, of the concept habitus allows me to talk about the relationship of the objective structures and subjectivities in what may usually be meant by 'culture'.

Symbolic violence

By symbolic violence, Bourdieu means a non-physical sort of violence which is exercised upon a social agent with his or her complicity (or to use Kumaravadivelu's [2003a, 2006] term, 'self-marginalisation'). For example, in the IELEPs the Australian project teams and the donors carry out symbolic violence (marginalisation) by imposing meanings as 'legitimate by concealing the power relations which are the basis of its force' and at the same time communicating a logic or rhetoric of disinterest (Bourdieu & Passeron, 1977: 4). Therefore, when English education goes about teaching English or EL teacher education, it is fundamentally trying to impose 'culturally arbitrary' conditions by an arbitrary power (p. 18) under the guise of legitimate order. The consequences in the IELEP, which are beneficial to the dominant players in the project, are numerous. First, the teachers and lecturers coming from the donor and/or provider countries find the project's approach to education comprehensible and show skill and excellence. Secondly, the culture of the dominant players, Australian universities, the donors or providers, is shown to be the most superior. And finally, an act of 'symbolic violence' is perpetuated on learners coming from the host countries by forcing them to support an alien education culture.

Mapping the Fields

Here I help the reader visually to see how I have used Bourdieu by mapping out the three distinct though not hierarchical levels of the IELEPs. The three levels are:

Level 1: Analysis of the position of the IELEP field vis-à-vis the meta-field of power (see Figures 2.1 and 2.2).

Level 2: The map of relations between the agents in the field
I map out the objective structure of relations between the positions occupied by agents who compete for the legitimate forms of specific authority in the field. What are the forms of economic and cultural capital that are specific to the field under investigation? How are they distributed relative to other forms of capital? This means identifying the dominant and subordinate positions of all the participants in the field (see Figures 2.3a and 2.3b).

Level 3: Analysis of the habitus of agents
That is, the systems of dispositions they have acquired by internalising a determinate type of social and economic condition (Bourdieu & Wacquant, 1992: 102) (see Table 2.1).

The three levels of analysis must be considered interdependently. However, it is not possible here to present a cohesive integrated analysis of all three levels. The stories in this book focus on Level 2 to investigate the way capital and, consequently, benefits are distributed in the IELEP field. Related to this analysis are the positions taken up by or assigned to the project's participants. In subsequent chapters these dominant or subordinate positions are investigated within the themes of: struggles in the field (Chapter 3); project practices (Chapter 4); language (Chapter 5); and culture (Chapter 6). It is within Level 2 that one is able to see the interactions between field and capital and to gain insights into the behaviour of participants in the project world, for instance, the role of different languages in the project, the practices of the stakeholders and the interests and investments they have in the field.

Level 1: Analysis of the Position of the IELEP Field vis-à-vis the Meta-field of Power

Here I locate the IELEP within the meta-field of power. This analysis is termed Level 1, which can be represented by Figures 2.1 and 2.2 (in the sub-sections below) depicting the broad distributions of capital within the field of power. The mapping of the institutions and projects in Figures 2.1

and 2.2 presents an overview of the field and provides a way to represent the inter-relationships between the institutional bodies. In creating these figures I have drawn on Swartz's (1997) and Grenfell and Hardy's (2003) work from the art field.

The projects are situated at particular times in international economic and social relations and the particular interests demonstrated by dominant stakeholders need to be contextualised within the broader realm of these international relations. One group of dominant players, the aid agencies, are informed and influenced by world economic, military and social events. This scenario of changing frameworks and priorities means that the bidders and tenderers must maintain a current knowledge of the role of projects and flexibility in the way they respond to the project designs. Sammels' (2006) critique of Australian aid policy points to how Australia's interests dominate in decisions about aid funding (see Chapter 1, p. 9).

Firstly, Figure 2.1 (from p. 42) maps out connections between the IELEP field and other fields and shows how it is located within fields. The mapping of the project field is significant for this story as it demonstrates clearly the struggles within the field of power between economic and cultural capital. The arrangements suggested by the figures are a way of demonstrating where the IELEPs lay in relation to the field of power, that is, they are located in the areas where, for P1, the university overlaps with both the aid agencies and the commercial enterprises. P2, the fee-based project, is located where the commercial enterprises overlay the universities.

The principal field in Bourdieu's work is the field of power. Its most significant usage for my study is its function as a 'meta-field' that operates as an organizing principle of differentiation and struggle throughout all fields concerned with international language education projects. Bourdieu (1998) depicts the field of power as delineated by the struggle between the two principal forms of capital, economic and cultural.

Figure 2.1 maps out the connections of the relevant fields of the international language education projects and illustrates the formal socio-political relationships in society.

These connections are drawn from the stories collected for this study, the interviews, 'insider' accounts and the various documents. The purpose of this diagram is to show how the three fields, education, commercial enterprises and political power, intersect and to prepare the way for the explanations which follow from the data. This broad collection of information has allowed me to make connections between the international language education projects investigated for this story and other

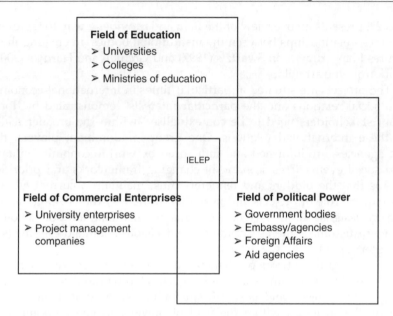

Figure 2.1 Analysis of the position of the IELEP field vis-à-vis the meta-field of power – connections across the fields

education fields and, ultimately, the fields of political power and commercial enterprises. The data reveal, as already noted in the previous paragraphs, that the field of international language education projects holds a dominant position within the field of power. A chief explanation for this is that the existence of the projects depends on the direction and interests of the Australian Government.

Lee, an Australian university lecturer, described the Australian aid agency's changes in priorites (as expressions of interest) throughout the last decade. His view reflected the way that the aid agency's focus shifts according to the government's political policies:

> we had a period back in the early 90s where it was explicitly an aid/trade relationship;...That moved in the mid-90s to aid for its own sake, so to speak, although everyone knows that that aid does lead to trade. It's just a question of focus. So the Australian aid agency wanted the project to run smoothly and to lift Australia's profile.

Along with increasing Australia's profile, Lee described the aid agency as having a genuine desire to 'help a poor country' and how the bidders must subtly reflect the aid agency's shift in priorities and yet demonstrate their own institutions' capacity to meet the enduring needs of the host context. The notion of helping, as in the above quote, is contentious; like Gronemeyer in Sachs (1992), many (Porter, 1995; Porter *et al.*, 1991) see aid and development initiatives offer help only when the helper (usually the dominant players) will benefit.

The aid agency donor that Lee referred to demonstrated 'grand interests', national interests in terms of Australia. Lee spoke of Australia's interests as multiple; the economic gains for Australian services and industry, through the export of education aid services, are immense.

The characteristics of interest in the fee-based education project did not vary greatly from the aid one, except that the national 'profit' from the export of education to an industrially developed country is predicated on an increased return on investment with possible spin-offs to other sectors, for example, tourism. The university's investment projects are usually carried out in collaboration with a private sector company (this may be a centre within the university). In P2, the investment organisation is based in Japan. On a macro level the university as a whole may have had grander visions of establishing links with tertiary sectors internationally (as expressed in University Critical Development Themes) while the individual faculty's interests centred on the number of enrolled fee-paying students.

The auspicing body of the fee-based project embodied the grand interests spoken of above. This agency was positioned somewhat differently from the large, often multinational, aid donor bodies; it did not have the economic capital but it did have the social capital, the connections, with key stakeholders. Murray (P2AM1), the Director, is quoted at length at the beginning of Chapter 1 where he put forward the idea that the purpose of the project was not to develop and deliver high-quality ELT teacher training programmes. This was in direct contrast to how the goals of the project were spoken about by the participants. He explicitly revealed that a purpose of the project was to enhance Australia's interest. This resonated with Lee's comments about the Australian Government's aim of 'lifting of Australia's profile' through the funding of education aid projects. It seems doubtful that the 'grand interests' of P2 were made public to the universities involved during any stage of the development of the project. From all accounts, the impressions given by the AGA in its public presentation of the project were its concern to assist the Ministry of Education (MOE) lift the standard of the teaching of spoken English in secondary schools. In another part of this interview, Murray explained further the interests of his agency by saying that although not having started, the project had in fact achieved its aims:

> While I do care about the quality of the project, my role isn't really to worry about English language teaching – how well the teachers do it or how well the students learn it. My concern is how well the project represents the Australian higher education sector. After all, the project is about Australian universities, not three independent universities...as far as I am concerned the project has already met its objectives.

In discussing the agency's interests in this way, I am concerned with the ways in which the multitude of interests are made transparent or not to the project's stakeholder groups and how particular interests take dominant positions within the field of power. In the above extract Murray talked about how, from his agency's point of view, the project had already met his agency's goals. The project had not at that time been promoted or enrolled students into its courses but it had effectively presented itself and impressed the MOE officials and had demonstrated that Australia's higher education sector is capable of delivering the sort of programmes that would meet the needs of the ELT teachers in this country's education system. Murray illustrated the complexity of the notion of 'interest'; in his assessment of the field, the central goal is satisfying Australia's national interests. He had a limited resource capacity and directed this capacity to where he saw the greater benefit for his agency and subsequently Australia's profile in this international context. The seeming abandonment of the Australian academic institutions, the resources they had already deployed and planned to deploy in this project, the staff whose positions may have depended on the planned project work, the 'assessed' needs of Japanese ELT teachers and the students and their families are all secondary to the dominant national interests.

The interests expressed by the dominant players in the aid world or by other Australian Government institutions are not surprising. The dynamics of the particular projects under discussion here again echo the international field, especially the international aid field. A well-documented perception of major aid donors (with projects in diverse contexts, for example, Burma, Cambodia and South Africa) is that they are relatively disconnected from the particular work and goals of the projects they fund (Abdul-Raheem, 2000; Kenny & Savage, 1997; Murphy, 1999; Smith, 1998). Yet the rhetoric of the development/aid field is that it is for the public good (an explicit position of a major Australian aid agency [AusAID, 2001]). This field could well fit the description that Bourdieu (1998) gives of the bureaucratic field in relation to the concept of interest. He describes the bureaucratic field as one 'constructed on a base of disavowal of interest – it represents itself as the image of the universe whose fundamental law is a public service; a universe in which social agents have no personal interest and sacrifice their own interests to the public service and to the universal' (Bourdieu, 1998: 78).

Other factors in positioning the field of international language education projects within the field of power include the following:

- wide circulation of university products from the various faculties and private centres within the university;
- connections with politics, through the national aid agencies, Australian embassies and Australian Government organisations situated overseas;
- political and social position taking associated with key individual field participants, for example, the vice-chancellor of the university expressing views on government policy;
- commercial partnerships with national project management companies;
- connections with a variety of national industry and entrepreneurial organisations who have interests in offshore ventures.

These factors illustrate internal and external activities of universities in the academic field which give rise to the internal differentiations within the field referred to in the preceding paragraphs. That is, how well-connected universities are to the major players, the national (or multinational) aid institutions, commercial project management companies or other public/private sector agencies that have a dominant position in the field.

Figure 2.2 illustrates a mapping of the field of power relative to education in general and, specifically, to the IELEPs. The field of education at its most general level is depicted as a two-dimensional space structured around the axes of volume (axis Y) and type (axis X) of capital. The choice of axes in this diagram may appear to imply claims about the way the different types of capital are accumulated; for example, if an institution has a high level of economic capital then it cannot hold a similar level of cultural capital. The positionings of the institutions is more complicated than this and the limitation of diagrams such as these are perhaps obvious and the role of such representations is limited to an attempt to understand the major tensions, that is, between accumulating economic and cultural capital in the field.

The field of education (rectangle 2) is situated above the X-axis, in that portion of the social space with the greatest volume of capital, and is itself

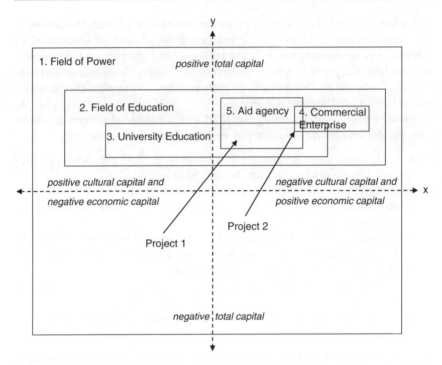

Figure 2.2 Analysis of the position of the IELEP field vis-à-vis the meta-field of power

internally differentiated according to the poles of economic and cultural capital. Within the field of education, the university education field (rectangle 3) is situated in an intermediary position, above the X-axis. It thus occupies a 'dominated position' within the field of power but a 'dominant position' within the broader education field. The university field is itself internally differentiated by the cultural/economic capital struggle, with the administrative functions being closer to the economic capital end and the teaching and research being closer to the cultural capital end. This is shown by the location of the projects. The projects are located towards the positive economic capital end of the horizontal axis because the main aim is for the university to gain economic capital. This depiction would vary of course with the different activities of the various sectors of the university.

Rectangle 4 represents the commercial enterprise field; this is situated in the upper right hand quadrant and rests almost entirely at the economic end of the quadrant. The private sector project management companies and private language teaching wings of universities are of a central concern to this study. P2, a revenue-raising venture for the university, is situated in the intersection between the university and the commercial enterprise fields. The project is in the lower section of the commercial enterprises field.

The aid agency field is represented by rectangle 5 and is in a slightly more intermediary position than the commercial enterprise field. This internal differentiation represents the practices of aid in terms of its obvious economic imperatives but also its smaller commitment to educational activities that are not administered by project management companies. P1 is situated in the intersection between the aid agency and the university fields.

The mapping of the fields in this way is not the only possible way to lay claim to the dynamics of the field, but the diagram is a useful way to demonstrate the inter-relatedness of the powerful institutions involved in international language education projects. Fields vary then according to their respective proximity to the competing poles in the field of power. At one end stands economic activity, where economic activity predominates. At the opposite end lie the teaching and learning activities centred around cultural capital.

Stakeholder interests: The university

In Figure 2.2, the universities are shown to hold a mult-dimensional position in the field and represent a myriad of interests. The institutions themselves are not unitary entities; the lecturing staff is distinct from faculty management which is distinct again from the university management. Also within the universities there are private entrepreneurial centres and organisations which bid independently for projects and contracts. Australian university staff spoke of the institution's persistent quest for economic capital and the impact of this aim on project work. A feature of the field is that the language education sectors of the universities are engaged in an area of work in which they have had little experience and yet they seek to hold a dominant position in the field.

Lee, an Australian academic, described the interests of the major stakeholders in P1 as a struggle between the dominant Australian-based players' economic interests and the educational goals of the project. The faculty project staff group consisted of a small number of lecturers in the faculty who were interested in working in the particular region. The interests of the different players cannot be neatly delineated; the faculty staff, while not holding overt pecuniary interests, had interest in accumulating other forms of capital which could be converted to economic capital. For example, two-thirds of the university staff working on this project were either casual (hired for the specific teaching duties on the project) or contract staff (on 1–3-year contracts with the faculty). These non-tenured lecturers were perhaps hopeful that the cultural and social capital perceived to be accumulated by working on the project placed them in a favourable position for academic tenure. This depended of course on the recognition of this accumulated capital as valuable. The faculty management clearly had interests to profit from the project. Faculties in universities have had greater responsibility for raising revenue than they have had before and as it is revealed later in this chapter, its interests may well have been aligned with the project management company.

P2 presented an intriguing case in terms of 'interest'. The interests of the universities were unusually complicated. Ordinarily this would be so for one university but an added complication was the formation of the consortium. This particular way of organising, while essential for winning the tender, brought with it explicit forms of competition between the universities for the potential economic capital. The micro-politics of the design team in P2 could be described as competitiveness in collaboration. The struggle within the consortium was also complicated by the status hierarchies of universities in Australia. The member institutions were differentiated by the academic hierarchy within Australia and their own historical development. Chris, an Australian academic, gave voice to the competition between the dominant stakeholders, the competition centred around the number of students each institution would enrol. She also talked about the initial interest the universities had in this new way of organising but had doubts about whether the relationship would work:

> a lot of people when they met at the consortium were very interested just purely because it's a consortium, because they knew of no other instances where universities had worked together successfully. This may not be one.

Chris described the Australian universities' interests as partly disinterested in the economic gains, in the sense that this was a new and possibly profitable intellectual experience. She expressed serious doubts about the possible success of the project even in this early stage.

Murray (P2AM2), from P2, expressed the concern that the universities did not seem aware of the benefits in forming a consortium. Chris mentioned above that the participants were initially interested but not in the details of how the project would be implemented. This collaboration was far outside usual university practice; most commonly, universities gain benefit from the competition between themselves. The international project field is usually one characterised by struggle between universities vying for project tenders. Murray talked about how he had to 'sell' the idea to the Australian universities that it was in their interests to act as a consortium. The agency had conducted its research into what would work in this particular country and, although against the current academic tradition, insisted that the course providers would work in collaboration.

> I think it's really quite important to note that this was market analysis done in, you know, in classic market analysis terms that actually... identified needs before we even decided to launch it. So I should also say that there was a sub-theme going that we also wanted to convince Australian institutions that it was sensible and worthwhile and long term profitable operating a consortium rather than to operate individually. Because to my understanding that's the first time that's actually occurred so we wanted to demonstrate that that was possible.

Murray described a complicated field. Earlier in this chapter he had explicitly stated that the project is to 'enhance Australia's interests' in Japan. It was more in the Australian Government's rather than the universities' interests that they formed a consortium. It was a way of selling Australia, the regional diversity and wholeness of the nation. In the tender document, the successful bidders had to demonstrate a regional spread across Australia. On further analysis this regional spread perhaps gave another dimension to the project. Australia was a prime tourist destination for Japanese people, and an educational project that also offered a range of locations around Australia had added value. In designing this project the AGA hoped to gain more recognition of the educational capacity Australia offered.

The interests of a university may be perceived to be different with aid-funded projects and fee-based projects. Lee (P1/2AU2) observed that there was a more pragmatic relationship with the fee-based project: he described the different interests and tensions of working in aid-funded projects and fee-based projects:

> a lot [of people] are working in the development context because they actually care for humanitarian qualities and equity and social issues. And so you have this moral, if that's the right word or ethical dimension... And there's quite a bit of tension there. If you're running a project which has to be financially accountable from the project management view, [and]... you also really care about the people you're seeing everyday, whose lives are very, very poor financially, I felt

I had this real tension. I was supposed to be balancing the books and save money here [in Australia] and I could see that over there, there's a real need. I think that probably for me, that power differential was the biggest characteristic when you compare to . . . fee-for-service courses. I think the fee-based project tends to be more of a direct relationship between the university and the students, it's a much more clearly marked exercise where you try to hang onto education principles.

Lee's personal values strongly resonated with the professed aims of aid agencies and development organisations in both the government and the non-government sectors. The conflict between meeting both the host country's and the faculty's economic needs was an area of tension and difficulty for him in P1. He referred to a 'power differential' in his position with P1 and it was clear that he was referring to the authority he held in the project field. He described P1 as having potential to fill a 'real need'. However, he described a more straightforward relationship with the fee-based project; his concern as an academic in P2 was about the quality of the educational content. The discourse of aid as being for 'social good' masks other significant relations in the field and the subsequent homologies within aid-funded projects and fee-based projects. The central economic relations and power differentials were very similar in both projects. Lee went on to discuss the priorities given to the 'economic profit' potential of the fee-based project. It was explicitly focused on the income it would generate; the other 'internationalisation' strategies were given a lower priority and would have to wait. Lee clearly outlined the priorities for the university.

It was fee-driven . . . The need to make money to survive, which is being imposed upon us by various federal government cuts to funding, we haven't had much choice other than to go this way in the last five or ten years. On one level, yes, it's money-driven, it's trying to get a share of the market and putting that first. I guess another side of it is that working collaboratively and trying to understand the other culture takes time and money, so that's not a desirable choice for the faculty.

The universities embody the economic motive of the field; this aspect is also complicated: some universities are better positioned than others to profit from so-called internationalisation strategies. Another possible map is one that positions different universities in relation to each other; this would make explicit the power differentials in the field.

Level 2: The Map of Relations between the Agents in the Field

This level of analysis maps the field of the international projects themselves. Such a map shows the structural connections between those involved, for example, the students, the teachers, the teacher trainers, the expatriate 'experts', the 'counterpart' trainers, the MOE personnel, the Australian university staff and managers, the project management personnel and the relevant Australian Government representatives. It is in this level of analysis where I identify the dynamics of the field in a Bourdieuian sense. I map out the objective structure of relations between the positions occupied by agents who compete for the legitimate forms of specific authority within each project. What are the forms of capital in the fields? How are they distributed relative to each other? Using the Bourdieuian analytical tools I am able to identify the dominant and subordinate positions of participants in the field and also identify the positions that the research participants hold. Such relations therefore occur at the personal and institutional level and at the formal and informal levels. The medium for these relations can be understood in terms of economic, cultural and social capital.

Figures 2.3a and 2.3b illustrate the respective positions of the interviewees and other project positions in relation to the axes of economic and cultural capital for each project. As in the diagrams for Level 1 analysis of the IELEP field to other fields, this is only one way of viewing the relationships between the agents in the field. The lines of communication and involvement are represented by either full or broken lines. The full lines represent a direct relationship in the project field whereas the broken lines are where the relations are more tenuous or distant. The representation of these relationships is drawn from my notes as research participant and from the discussions with project participants. Another way that such an analysis at this level could be approached is to take an individual project participant and identify where they are placed in the field, who and what they are connected to, their educational and work trajectories and their relations in the field. This could give more detailed information about which attributes of a project participant lead to certain positionings in the field but due to the necessary confidentiality of the interviewees this was not done.

Stakeholders: Agents in the field

The participants/stakeholders of each project are located in Figures 2.3a and 2.3b, and below I outline their designated roles within the

(a) Project 1

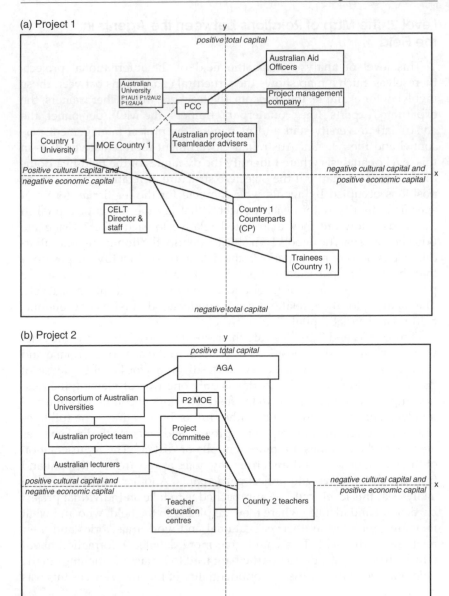

Figure 2.3 The map of relations between the agents in the field. (a) Level 2 analysis of Project 1 (Laos). (b) Level 2 analysis of Project 2 (Japan)

projects. (I choose to use the terms stakeholders, participants and agents interchangeably throughout the remainder of the book.) These profiles should familiarise readers with the main players who will be telling their stories in the rest of the book.

In P1, Laos, the participants (agents in Bourdieuian terms) were: host-country MOE staff, host-country university staff, Australian university staff, Australian project team members, host-country project staff, host-country course participants (teachers and teacher educators), host-country school students, project management company staff and Australian Government aid agency staff.

In P2, Japan, participants were: host-country MOE staff, host-country university staff, Australian university staff, Australian project team members, host-country project team members, host-country teachers, host-country school students and Australian Government agency staff.

The agents in the international language education project field are referred to as 'stakeholders' in current project discourse. Stakeholder describes all those who have a 'stake' in the project. The notion of the stakeholder is a complex and slippery one and can be easily manipulated, as demonstrated in the literature on projects (Coleman, 1992, 1995; Holliday, 1994; Kenny & Savage, 1997; Morris, 1996; Murphy, 1999; Phelan & Hill, 1998; Phillipson, 1992b; Pottier, 1993; World Bank, 1998). Stakeholders and their relationships, while slippery, are also broad ranging, Kaplan (2000) depicts a complex web of politicised relationships within the field of ELT. His depiction is equally applicable to the IELEPs in this study. His list of stakeholders clearly demonstrates 'crisscrossed power lines' within the field of the projects and also shows the relationships of stakeholders within and across national boundaries. The relationships in the field of ELT (according to Kaplan) are numerous and varied: teachers and students; students and students; students and parents; teachers and parents; schools and parents; teachers and teachers; teachers and administrators; administrators and the state; schools and communities; schools and society; languages and students, parents, teachers, administrators, schools, communities and societies; teaching materials, curricula, assessment instruments and the individuals who create and buy and use such things (Kaplan, 2000: vii–viii).

Key stakeholders in P1: Laos

The host-country staffing is complicated. Participants in P1, in particular the host-country staff, commented on the specific issues related to the Lao teacher training and programme coordination staff. Part of the contribution of the host country to the 'bilateral' project was in the form of trained personnel. Lao participants in the project were mostly designated as 'counterparts'; the particularities and peculiarities about this designation are discussed more fully in Chapter 4. What is relevant here is that there was an ongoing struggle between the Lao MOE and the Australian project team about which Lao staff would be attached to the project. On the one hand, the (Australian) project management wanted the host-country MOE to arrange for their most skilled and qualified people to be involved at a management level in the project but, on the other, these same people were to be counterparts of the Australian team. A key point to note is that if a trained person is assigned a role as a counterpart that immediately places them in a less powerful position in the project.

The Australian project management expected to draw on trained staff but Lao tertiary institutions and teachers colleges also needed these staff to manage and deliver their programmes. The personnel (trained teachers and teacher trainers) in question were a scarce resource and there was intense struggle over the staff; and this struggle gave much insight into how particular agents dominate the project field. The struggle also drew on tensions within the host country's MOE. Each post-secondary and tertiary institution was under a different MOE department and from the way that both Lao and Australian participants described their experience of working with these institutions and departments, it appeared that the departments were in competition with each other for resources and the autonomy to determine how they ran their education services.

The departments may not have appreciated the aid project dictating how their staff were to be deployed. The departments may also have wanted to protect their staff as many did not want to work with the project (see section on Unwilling participants). The project's work practices did not allow them to fulfill other work obligations and, if they were seconded beyond a certain amount of time, they might have lost their MOE positions. This reluctance on the part of the country's lecturers and teachers was not taken seriously by the project management. Sol, a host-country project participant in P1, expressed her concern about working with the project:

> One problem that could happen for me is that if I stay too long with the project I will lose my position at the university; this is a big problem for me and I don't think the team leader understands this.

In P1, the Australian project team estimated that in the initial years of the project up to 40 counterpart teaching and teaching coordination Lao staff worked on various activities.

The host-country participants fulfilled one, and sometimes two, of the above roles and all were involved in the projects. They talked at length about the 'benefits' or not of the programmes for the teachers of English in both host countries. There were often conflicting comments about the impact of the programmes. What clearly emerged was a lack of attention to the school or university students and their interests in the ELT classes.

From the start the teachers had a conflict of interests; they had to attend to their substantive work commitments and there was a high expectation by the donors and providers that they would prioritise their work with the projects. There were many comments about the 'benefits' to the teachers and the cultural capital that they were assumed to have accumulated through involvement with the projects and completing the programmes. Weng (P1LM2) from P1 was a member of the teacher training department in the MOE and also a counterpart lecturer with the project. She had been an EL teacher in secondary schools and taught English at the teachers' resource centre in the evenings. She was closely involved with EL teachers' professional development and estimated that at least half of the teachers believed that their involvement with the project would be of benefit to their future careers.

An underlying assumption was that the benefits, the cultural capital offered by the project, were distributed fairly and equally. The participants bought into the game. The participants believed that the end result would lead to a more 'profitable' future, a pathway provided by having completed an Australian university ELT degree. In this sense the teachers saw themselves as participants in the broader economy of the country and its future directions.

At the level of delivering the project teacher training programmes most Lao participants perceived that the interests for the host-country teachers have been neglected. In her first response, Weng (P1LM2) was reservedly positive in her summation of the course; she saw that the teachers themselves would benefit in a number of ways but she then discussed what she saw as a gap in the work of the project, that the project did not fully grasp the interests of the participants. She expressed a concern in relation to a component of the project which produced an English curriculum that was echoed by other members of the teacher training department of the MOE. She acknowledged that the project produced a curriculum for the secondary students where one had not previously existed and that this was a much needed resource. However, she was concerned that the project had produced a curriculum but did not have a coherent and comprehensive plan for training the teachers to use it. Her department was seriously under-resourced and had the responsibility for all levels of the school system and the task of building a viable education sector.

Trong (P1LM4), a high-level official in the MOE, similarly believed that right from the beginning the project did not take into account the interests of the country's MOE. He talked about the project being limited in its design. He elaborated on this to say that the project design team did identify a need, that is, an ELT curriculum, but did not identify who was going to teach it; this is what he calls its 'weak point'. He emphasised that the training for teachers who would use the curriculum had to be carried out in the host country's teacher training institutions. The Lao teacher training department and MOE members were surprised that the project had not assisted the teacher training department to develop the infrastructure to train its own teachers. Trong said that while it was not completely misdirected and at first 'we were excited to see this project implemented, but when it came to the time, we sat down and realised that we hadn't included that part, the formal teacher training.' This dimension of project work reflected the relative positionings of the field; the teacher training department's main interest was that teachers be trained in using the book but the project's main interest was that the product was produced. In the end, the product was produced.

Sol (P1LU4), an EL teacher, raised a related issue concerning the number of teachers who were given the opportunity to gain post-graduate qualifications. She asked a lot of questions about this process and seemed to express concern that the project management had not really focused on EL teachers, noting that since the selection criteria had restricted the number of teachers, 'not many people are able to have the opportunity.' She seemed to feel that the English entry levels were too high for the regular teachers and consequently those in need had not had access to training. Weng (P1LM2) from P1 felt that the English language selection excluded particularly those teachers from outside of the main urban centres. She would have liked to see that 'they got more'.

Key stakeholders in P2: Japan

The host-country and Australian participants in P2 are difficult to map. On the Australian side many staff were involved in the larger project meetings but not in the day-to-day running of the project. The more senior academic staff were the decision makers, although this was not obvious from the ways in which the meetings were conducted. The structure of the project team was similar to the one of P1 in that there was a director, a project manager and a curriculum development team, but the similarity ended there. Each project had its unique characteristics and P2 spanning four tertiary institutions was a complex terrain.

The teachers from P2 made poignant comments about their professional development needs and pointed to ways that teachers were already serving their own professional interests outside of the project parameters. This indicates that early in the project's life there was already a clash of interests. Lan (P2LT4) below referred to what she saw as a general improvement in the skills of EL teachers but not a commensurate increase in their oral English proficiency. She discussed a training innovation which she had set up:

> ...in my school we had 10 English teachers last year and I was in charge of ALTs [Assistant Language Teachers] so I thought it would be interesting to have just English classes for English teachers. So I scheduled two English classes a week and I asked the other English teachers to come but they are kind of afraid of coming because they are not used to listen to and speak English. They don't want to be embarrassed. So maybe like three or four teachers usually came.

Lin (P2LT1) also believed that the skill level of teachers was more advanced than in previous times and that teachers were highly motivated to undertake professional development. She saw more teachers seek information about teaching though the grammar translation approach was the preferred approach for many; she did not make a judgement as to the desirability or not of this style of teaching.

She continued to discuss the skills and needs of teachers:

> teachers use English in the classroom more than before and they know some knowledge of communicative teaching and some teachers belong to some study groups. But, I say that the level is getting higher and higher... Actually I'm in one of the study groups; there are seven members in the group.

Lin was measured in her estimation of how much English teachers have improved but pointed out that the teachers were motivated to form self-study groups and she was a member of one of these groups.

Lin was keenly aware of what did not meet EL teachers' needs and described how some IELEP projects fail; these projects were ones that included short-term visits to English-speaking countries. Lin gave three reasons as to why teachers might not be interested in these courses:

> first of all we have to take a long vacation [to do the course] and second thing we have to pay a lot and third thing is that the course is not

so highly programmed. That's why many of this country's teachers don't go overseas for short-term courses.

She was quite critical of those courses that included a lot of tourist-like activities:

> how shall I say it is OK? . . . there are a lot of sight-seeing activities in the course so if we really want to study something it's too short to study. It's not so serious.

Shor (P2LU2), a university professor from P2, a widely published writer of ELT texts for Japanese teachers, described teachers' interests in professional development:

> there's the many individual English teachers who have tried to brush up their abilities by attending the special circle which was organised by themselves. I mean, their own group. The senior high school teachers living in the vicinities gather together once a week and find someone to speak English like an instructor and pay maybe a small amount per month each so 8 or 10 person gather.

The teachers from P2 discussed how teachers in Japan cannot really afford the time and money to undertake external study, especially overseas study. Another factor which deterred teachers in Japan from investing in further qualifications was that a higher degree, the accumulation of cultural capital, did not change their position in the field, that is, they were not necessarily offered a promotion or other benefits within the school education department. Promotions were most usually gained through seniority. However, Ken (P2LU1), an MOE official from P2, believed that the ministry will change and soon recognise the value of higher education qualifications.

Ken (P2LU1) identified competing and conflicting interests between EL teachers, Australian project goals and the Japanese MOE in relation to the issue of qualifications and international study; his quote below seemed to contradict his previously stated optimism about changes within the MOE. The Australian project was predicated on the belief that Japanese EL teachers, supported by the MOE, had an interest in gaining an Australian higher degree. However, according to Ken, the MOE did not want the teachers to gain a formal qualification. He gave an example of an international EL professional development programme organised between the MOE and the Learning Council (this British organisation is also referred to in Chapter 3):

> These six months programs and twelve months programs are what we call tailor made programs and they do not fit into the existing courses of the participating countries. So even though they (the

teachers) stay in Britain or America or in Australia or in New Zealand for 6 months or 12 months they are not expected to get any diplomas or any qualifications at all. And this is one of the drawbacks of the programs we have but this is what I heard from my predecessors that if you give formal qualifications to the participants then they would soon be eager to find jobs at the tertiary level.

According to Ken (P2LU1), the MOE's interests prevailed. The MOE wanted to keep the teachers in their teaching positions within the school system. If the teachers gained post-graduate qualifications then there is a possibility that they may move to more professionally and financially lucrative positions.

The self-interested teacher

One interesting proposition that emerged from the data was about the host-country teachers' self-interest in undertaking the programmes. This was frankly spoken about by ministry officials from P2. Ken (P2LU1) discussed how teachers were selected (or otherwise) for the overseas courses. He described a complex relationship between the national MOE, the provinces and city councils. He put forward an argument against making study opportunities open to all teachers. He posited an interesting view of teachers, describing a group of them as quite self-interested, wanting to improve their own skills, not necessarily those of the students:

> some of the prefectures just pick out some participants according to their own criteria because . . . In a way they are very keen on improving themselves but they are not so much interested in teaching school students so they are always interested in improving and learning new expressions, new vocabulary studying on their own but they are not keen teachers. They are not enthusiastic teachers so, if you make the whole program open to the participants and select them, maybe best users of English, then those teachers who are only interested in self improvement can be selected. And local boards of prefectures and boards of education do not like this so they select good English users and also they want to select good teachers as well.

In discussing who should be selected for professional development opportunities, I wish to explore the way particular interests were talked about. In the above extract Ken (P2LU1) depicted teachers' interests in a particular way in how they took up the beliefs and values dominant in the field (doxa) even though this may not have changed their position. Ken has already explained that, higher qualifications did not guarantee a person a high-level work position in the education field. Rather it is experience in the area or the social capital one accumulates in the particular field. But the dynamics of the field are changing, and at the time of writing, higher qualifications could possibly give access to more specialist and higher-paying positions:

It's hard to tell but still in this society . . . even though you have a MA degree or a PhD degree you may not be employed as a curriculum specialist or as a university professor. But things are changing very rapidly and especially for teachers teaching at senior high school level and teachers who are interested in applying for the programs that you develop with the consortium. They have very good English abilities and they have lots of opportunities now to improve their own English skills even in this country. They listen to the radio or use the internet. So, I think the main reason that they would apply for the program would be to improve their qualifications so in order to satisfy their interest, needs.

Similar to teachers in Laos, the teachers Ken described were keen to reposition themselves in the field. This is a key struggle in the IELEP field; the teachers' strategies to accumulate more cultural capital can be seen as an attempt to change the dynamics of the field. In one sense this struggle can indicate the desire of the teachers to 'relocate TESOL' (Kumaravadivelu, 2006: 17); a relocation of the field would necessitate repositioning of participants and a more equal distribution of resources. Yet the teachers are buying into what was offered by the dominant stakeholders, dismissing their own expertise and indigenous knowledge, engaging in the practice of self-marginalisation.

The absent stakeholder: Learners of English

The EL learners were not formally positioned in the field. A significant question underlying this story is the notion of an 'ultimate beneficiary': does this group exist and what is its composition? It was evident in the data, in particular the project documents, that those who were presumed to benefit from the improved provision of ELT are the school students. This group, with their improved English language skills, was also seen as the one which will lead the host countries into a stronger position in international relations. However, this group was conspicuously absent in the interviewees' discussions about 'interest' and 'benefits'. This stakeholder group was referred to obliquely by the MOE officials; when the officials (from both projects) discussed the increased and improved provision of ELT in the schools I can only assume they were referring to improving the students' experience and skill development. Min, a project official with the national university (P1LM3), from P1 spoke candidly about the interests of the students, 'the first priority, the student must be the first beneficiary and not the teachers. The teachers come after.'

The issue that's important here is how the purported beneficiaries of the projects' activities, the school students, articulate and negotiate their interests. Interviewees from P2 talked about a general disinterest in English language study in schools. How does a project reconcile the interests and desires of the ultimate recipients of the projects' activities with the interests of the donors and providers? This central question underlies the story as it continues its investigations of the dynamics of the field in the following chapters.

Unwilling participants

One complexity that is not often spoken about in the project literature but was raised by interviewees in this research is that some stakeholders do not work voluntarily with projects. While competing demands of multiple roles is investigated more fully in Chapter 4, it is important for the reader to be aware that not all participants shared the same degree of engagement with their assigned roles within the projects. The ministries of education in both Japan and Laos seconded teachers and teacher educators to work with the projects and a number of interviewees raised this issue in their discussions. While I cannot draw any firm conclusions on the effect of 'unwilling' participation, it clearly has impact on the way an IELEP plays itself out and bears out a central premise of this book, that the dominant agents in the IELEP field reap most of the benefits.

Morris (1996), in his examination of the tensions in bilateral aid projects in Vietnam, critiques the premise that all stakeholders have a desire for the project to 'work'. His critique uncovers a central dynamic of aid and development projects where the interests of the dominant agents subjugate the indigenous knowledge and skills of the 'recipients' while at the same requiring that the 'recipients' (through funding agreements) participate in the unequal exchange of ideas and practices. My data suggests that while each stakeholder contributes in some way to the project, they have disparate interests and for some stakeholders the success or not of a project bears no relationship to the success or otherwise of their individual involvement in the project. This was highlighted by the interviewees' (in both P1 and P2) comments about the particular ways that project stakeholders saw their role and project goals. These comments allude to how some stakeholders gain promotion or prestige from their involvement with the projects regardless of how well or otherwise they contribute to stated project goals (this is explored more fully in Chapter 4).

Level 3: Habitus in the Field of the IELEPs

The Level 2 analysis above of agents within each project shows how vastly different capital backgrounds can come together and work under a form established across and within national boundaries. Of relevance to this story is an understanding of the effect of key players' habitus in the field and to see if new arrangements such as the IELEP are replicating established configurations of resource distribution in the field. Is it a new form according to an old process or are the projects enacting change and enabling new players to accumulate capital? The rhetoric of most projects (e.g. the goal of *capacity building* in the case of P1) claims to be enabling but, as I show in subsequent chapters, redistribution of capital rarely occurs.

Bourdieu's habitus has been used extensively to investigate the tertiary context (Delamont *et al.*, 1991; Grenfell, 1996; Krais, 1996; Kramsch, 2008; Robbins, 1993, 1998). These researchers looked at the ways in which students and teachers engage in and understand the practice of their particular disciplines and the way higher education represents itself. Their research has informed my story in the way I have chosen to identify the generative aspect of habitus, how the habitus appropriate to 'play the game' in a specific field of practice has two components:

(1) the body of knowledge of regularities of problem-definition and problem-solving that is specified – in this case, the different procedures of project work;

(2) the competence of moving in a field of practice, of identifying power relations, of speaking the language (of project work) and of bringing the agent's own interests and qualifications to bear. (Krais, 1996)

Habitus allows me to investigate the ways in which stakeholders act and the interests which motivate such behaviour. It also provides clues about the ways stakeholders legitimate new ideas and respond to those non-hegemonic innovations.

Table 2.1 maps the interviewees according to the basic signifiers of age, language background, formal education, work position outside of the project, project position, gender and geographical location. These signifiers relate broadly to habitus and give some information about the interviewees' dispositions; for example, dispositions inculcated through particular educational histories, work experiences or positions. A significant feature of this map is that most of the participants have multiple

Table 2.1 Interviewees – basic signifiers of habitus

	Host-country interviewees		Australian staff
	Project 1 – Total 12 participants	Project 2 – Total 9 participants	Projects 1 and 2 – Total 4 participants
Age	6 aged 40–50yrs 2 aged 30–40yrs	7 aged 40–50yrs 2 aged 20–30yrs	3 aged 40–50yrs 1 aged 30–40 yrs
Language background	10 – Lao language (L1) 10 – bilingual – Eng 7 – bilingual (Lao, English and another language) 2 – English (L1)	8 – Japanese (L1) 9 – bilingual – Eng 1 – English (L1)	4 – English (L) 1 – bilingual (Lao) 1 – bilingual (Japanese) 1 – elementary proficiency (Lao and Japanese)
Formal Education	6 – MA TESOL (from Australia) 2 – Grad Diploma TESOL (from Australia)	6 – Diploma Education 2 – Master's degree	8 Master's degree in TESOL and/or Education
Substantive work positions	6 MOE officials 4 university lecturers 2 project team members (Aust)	4 school teachers 2 university lecturers 2 MOE officials 1 AGA official	4 university lecturers
Positions in projects*	4 MOE project coordinating committee member 4 project counterpart staff 2 local university project liaison staff	4 MOE project committee members/project liaison 4 project targeted teachers 1 AGA official	4 project team members
Gender	8 female 4 male	2 female 7 male	3 female 1 male
Geographical	12 city	4 provincial city 5 state capital city	4 Australian state capital cities

* Some participants have multiple roles in the project.

roles in the ELT field; for example, an MOE official would have once been a teacher of English in a secondary school, is now a part-time teacher of English and also a member of the project team. It is important also to recognise a hierarchy of habitus and this is how habitus shifts according to what role the agent is taking up. That is, while some dispositions may be more powerful in some contexts, for example, in P1, a Lao ministry official has a dominant position among Lao staff, this hierarchical position does not necessarily transfer to the IELEP and this project member's habitus may not be recognised.

Table 2.1 demonstrates a remarkable homology in terms of age, educational qualifications and positions of employment between the groups of interviewees (a full description of the interviewees is given in Appendix). The major differences between the groups seem to lie in the linguistic skills held by participants from P1, gender balance in P2, age balance in P2 and that half of P2 interviewees live outside of the state capital cities. However, on the latter point, the provincial cities in this country are large, industrialised cities.

This is only a snapshot of the habitus in the field, yet I contend that the individuals detailed here, according to the basic signifiers of habitus, would share similar characteristics to other project participants. Of major importance to the central theme of this story is the fact that the project coordinating committee representatives and government officials from P1 and P2 have similar attributes with regard to age, education and positions of employment. However, as my analysis of power relations unfolds throughout the rest of the book, it becomes clear that the accumulated capital held by the Australian individuals in this group (project coordination/government officials) is legitimated and they occupy a dominating position in the field (see Figures 2.3a and 2.3b).

The interview data exemplified the premise of this chapter: the notion of beneficiary is multi-faceted and the identification of the beneficiary is dependent upon the interests of the particular stakeholder. The striking feature about the project case studies is the unabashed way in which the interests of the implementers operate to dominate the procedures of the project. These interests have not necessarily related to the project goals or outcomes and are not necessarily been a result of a rigorous appraisal process. Bourdieu, in his book *Practical Reason* (1998), claims that a disinterested position is not possible, that the critical issue is the repartitions of power which are determined by the accumulation or not of various forms of capital.

How would Bourdieu see the particular interests shown here operating in the field? My reading of the data reveals that the accumulation of symbolic capital by those in dominant or decision-making positions expresses their interests in grand terms: the nation's interests are central; the project management company while meeting the nation's interests are getting their cut; those agents who accumulate little capital, symbolic or otherwise, in this case the teachers, are much more self-interested. The students' interests, which in the project rhetoric are positioned as the ultimate beneficiaries, are not represented.

The above analysis exposed that the interests are not what they are said to be, that the benefits accrued through the project work may bear no relationship to the beneficiaries assumed in the project's goals. In the light of this analysis all stakeholders are beneficiaries to some extent. All stakeholders have interests; it just depends how well their interests are negotiated and represented. Benefits accrued through the work of the project may better position stakeholders in future international or national markets.

The analysis and diagrammatic illustration of the multiple fields, agents and interests operating in both projects presented in this chapter hint at the potential for clashes/struggles to ensue. In Chapter 3, I outline some key struggles that frame the IELELP field and explore how the notions of success and failure emerge through these struggles.

Chapter 3
Struggles in the Game of the IELEP

The story now focuses on the overarching struggles in the field. In Bourdieu's terms, a field is a site of struggle; it is clear in the IELEP that the struggles are around the main forms of capital: linguistic, cultural, social and economic. These forms of largely symbolic capital are realised through language, qualifications, connections and money. I turn to some pervasive sites of struggle to emerge from the study, economic capital and winning the projects and clashes over the valued resources in the field: (1) forms of capital and exchange rates and (2) struggles over cultural capital in Project 2. Subsequent chapters will then examine struggles around language and culture in detail.

All the struggles in the IELEPs underlie the themes of success and failure. What accounts for a successful project? I navigate through the complexities of success and failure and address the ways in which a project may or may not be perceived as successful by particular stakeholders.

Different stakeholders may feel different levels of ease about their participation in the project, and this is not simply due to whether the participant is from the donor/provider's country or not. Stakeholders may have cultural capital outside of the project from being known as language specialists, ministry officials, teaching professionals or prominent university lecturers or professors but these same qualities that brought cultural capital outside may carry no status within the project. Students may respect the professional qualities or the standing the project stakeholders have in their particular discipline or area of work and these qualities might be essential for bringing in students, but they cannot necessarily be traded for cultural capital inside the project field.

A pivotal struggle in both projects is around who defines the value of the capital one holds. In general the effort to convert one's specific cultural capital through symbolic capital to economic capital may, on the one hand, be a fruitless exercise or, on the other, very rewarding depending on which field and what capital one starts with. An obvious example from this research is the cultural capital host-country teachers hold in their teaching qualifications; by their very definition the projects invalidate the host countries' teachers' training in order for the cultural capital held by the Australian providers to be more highly valued (or validated) and to be converted into economic capital through the activities of the projects. Interestingly, the reverse, that is, taking one's economic capital and trying to convert and exchange your way into a field, is much more likely to meet with unmitigated success. For example, the Australian project management company participants (in both projects) do not hold a lot of cultural capital in the form of academic qualifications but they do hold the economic capital which accumulates the symbolic power in the field. Clearly, economic capital is highly significant in project work and in this research operated somewhat differently in the two projects: the economic capital held by the donors in Project 1, the aid-funded project, delineated the power relations in this project.

Because the IELEPs are bounded by the rhetoric of 'partnership and collaboration' and the recognition of the host-country contributions, one might assume that the linguistic capital accumulated by the bilingual project participants would place these participants in a powerful position in the field. But as I reveal later in this story (Chapter 5), this is not the case. The participants' mother tongue (L1) is invalidated and the dominant language, English, is validated (Skutnabb-Kangas, 1998, 2000); the value of one's linguistic capital is far greater if you are a native speaker of English; this then accumulates a greater amount of symbolic capital which converts to economic capital. Table 2.1 in Chapter 2 demonstrates that the participants have similar attributes of habitus but their position in the field was determined by the unequal amounts of capital they accumulated.

Struggle to Win: Project Tenders, Bids and Proposals

In all respects the IELEP is an economic exercise. The central activity, selling English language, corporatises and commodifies ELT. Phillipson (2003) paints an insidious picture of the ELT field as he describes its 'narcotic power' and as one with 'major commercial interests involved in the global English language industry' (p. 16). The central premise of this book is that the design and implementation of IELEPs are governed by pecuniary interests and a key struggle is how universities, project management companies and private language education providers position themselves in the field. While this story focuses on two Australian university projects, agents in the field may be transnational, multinational or national companies and universities. Economic capital is not bounded by national borders and multinational companies share regularities across these borders.

Both projects were realised through a tender process: the project teams were required to put forward proposals which demonstrated their ability to more expertly meet the goals of the proposed project than their competitors. Although the conditions and processes were different for each project, there were many similarities. Universities and companies have to demonstrate their suitability and superiority over other competitors. The competition is fierce as for the ultimate winner, the profits are substantial. The struggle to win is framed by how well the bidders know the market and their competitors and requires a significant investment of time and money. This is a field that Australian universities (as briefly described in Chapter 1) are not necessarily familiar with.

Project 1 was established under the regular conditions of the aid field. The Australian Government aid agency asked for tenders to carry the ELT project in Laos. The Metrop University partnered a private sector project management company and as partners they contributed to different sections of the proposal; the university developed the ELT education components while the company provided the management plan. The project was conceptualised as having a 'bilateral' relationship with the host country, which was intended to mean a mutually negotiated and managed project. The partners in this project were the host-country Ministry of Education (MOE), Metrop University (Australian) and an Australian project management company. The Metrop University and the project management company were highly motivated by the financial gain the project would bring to both institutions. In writing the proposal for Project 1, the writers were keen to demonstrate their knowledge and expertise of the host-country needs but in the end it was the financial management and expediency plans that won the bid.

Project 2 was established under a similar process. The Australian Government Agency (hereafter AGA) in Japan was involved with many public and private sectors. Its main aim was to encourage trade and international relations between Australia and Japan. The AGA put out a project tender asking for proposals to deliver post-graduate EL teacher training qualifications to Japanese English secondary school teachers. The tender document required that a national consortium of Australian universities produce the proposal and clearly outline how the project would deliver the courses on a national basis. A consortium was formed between three universities and a private language teaching college (see Chapters 1 and 2 for more detail).

The proposal for Project 2, while significantly different in terms of sources of funding from the aid-based project, was similar in terms of the expected recipients and teaching traditions. The proposal reflected the concerns the main academic writers had for high-quality ELT and social justice issues: access to the programmes, concerns for the students, importance of contextualising materials and suitability of approaches. The proposal promised that the subjects offered to Project 2 country teachers of English would be developed with their particular needs in mind. A unique feature was the proposed inclusion of bilingual materials and English language focus activities at the post-graduate certificate level. This meant that key terminology and theoretical concepts would be translated into Japanese. The proposed programmes were innovative in terms of the pathways and options available and the process was creative in the sense that three universities and a private sector language college were forging collaborative relationships and pooling intellectual resources.

While the dynamics of the two projects in this study were similar, some aspects of the implementation process were necessarily different in the aid and fee-based projects; in the latter, market forces more explicitly impact on the approach taken to setting up the project activities. Murray talked about the way the field worked and effective implementation procedures for the fee-based project (Project 2). His strategy for implementation and the importance of timing and quality of the product was based upon the experience of developing and implementing numerous projects in Japan. His suggested strategies for delivering a high-quality project and appropriate timing ran counter to the Australian consortium's timelines and project production. Contrary to what was specified in the proposal, the consortium members wanted to run with their existing programmes and, from Murray's account, were mainly concerned about enrolling students. The consortium members prioritised the accumulation of economic capital over the ethnographic advice of a key stakeholder in the project. At this point the struggle intensified as the different stakeholder interests became clearer.

Murray detailed the steps he took in thinking through the implementation of a project. Murray (P2AM1) explained the thought given to the process:

in the delivery of anything like this there's a couple of factors that run in the background . . . when we're considering any sort of project. One is, what's the competition doing. I know I sound overly sort of private sector oriented or but I believe that we've got to aggressively pursue the projects that we've engaged in so that we achieve results that add to Australia's interest in the Australia–Japan relationship. What can we do that's different that allows us to stand out and allows the product to be highlighted? That's the first consideration.

In the next extract he contextualised the project in the broader market place. He discussed what external factors may be putting pressure on the particular field and what strategies one needs to take in implementing a project:

> Second is, what's happening in the market place in terms of market dynamics? The debate that we have running at the moment in this country about English Language teaching in schools is the typical sort of dynamic that I am referring to. But it would be almost foolish to try and roll it (the project) out while a debate about language teaching is running in this country. It is far better to try and influence the debate and then present the product as a solution to the problems identified in the debate. So I think understanding market dynamics is really very important.

Murray identified the timing of the project as one of the key strategies in the implementation process. He expressed concern that the universities were not necessarily sensitive to the dynamics of the market place, for example, the timing of when a new course is introduced to the potential students. Are the students available to start a new course? Has the product been assessed and presented in a near perfect state?

Murray then gave an example of what he perceived to be a success-ful implementation process. His foundation had developed a teacher's kit, for teaching about Australian society and geography, designed for all Japanese secondary schools. He talked about how he considered the various external factors; he explained why he sent it to schools in the third week of the new school year. The first and second weeks are full of administrative and organisational tasks for teachers, so there is no time to generate interest in a new teaching product. He then explained how the launch will take place a month after the product has been in schools; this will give teachers a chance to try out the teaching kit. Murray described the elements and processes of successful project implementa-tion and while this is described within a fee-based context it is a useful framework to consider for an aid-based project. He was focused on the context and understands the issues facing teachers and the MOE in Japan.

What insights can we gain from this struggle? The clashes were clearly between the dominant stakeholders, the Australian universities and the AGA, and they were over two issues: (1) money and (2) project imple-mentation strategies. In this particular case, pertinent ethnographic advice was available from the provider; why was it ignored? An astounding feature of this IELEP was the extent that it conformed to a well-documented regularity of the IELEP (and other international education type project) field: ethnographic advice is readily available but the pursuit of economic interests blinds the dominant agents to its importance.

Struggle over Resources in the Field: Forms of Capital and Exchange Rates

The amount of capital one has (regardless of type, that is, the vertical axis of a field) (see Chapter 2, Figures 2.3a and 2.3b) converts to a relative amount of power, which can then be converted into economic capital. The transferability of capital and the 'exchange rates' between different kinds of capital are a focus of struggle in themselves. Capital is never absolute: the value of capital varies according to the particular situation or the ways of seeing it. For example, in Project 1 the course participants, from the project management's perspective, may be viewed as holding negative economic capital (in terms of money) and low or negative cultural capital (i.e. low English language and perceived low teaching skills). However, from another view, the course participants hold the 'potential' (this converts capital) for positive economic capital as the project companies and universities were funded for the purpose of their ELT training.

As one would expect in this area of work, the accumulation of economic capital is a particularly powerful stake and many of the struggles in the project field are over the accumulation of this form of capital. This struggle was referred to repeatedly in the data, particularly in relation to Project 1, which was firmly situated in the aid and development context. References to this struggle included the issue about disparate financial situations of the host teachers and the expatriate advisers. Many of the participants from this project made the point that there was difficulty in meeting some of the project goals because the host-country participants, teachers and teacher trainers needed to work outside of their primary job in order to survive and could not devote the time that is perhaps needed to the project activities (this is a reason why the project might misbehave). These comments resonate with Peter Medgyes' (2000) description of the different economic realities of host-country teachers in a British Council project in Hungary:

> Many of these experts have been employed under British Council terms and conditions, which seem to us to be fairly generous, and have been able to give their full attention to their institutional or

project related obligations. In the meantime, teachers in my own institution and, I guess, throughout the region, are so poorly paid that they have to hold down two or even three jobs simply in order to earn a living. As a consequence, they regard their main job as a part-time occupation too. As soon as they've done their classes, they're off. You can't build an institution on the dedication of its employees alone. Certainly not in the long run. You've got to pay them according to the level of their commitment. But this is wishful thinking in Hungarian universities for the time being. (Bolitho & Medgyes, 2000: 381)

Strategies to gain economic capital underpin the IELEP field; this is often more overt in aid-funded projects. Projects such as the British council one described above, the Lao IELEP and others referred to in this study abound with stories of how struggles for economic capital delineate the field. As mentioned earlier, aid-funded IELEPs are most often located in poor countries, and the project is a source of income to host-country and expatriate participants; however, from the start, economic capital is unevenly distributed. The story Peter Medgyes recounts in the extract above speaks of a disturbing regularity in the IELEP field; the example of disparity in income is an explicit process of marginalisation (Kumaravadivelu, 2006).

Fee-based project fields attract investors; in this case study, it was Australian universities. In other parts of the world, universities may originate from the USA, the UK, New Zealand or Germany (to name a few); the motivation is to offer courses to international students at a vast cost. Host-country students come from relatively wealthy or poor backgrounds; those from poor backgrounds have often left a huge debt in their home country (Marginson, 1997b). Struggles over economic capital take the forms of competition between universities to attract students: students demand for quality, support, assistance and career aspirations and are pitted against the institutional regulations and regularities. Another is the struggle within the university, among faculties and staff, to accumulate the economic profit.

Struggles over Cultural Capital in Project 2

Agents in the IELEP struggle to accumulate cultural capital that demonstrates their accomplishment, and this is able to be transferred to other parts of the field or other fields. In this story the Japanese MOE was driving change in the EL curriculum, particularly in the areas of method and content; the AGA was providing a product. These key agents at times clashed with each other and their struggles with the universities, teachers and students delineated the field.

In Project 2 the project products were designed for Japanese secondary EL teachers, with a focus on methodology, improving the skills of the teacher. My discussions with interviewees revealed a complexity that is not really addressed by the project design documents, project proposals or implementation documents. From the interview accounts, the MOE in Project 2 desired that teachers introduce more oral language into the classroom to improve the students' speaking skills. To do this the MOE wanted teachers to use more 'communicative language teaching' (CLT) methods. However, the compulsory university entrance exams tested mainly reading and writing; a limited listening component was included by some private universities. The students wanted the English language skills to pass the exams; hence they wanted a focus on written English, not what the project has been designed to do. Further there was variable interest in studying English among the students; the motivation appeared to be influenced by the educational, economic and social class of the students. Students in high-status secondary schools had a better chance of succeeding in the university entrance exams and were therefore more motivated to study English. These high-status schools had less interest in changing their teaching approach/methodology as their focus was on teaching to the university entrance exams. From the interview accounts from Project 2 and my own observations, the lower-status schools were more open to adopting a communicative approach (as described by the EL teachers) with a focus on spoken language. However, the students' motivation to study English was lower than in the higher-status schools and the teachers, while very interested in innovations in teaching methods, were less confident about their English proficiency.

A general response from the interviews with Project 2 Japanese teachers of English was that the teachers' skills in EL teaching were sufficient; they were well trained to teach. The skill that needed to be addressed by the project was that of English language proficiency. This presented an inherent difficulty for the project. One of the components was focused on English language development but, as mentioned in the previous chapter, most teachers would probably seek language proficiency courses in-country. These were probably less expensive and more accessible (among other benefits). Yet this area of professional development was of immense importance to foreign language teachers and I suspect the project was trying to reflect its awareness of the needs of English teachers in this context by including this component. Improving and maintaining proficiency in the target language are consistently identified as two of the major professional development needs of foreign language teachers in Australia and I would suggest that this need was similar for foreign language teachers elsewhere.

The Japanese MOE (in Project 2) did see the students as one of the ultimate beneficiaries, in terms of improved language skills, and therefore had the students' interests at heart. However, the teachers interviewed were much more aware of what benefits may be available to teachers (as discussed in Chapter 2). In their conversations most teachers felt that they were more than competent in preparing students for their future needs, which, for the majority of students, was to pass the university entrance exam (mainly written).

Lan (P2LT4) from Project 2 stressed that Japanese teachers know how to teach the English that they know their students need. She talked about how her society has had a long tradition of teaching English in a specific way, using the grammar translation approach. She also emphasised a point that many of the Project 2 interviewees made: students do not need to use English outside of the classroom and because it is not necessary to use it socially, they do not understand how to use it as a means of communication. Students and parents wanted to study the type of English that will be tested in the university entrance exams.

Lin (P2LT1), also from Project 2, discussed what Australian lecturers needed to know about the country's education system to make the course relevant:

> They have to know about the country's education system ... Most of the high school students will take entrance examinations to the universities and in the entrance examinations universities ask their students a lot of grammatical questions, compositions and reading comprehension ... I want Australian lecturers to understand the system and let us know how to teach the students to use English as a tool.

She echoed similar statements by other interviewees from Project 2. This of course was a multi-dimensional situation. Schools must necessarily be responsive to the MOE, and from my observations and data it appeared that there was a lot of pressure for schools to perform better in preparing students for examinations. At the same time, various Japanese universities proposed to revise their examinations to involve more communicative skills, and it looked like this would happen. Along with these purported changes were the reported experiences that teachers have in schools and the types of professional development courses that may interest them. Clearly what the interviewees were saying is that many of the courses offered by foreign universities did not take their teaching context into account, specifically the issue of why many of their country's students were studying English.

Yet the Australian focus was on selling their product – a product that focused on CLT with an oral component, despite contrary needs outlined above. As Murray (P2AM1), Director of the AGA, Project 2, said, 'we have this product – this is what we will promote – we will do this in spite of what the teachers say they need.' The Australian universities had undertaken minimal investigation of the needs of teachers and we can see by the comments of the auspicing body (AGA) that it really had no role in pushing these universities to find out more for as far as the auspicing body was concerned the project had met its goal.

At the time of this study English was a compulsory subject in secondary school and university in Japan and the MOE had plans to introduce English into the primary curriculum in the near future. The teachers in Project 2 felt that upgrading their qualifications would benefit them for their future positions as ELT teachers. These teachers, when they discussed their students' interest in English, presented a diverse student body. There were students who were in the position to travel to English-speaking countries, but in general the teachers felt that the majority of their students had little desire to study English other than for the university entrance exams. Lan (P2LT4) below acknowledged that she had a group of high-achieving students who were very interested in studying English, but in other parts of her interview she had stated that this was not a common situation:

> My students are interested in English, but I have the best students – a lot of them spend their holidays in English-speaking countries and will probably attend a language school in the US or England before they go to university. For students in the lower classes or the not so good schools it is different, they do not see the need for English other than to pass the exams. They do not think it is important; it is a difficult subject and not too interesting for them.

The interviews with the Japanese ministry officials revealed their interest in the content of what the Australian universities had to offer teachers. It was interesting at this point to recognise that very little discussion had occurred between the providers, the Australian universities, and the Japanese MOE.

> I am unsure of exactly what the programs will be . . . there is now a lot of pressure for this country's teachers to upgrade their qualifications.

In this society, experience is highly regarded; even with high academic qualifications a person may not be employed. But now things are changing and teachers are interested in improving qualifications and most want to study for an MA. (Ken P2LU1)

The ministry officials' interviews produced a complex picture of the beneficiary; the MOE was undertaking a process of immense curriculum change. In particular, the English language curriculum was being rewritten to reflect current policies of internationalisation which had been interpreted as the increase of English language skills (Hashimoto, 2000). In Japan the nature of the English language curriculum had largely been determined by the university entrance exams (Gorsuch, 1999; Okada, 1999), which focused on reading and writing/translation skills. The curriculum in turn influenced the type of teaching in EFL classrooms. The ministry was driving the universities to change their exams to include oral/aural tests which would then necessitate the teaching of more oral communication skills. Ken (P2LU1) invalidated the Japanese school and university teachers' knowledge and skills in the area of examination writing and development; he suggested that the teachers would not be able to write an exam to test communicative skills. His hope was that the project would provide the skills to write new examinations:

> ... the thing is that senior high teachers and university professors don't know alternative ways of making problems in exams for senior high teachers. Most of them don't know the alternative way of teaching. For example, most of them say they are interested in studying the communicative approach but they are not well versed with the new ideas. So, even though they criticise the university entrance examinations, they can't provide alternative exams. . . . So, the main point is to for you to provide what is the ideal examination in terms of communicative approach . . . how we can improve the present university programs toward in the direction of more communicative problems.

Ken disagreed with the views put earlier by Lan and other participants from the same project. He did not depict teachers as competent in EL teaching methodology and as only in need of better English proficiency. He felt strongly that teachers needed to have a much better understanding of ways of teaching English and how to test students' communicative proficiency.

In terms of who will benefit from the Australian university project, the MOE perceived that the increase in English language teaching skills would ultimately assist in the development of this country's internationalisation process. The MOE officials presented a demographic scenario similar to other industrialised countries: in general the population is aging, fewer students are entering schools, there are fewer younger teachers and for those aging teachers there is little motivation to change the content and method of teaching English. In the near future teachers will need to upgrade qualifications to meet the MOE requirements. The MOE was encouraged by the Australian donor to believe that the Australian universities' project would provide appropriate training.

The intriguing aspect of the above comments from the perspective of implementing a project is how the interests of the various stakeholders are represented and negotiated. The interests of the in-country Australian Government body (AGA) did not align themselves with the interests of the Australian universities who were providing the product. What was particularly worthy of note about the AGA's position was its almost cynical attitude towards the universities and their field of expertise. The AGA had the in-country expertise, the Director was bilingual and had extensive networks in a range of fields both private and public sector. The universities, or at least at the level of the project staff, seemed unaware of the interests of the AGA.

Murray (P2AM1) from Project 2 clearly identified the Australian Government as beneficiary. He surmised that the success of the project was determined by how much it was able to raise the perceived quality of higher education in Australia and generate economic capital for Australia:

> As I was explaining to you earlier, the AGA's objective in this particular activity is not to improve the standard of English Language teachers in this country. Our objective is to demonstrate the excellence of the Australian Higher Education sector and we believe that the mechanism best suited to do that is the mechanism of high demand in this country and relatively high quality supply in Australia. [And] when you do those sums, you either come down to medicine, particularly some of the specialities of medicine, or English language.

The AGA wished to construct the Australian higher education sector as a source of cultural capital for Japanese students. It wanted to attract more Japanese students to the higher education market and could only do this if the quality of the institutions is seen to be equal to those in the USA and in the UK. The Japanese MOE was similarly in the game to gain cultural capital that would continue to 'internationalise' the education programmes within the school sector. This struggle over ELT qualifications as the valuable stake deepens the divisions of domination and subjugation within the international language education field.

Constraints in the Field

The IELEP as a site of conflict is constrained by the inequities and uneven distribution of resources; it is important to name what is difficult about operating in this particular field. The study investigated the constraints that the interviewees/agents face in their own institutional settings and/or social settings and how the constraints work to limit or enhance the way that they can operate in the project field. It is an assumption of this research that the field offers restricted choices/models for the way the agents can operate. Bourdieu (1991) gives the example of how the material structures of teaching and the physical position of the professor can structure or govern the behaviour of the agents in the field of education. The concept of a normative ideal provides an additional level of understanding how the behaviours of agents are structured and perhaps constrained within the field. The normative ideals that govern a field are absorbed through social and cultural texts (including media) circulated by the major institutions in the field; these texts help to shape the agents' way of being, their habitus in the field.

The chief constraints operating in these projects included the dominant position of economic capital and the lack of experience (cultural capital) in IELEP work. Lee (P1/2AU2) and Yvonne (P1AU1), Australian academics, were conscious of the way they were constrained by their internalised discourses (normative ideals) about how things are supposed to be from doing what they may ideally have wanted to do. For example, Lee talked about how he believed he made choices about the content, staff and delivery of the courses because he was driven by the dominant discourses in his faculty about making a profit. He felt that he would have made what he terms 'more appropriate decisions' if these discourses of profitability were not so powerful. Yvonne discussed how she was constrained from carrying out what she thought was necessary preparatory work because as an academic it was expected that she would be in control of whatever work she was assigned to do.

The operation of a field both rests upon and regenerates belief in the value of the capital at stake in the field (or an absorption of the normative ideals). In the early interviews I collected from the participants in both of the projects, though more particularly for Project 2, it was evident that the interviewees were quite new to project work; some teachers and ministry officials had been involved in projects but not these particular types of IELEPs. Also the majority of the Australian university staff had not worked in either Laos or Japan before or with an IELEP. They therefore had to use other recent experiences that they judged to be related to their activities in the projects in order to reference their opinions. These agents had not been exposed to the main social and cultural texts that defined work in an IELEP; they had to construct an ideal notion of an IELEP. A struggle that constrained work in the IELEP was how to best construct the ideal pictures of bilateral, collaborative work that was called on to guide their participation (this is a well-documented problem that often affects project workers). These participants were perhaps not yet acquainted with the valued stakes in the field. They had not developed a sense of the game as constructed by the dominant participants, or a sense of a particular reality. The participants were possibly resisting or challenging the dynamics of the field in ways that were not recognised by the dominant participants.

Notions of Success and/or Failure

The previous sections have mapped the key disparate interests and struggles in the IELEP field. Success or failure seem at first glance surprisingly transparent, that is, there are specific criteria available to clearly measure project outcomes. However, how can one measure success or failure from among the plethora of often-conflicting interests and struggles described above. This reality of diverse interests makes it difficult to understand whether a project has succeeded or failed. I mentioned earlier that Project 2, from Murray's (the director of the AGA) point of view, had already been seen to meet its objectives (of national interest) before it had enrolled any students. However, the criteria for measuring its 'success' were not shared by all of its stakeholders. So, in this type of scenario, what are the effects of applying the concepts of success and failure to the projects? How are they perceived by the various stakeholders? Another complicating factor is that notions about what is successful change over time. For example, in the aid sector, at one time sustainability was not seen to be as important as other indicators (Brown, 2001; Cornford, 1999; Cornford & Simon, 2001; Gunning-Stevenson, 2001).

As I have already shown in Chapter 2, the success or otherwise of the project may be irrelevant to the success of the dominant stakeholder(s). A failed project (however that is determined) does not have to be represented as such on the curriculum vitae of the academics (or other project staff) in the Australian universities. Some of the host-country interviewees from Project 1 spoke of their disappointment that the project did not fully train appropriate staff to use the project products (curriculum materials).

They maintained that from their point of view the project did not fulfill its goals. However, from the project management company's (funded by the donor government) point of view, it could be said that they did fulfill the requirements of the project contract. The curriculum was produced, and they had no obligation to respond to the local circumstances, that is, the training needs of teachers. They operated within budget guidelines and delivered adequate reports which constituted success. Recipient organisations may also characterise a project as successful simply because to do otherwise may jeopardise the chance for future funded projects.

Describing a successful project

Success, like many concepts in this story, is a perilous word: success to one agent may mean failure to another, and dominant agents ride the waves of documented successful projects without having to necessarily be accountable or transparent to the host-country participants. On the ground, in the project, success is also a risky term. In my discussions with participants there was little consensus on what constituted success; for one it was the extent of 'true' collaboration that measured success while other agents put forward the measurement of unstated and underlying criteria, such as building relationships in the field as indicators of success.

The necessary strategies to survive and succeed in the work of the project were also seen differently by different stakeholders. Son (P1LM1), a key official from the host-country MOE for Project 1, made this point eloquently in describing what she identified as necessary for the work of the project to be successful. For her, the main criterion of success was the extent to which all the parties involved in the project development collaborate and exchange ideas before writing the design document. She was quite critical of the process that the aid agency undertook in setting out the parameters of the project. She described the procedure as one where documents went back and forth between key stakeholders and she expressed discontent with the process on a number of levels. The first point was that 'we didn't know each other.' The second point was that the mission visits that the aid agency sent to conduct some fact-finding field work were of a very short duration (a matter of days) and there was no time to 'sit down to carry [out] the conversation to understand the real situation of each country and find out what the host country could expect from the donor country'.

The sentiments expressed by Son – calling for collaboration and understanding of where each party is coming from – will have little impact on the way the donor-dominated project works. Work practices are shaped by and shape the field (as shown in Chapter 4) and in the case of IELEPs the project approach has a major influence on relations in the field. Integral to the model is the maintaining of the donor/provider's dominant position (Smith, 1998). This choice of project model in aid-funded ventures precludes collaborative interests; the expectations of stakeholders such as Son were doomed from the outset.

Lee drew attention to the complexity of interests, success and benefits in the field of Project 1. He put forward the generally accepted idea that only 50% of projects 'generally work' in Laos. As revealed in this book, there are many factors which influence success and failure. Lee talked about an aspect not yet addressed: the features and characteristics of intercultural work within the project; he believed that some expatriate staff's behaviour was culturally inappropriate to the host-country context and that this affected successful relationship building and intercultural learning within the project. He accepted that the Lao stakeholders generally tolerated some of the expatriate's inappropriate social and work behaviour because their greater interests centred around accumulation of economic capital:

> So I think at one level, the country's government is a bit cynical about project outcomes, but only on one level. On other levels, I think, the country's government wants any foreign capital, any influx of Western capital, it's still one of the poorest countries in the world, there's a level of personal gain for some of the members.

In discussing this aspect of the project further he alluded to the different ways people worked to ensure the success of the project. Playing the game successfully, that is, looking after one's own interest, gives some assurance of personal gain. On the other hand, many staff 'were absolutely committed to raising the professional levels of English teachers, and I think for a number of people, there was a real desire to see that happening, and particularly amongst women, and minority groups'.

In his explication of the field Lee talked about different unstated criteria for measuring success or failure. He described the different interests within the host-country project management and concluded that there were people who were more 'authentic', or, to use Bourdieu's term, disinterested than others, presumably those who had an interest in providing training for as many teachers as possible. The use of 'authentic' refers to the ways in which the person embodies the notion of 'aid for social good'. There is an unspoken assumption that the prioritising of ELT training is a positive move for the country and it is a way to build in some social justice principles.

Implementing for success

Project success is often linked to the way a project is set up, and many in the education project field believe that the way negotiations are managed, how paramenters are set and how infrastructure is built are important indicators of how well a project will fulfill its goals (see Romiszowski, 1989 for such views). This rather technicist view prevails in the aid and development sector and does influence private sector projects. A number of participants in Projects 1 and 2 offered their perspective on the type of project implementation procedure that leads to a 'successful project'. The indicators of success noted here are broad-ranging and while including the more technical aspects such as timing, administrative procedures and structural matters, participants also pointed to indicators such as relationship building, equity, sustainability, communication and the relevance (of project work) to the local context.

The first two quotes from Australian interviewees with considerable experience in the international context speak typically about the field, that is, the importance of approaching the project as a logical entity. In the first data extract Lee spoke about aid-funded projects and drew on his experience with Project 1; the aid agency set out the measurable outcomes but, as he importantly pointed out, this design can 'only really be a skeleton of what you're meant to do in terms of relationships and longer term'.

Lee identified equity, sustainability and participation of minority groups as key indicators of a project's success. He noted that Project 1 had not fulfilled part of the original design: the sustainability goals. Lee's comments alluded to the importance of a deep macro-level understanding of the local context, that is, the social and material conditions of the host country. Lee described the project design document as an instrument which adequately outlined the parameters of the project and then it is up to the project managers and team to establish the practices of work and to develop ways to meet the broad goals, for example, sustainability. The latter goal is a vexed point; as Lee noted in Project 1, the host country was very poor, aid funding comprised 70% of its national budget and the goals of sustainability were predicated on the project establishing an entrepreneurial arm in the context of a public service.

Murray, a key stakeholder on Project 2, described what made a successful project from his point of view:

> Firstly, ... one should never make a decision about whether one's going to proceed or even run the proposal stage unless one is confident that one can marshal the resources that are necessary. The second is your ability to engage the target audience and to establish support

structures within that target audience. The third critical factor in any sort of assessment needs to be what levels of sustainability you are looking for and in a crude way that means, well, what contributions are going to come from the other side but those contributions could be in any one range of different areas.

Even though Murray's way of talking about projects was different to Lee's, the procedures and underlying concepts were similar. Murray talked about 'engaging the target audience'. While entrepreneurial in an outcomes sense, he spoke of the importance of building relationships in the field. There was also congruence around the concept of sustainability. Further on Murray emphasised how the Australian universities must understand the context of this particular environment (Project 2); he echoed Lee's comments from Project 1 where he was concerned that inappropriate behaviour could affect the outcomes of a project. Murray identified timing and quality as two significant factors in the success of a project in Japan. He described the people of this country as ones who do not want to be rushed. The Australian project partners had to be patient and be mindful of the correct time to introduce or launch the project. He stressed that this particular market is highly sensitive to 'quality' and he gave examples of commercial products that failed due to incorrectly understanding the social conditions of the country.

Murray candidly described what the potentially winning features of the project were and how he ascertained whether the project was a success in the universities' terms:

> The benefit of a consortium approach is that, A it provides a national face and a national unity to a particular product, B it provides all of the academic infrastructure that's likely to be necessary if it is a major project . . . I will define this particular one as a major success if it involves more than 200 students a year in the medium term. I think Australia would have difficulty in dealing with more 200 students a year.

Min (P1LM3) from Project 1 discussed what he saw as the essential elements for a successful project. He worked with the national university and helped to administer international projects. He considered that communication was at the core of a successful project and it was crucial that the project director should be able to contact the donor agency staff whenever he or she needed to. However, often the foreign project staff was dealing with another project half-way around the world.

In the extract below Shor (P2LU2), a member of the MOE committee which oversaw the development of Project 2, identified the relationships between the MOE, the project providers and the project participants as the component on which a successful project rested.

> They [the project providers] need to know the course of study and the national guidelines for education especially foreign language educa-tion. The MOE are now doing the translation work in this course of study and it will come out some time maybe after the summer vaca-tion. I would like overseas institutions to read the English language course of study and also if you have the opportunity I would like you to visit schools in this country. How about developing network with former participants . . . of your programs and regularly contact them and get feedback from them on a regular basis about what sort of developments they have made after they have returned home. Have some, you know, bulletin kind of thing newsletter or something and exchange information even among the ex participants would be good. So things can change all of a sudden but you have to have a regular kind of network amount of participants and the institutions.

He was very specific about the type of local knowledge the project providers should hold and how they might proceed to embed endur-ing relationships between all the stakeholders in the project field. Shor focused on the practices in the field, that is, what teachers actually did in his country. He was concerned that project implementers had information about the material conditions of the teachers, the course books, board of study information and so on. He also suggested how to further relation-ships in the field. He did not mention the term 'internationalisation' but described the type of international relationships that Australian universi-ties strove (and still strive to) to develop through such things as alumni. These he saw as two-way processes. In the first instance, the Australian project team should learn about the host-country educational context and then, the project providers should establish networks (enabling teachers to accumulate social capital in the field) among the host-country teach-ers and between the Australian lecturers and the host-country teachers. Shor (P2LU2) perceived these networks to be of benefit to the host-country teachers and a strategy to promote sustainability of the project. In the extract below, he then discussed the issue of why projects fail. From his point of view, international projects have not met 'our need'. He talked specifically about the way the projects did not address Japanese EL teach-ers' classroom practices. Shor stated that in Japan the EL teachers must use a MOE-authorised textbook and he believed that any professional devel-opment programme must use the authorised textbook as a basis for its courses. Below he talked generally about why international projects have failed in Japan:

> One of the biggest reasons that the international project has failed is that I think their project... did not meet our need and that is to say that they gave us a chance to speak out or to brush up whatever it is [English language proficiency] but they have not yet given them [ELT teachers] the chance to use their skills in our context in our high school context. I mean for example, they [ELT teachers] have to use the education ministry's authorised version of text books and although they have some ability or they have brushed up their speaking of English and listening abilities but they cannot utilise those abilities in their real context.

He continued to talk about the necessity for the project to understand the teaching conditions and he mentioned, in particular, class size (as mentioned by other Project 2 teachers). The project would perhaps offer an excellent methodology to teach classes of eight or 10 students grouped around tables in communicative situations but the majority of teachers will have 40 or more mixed-ability students in a class and the project would not offer the teachers ways of using more spoken language in this type of class. He raised the point in the above extract that the teachers may well have improved their English language proficiency in an Australian university project but this would not necessarily make it better or easier for them to teach English in their classes. He also brought up the issue of the limited number of English language classes/periods per week in Japanese secondary schools: 'only three hours; and in the near future junior high schools will have only three hours a week at the most.' These conditions were not addressed in project's courses – a very real constraint for the teachers and students.

Ken (P2LU1) from Project 2 discussed how the project could succeed and again focused on understanding the needs of the Japanese teachers. We discussed the issue of why teachers would apply for the programmes under the project and he raised a point about the type of qualification available through the project. The host-country interviewees were not familiar with the name of the degree offered within the project and this interviewee stressed that we need to make the pathways very clear to the teachers:

> So I think the main reason that they would apply for the project's programs would be to improve their qualifications so in order to satisfy their interest, needs. You have [to] make clear what sort of process you

have for them to go to the MA degree. If it is clearly defined in the project then they will show interest in your programs and you won't have so much problem in training those teachers any more. Because this is what I've sensed over the last eight years while I was working with the Ministry. Their English has improved a lot yes, and there are some very fluent teachers in the project's programs which you run.

The projects facilitated internal networks and social connections between host-country teachers and teacher educators. Weng (P1LM2) saw this as a way in which Project 1 was successful. Her comments focused on how the courses brought teachers together from all regions and institutions in her country. She believed that the successful aspect of this was the way that teachers with different levels of English proficiency, teaching skills and experience worked together. In her opinion this cooperative and collaborative work between the teachers helped motivate them to study and 'really improve the knowledge of how to teach English here'.

This building of connections within the project addressed how the participants amass some social capital in the field and how they build connections with other host-country agents/players within the field. In turn this raised a question about the relative value of capital within the field and where the agents are positioned in the field. Do, for example, stronger connections between local EL teachers in this country strengthen the position of these project participants? Are they more likely to have their interests recognised and negotiated within the project? Weng believes that it was in the country's interests to facilitate teachers gaining TESOL qualifications and that the accumulation of this particular cultural capital would help a developing country. The significant point for me in what Weng described is to try to identify what motivates participants to take part in the project. Is their interest in the accumulation of a particular sort of cultural capital, gaining a foreign university qualification in TESOL (from an English-speaking country), in the hope that this will give them the opportunity for a better standard of living?

Earlier in this chapter I called success a perilous and risky term; we can see how the participants hold multiple, and at times non-negotiable, meanings of success within the IELEP field. If a project is successful in lifting the profile of the provider/donor's country, how is success measured by the host-country participants? If the project deeply engages with the context of the host-country teachers, will the donor/provider value this accrued capital? I suspect that the danger with success is that the indicators for measuring the value of the project will stay in the donor/provider's domain.

Failing to succeed

How can we know if a project fails? The criteria for measuring success and failure as discussed above change according to who is speaking about the project. Already in this story host-country participants have pointed to reasons as to why a project has or may have failed. From the donor/provider's perspective the normally short cycles of projects make it easy for project advisers to move on without repercussions from work that made little impact or did not meet the contract goals.

The stakeholders who do not appear to 'profit' from 'failed' projects are the regular EL teachers and their students. In her position as an Australian lecturer, Yvonne (P1AU1) worked intensively with EL teachers in the provinces and the cities, including field trips to observe English language lessons. She gave evidence of the dominant and subordinate positions within the ELT field. In this extract she began by talking about the needs of teachers. Meeting their needs would ultimately involve a collaborative approach to developing more teaching resources and the project giving more time to teacher training.

> What they needed was support, collegial support to actually develop, I mean, what they needed comes down to finances, I think. They needed collegial support to be able to develop their lessons and programs and units that really would help their learners want to learn the language.

Her views echoed the earlier views of the local ministry officials where they questioned the project's lack of support for the training of teachers in using the new curriculum. In the extract below Yvonne identified the English language students as the core of the project's teaching and learning work and called for more thought and time to go into the professional development of teachers to enable them to respond to the needs of their students. She also made a subtle reference to the role of ELT in Laos and implied that it is only relevant for a small group of people. She questioned whether the solution was to fund large projects:

> Not just here's a million dollars, but they need more ongoing ways of investigating how to teach EFL...because I suspect that a lot of the time and energy and money that goes into English teaching in this country is wasted, literally wasted because so many of the learners don't really want or need the language. It seems as though it's more for the elite in business or government who want to get on in the global world...a lot of their learners were just going through the paces.

She continued to discuss the context of teaching English and questions the ways in which the benefits of English were distributed in the field (see also comment by Bruthiaux (2002) in Chapter 1), particularly in reference to the distribution of resources within Laos. Resource distribution was concentrated in the capital city and was filtered out to the provincial organisations. The country is ethnically and linguistically diverse, with the minority ethnic populations concentrated in the provinces. The provincial teachers and students had much less access to resources than their capital city counterparts had, and in the particular case of English language teaching, far, far less access to English as an international language. Yvonne raised questions about what was really needed in the provincial regions:

> But really and truly, out in the provinces ELT provision is for some people perhaps, to gain access to privileged knowledge or, strategies for how to get money. But really and truly, in terms of organic development of the local economy, no, looking at what really is needed in the local cultures and it's not English. The government is doing what they think they should, because it's going to better the country's economy. Well, it might, marginally too. But ...

The impact of the dominant interests in ELT projects was keenly felt in scenarios such as described above. Yvonne's comments resonated with a description of the recent provision of ELT in East Timor. A teacher on that project wrote about the impact of the Australian Government's decision to prioritise the provision of ELT for aid funding to East Timor. The decision was not a neutral one in terms of the infrastructure of the education services in a very poor country. According to Appleby (2002), the Australian Government had a major role in the future construction of education priorities in East Timor and the consequential effect on other areas of study. The decision to fund a major ELT project satisfied the interests of the elite. The resulting funding of ELT meant that other important areas of education were bereft of financial support (Appleby *et al.*, 2002). Yvonne (P1AU1) implied that the funding could have been better spent elsewhere and she identified the giving of collaborative, cooperative support as a key factor that would benefit the host teachers:

> what are the professional development needs of those teachers? If they must keep teaching, they need collegial support for how to actually go about it. You know, methods, using English, how to do it, in a context where the target language doesn't really have any great purpose.

The sentiments expressed in the above extracts indicate a dis-ease with the ways in which the project worked with the teachers and its priorities as manifested in curriculum production and post-graduate teacher training. Yvonne (P1AU1) intimated that the project had 'failed' the host-country teachers and students of ELT. These groups did not 'profit' from work of international education projects. Looking at this scenario in terms of the concepts of success and failure and the closely related notions of winner and loser, we can identify that the losers in this 'aid partnership' were the owners and producers of indigenous forms of knowledge, that is, contextual practices, traditions of education and organisation of work. Knowledge, skills and belief systems which have sustained local societies and contributed to global bio-diversity are often 'reduced' to inferior perspectives by the ways of carrying out learning and teaching processes and work practices offered by Western development experts (Maffi, 2002; Morris, 1996: 156).

Yvonne addressed what she identified as the major goals of the teacher training component: 'to train teachers and to train the trainer'. In assessing the success or not of the project she referred to the 'impressive numbers of teachers that have been trained'. This reference to numbers of course participants resonated with how Murray would assess the success of Project 2 earlier in this section. Yvonne's assessment of Project 1 is not purely a cost-benefit analysis as it was a significantly different context from Project 2 and teacher training provision is limited. But in reference to the goal of training the trainer she was much more cautious:

> perhaps the jury's still out on that one. I mean, there's obviously a lot of teacher training going on. How much of that's related to our input over the years is unclear. Obviously there must be a fair bit. But I guess in a way, it's hard to evaluate that, without really looking at the teacher training program on the ground in Laos. That's a really core question that goes to the very heart of outsiders coming in and doing something, and planning the way it should be taken over.

An implication of the above comments is that perhaps Australian universities and project management companies are out of step with the interests of ELT teachers internationally.

This chapter explored some key struggles around the planning and design of the IELEP, resources and clashes over cultural capital in Project 2. It also introduced the risky notions of success and failure in the field; these are contested notions: one participant's failure may be another's success. A common thread in the stories about IELEPs is that they have repeatedly failed to meet the needs of their host-country participants and in spite of this, recent activities by major international aid and private sector agencies continue to reproduce the same rationalist project model in new and expanding markets. The following three chapters examine the key struggles around project work (ELT in particular), language and culture in detail; the glaring inequities in the distribution of resources are nowhere more apparent than in the way certain knowledge and skills are deemed legitimate or illegitimate.

Chapter 4
Practices in the Project Field: ELT and Project Work

This chapter shows how a Bourdieuian approach to the study of practices in IELEP work opens up new ways of understanding activities such as ELT, project management, distribution of project tasks, relationships between stakeholders and the processes such as collaboration and consultation. My investigations reveal the different ways in which project work is legitimised; in Bourdieu's terms, how the game is played and the ways in which some agents are better players than others and how for some players everything about project work is 'natural'. It demonstrates how the organisation of work, the project, serves some interests better than others. The stories here speak about how some teaching and work practices are deemed either dominant or subordinate, legitimate or illegitimate; in Kumaravadivelu's (2003b, 2006) words, these practices undergo a process of either marginalisation or self-marginalisation. These processes give rise to a discontent with the project; the dis-ease with the project model is woven into this story about practice.

The two projects' goals and objectives are informed by the practices embodied by the Australian institutions within which the projects were conceived and developed. The practices, while imported from Australia, reproduce the regularities of project work originating from many other countries; the power relationships which delineate the field are international. The notions of teaching practice are drawn from those ELT specialists (usually so-called 'native' English speakers) who hold the social and cultural capital within the field. These specialists often have had a long history with the funding agency or the institution/auspicing body of the project. Projects are driven by the entrepreneurial notions of finding a gap in the market, and in the case of educational projects, they are usually aimed at those groups who are perceived to be disadvantaged and thereby suitable candidates for innovations in teaching methodologies, new technologies or different ways of thinking about an area of work. ELT is a good example of this. Aside from the target group being typified as non-expert users of English, they are also seen as non-experts in the teaching of the subject. The terms 'non-expert' and 'expert' are not entirely satisfactory. Throughout this story I try not to employ the binary definitions of so-called 'non-native' speakers and 'native' speakers of English. I am in agreement with Oda (2008), and Rampton (1990) before him, that the binary divide sustains the idea of a norm in ELT, the 'so-called' native speaking English teacher (these issues are taken up in Chapter 5). The values and philosophy of the Australian institutions manifest themselves in the approaches and strategies taken by key actors in the development of the projects, that is, the way information is gathered, how training is conducted and how knowledge from the projects is validated and disseminated. The recipients of the aid projects are required to change their behaviour and in the main accept and reproduce the donor's or provider's practices.

The practices of the projects' work are situated in a specifically international context and bounded by an organisational structure that is driven to engage in the struggle to accumulate economic capital. As noted in Chapter 1, the universities and the respective project management companies are engaged in work that is in a sense 'becoming', the entrepreneurial capabilities of universities have yet to be fully realised and the partnerships with project management companies are still in varying stages of development.

Construct of Project in the ELT Field

One of the most obvious and contentious constructs of the IELEP field and one of the first things to examine in seeking to understand success or failure is the concept of the project itself. The participants revealed confusion and frustration in dealing with the wholesale application of the project model in an educational endeavour. Essentially this way of organising work was borrowed from the private sector (Little & Mirrlees, 1974) and applied to the development and aid context during the 1960s. Abdul-Raheem's (2000) critique of aid and development in South Africa exposes the durability of this model and he summises that little has changed about the rationalist approach to project work that was used to replace the economic relations established under colonial rule. The project model was and is viewed as a way of identifying discrete areas of work with clearly defined aims and objectives and, because of its focus on small areas of work, is viewed as assisting in evaluation and assessment (Little & Mirrlees, 1974). The project model is outcomes-driven, which is perhaps suitable for the private sector where profit is a way to measure the success of an enterprise venture (MacArthur, 1993).

In his study of ELT aid-funded projects in Cambodia, Harvey Smith (1998) characterises the projectisation of ELT as a tactic to carry out more effective aid-related strategies rather than to support the provision of ELT. He discusses how the projects in his study focused on the donor's broad international aid objectives rather than the teaching and learning aspects of the projects' goals. He claims that this often unstated focus subtly disenfranchises some of the key stakeholders, either those from the host countries or those from the recipient countries. Therefore, while some stakeholders are working towards the explicit goals of the projects (of teaching and learning), others, most likely those 'more in the know of project work', are focused on the donor's/provider's national goals. Smith (1998) claims that this focus on the national interests of the donor distinguished aid-funded projects from fee-based projects. In the extract below Smith (1998) outlines how the project field shapes the dominant practices of project work:

> The project approach has provided a management model for the design, implementation and evaluation of ELT aid, and the use of the project (or 'logical') framework has made this a particularly disciplined model. There is a clear focus on the need to have strict time and budget limits and to produce results within these limits. While there may be doubts about the appropriateness of a strict project framework approach to 'people-centred' aid activities, in practice it has now been applied to ELT for a decade. The inputs-outputs-objectives framework and the time and budget constraints place aid-funded ELT very much in the field of management and it is acknowledged that ELT specialists now require management skills in order to be effective. ELT team leaders have now become project managers and other members of the team are also required to adhere to project-driven targets. These characteristics are peculiar to projects and do not pertain where aid or ELT support are delivered by other means (e.g., through the provision of an adviser to a ministry without specific objectives or time constraints). (Smith, 1998: 96)

So how suitable is this approach for the public sector? The public sector in Australia operates in general on a programme basis that is expenditure-driven. From the outset there is a mismatch of a private sector approach to the provision of a public service, education, where success is not as easily measured as, for example, in the sale of cars. In the tertiary sector university international projects are profit-driven. This makes for a complex field which displays different faces at different times, and particular faces are only available to particular audiences at particular times.

The project approach, as it is conceptualised by Australian institutions, determines certain practices, that is, ways of behaving and ways of deciding what is valuable in the project field. Murray, the director of the Australian Government Agency (AGA) in Japan, discussed the concept of the project in his particular context and how this organisational structure is not well received by the Ministry of Education (MOE) in Japan. Murray explicitly described the project as belonging to the private sector and that differs significantly from the way work is carried out in the education area: 'In fact public sector activity tends to be program rather than project based and tends to be expenditure driven rather than results driven. So we often have difficulty in explaining the way we do business because this agency does approach things from a project basis.'

The project approach did not sit easily in the international context in which Murray worked. This point is repeated by Tan, a member of the Japanese MOE project liaison committee; he was not familiar with the notion of 'project' in the educational sector. He was much more familiar with the notion of programme and how this fitted within his educational resource centre. Murray explained this to the Australian project team. It is worth quoting Murray at length as I suggest he identified a central problematic to the across-the-board application of the 'project' in the education sector. The MOEs of both host countries were established on the basis of providing a public service. Yet the 'project' is borrowed from the private sector.

However, Murray did concede a purpose for the use of the project approach to educational services. The explanation he gave was based entirely on the question of resourcing. The project approach allows for a narrow focus and an end date. The approach, from his point of view, was not seen as an approach that will particularly enhance or make more feasible an educational innovation. It was a way to manage the scarce resources in field:

> I guess . . . the public sector of Australia has learnt this model from the private sector and some of the more energetic international organisations. But we are no longer in the game where we can afford to spend all the money on all the activities that are suggested. What we've got to do is identify the critical needs. This sets our ability to respond to critical needs and divert and deflect limited resources, in order to be able to meet those needs in a timely yet terminateable manner. We've got to respond to the priorities that obviously need to be addressed by

the particular project but at the same time you want to have a sunset arrangement in it and terminate one day any sort of involvement in it.

Murray continued to speak in detail about the way the projects work in the international context. His contribution was enlightening as prior to this 'research conversation' I had not been able to ascertain this level of detail about the practices inherent in the project approach to work in international education. The project rationale and processes described from his vantage point galvanised the questions I had had about the suitability of the project model in the public sector. In the extract below he described what is involved in resourcing a project, that is, what makes a project viable or successful. Murray's account was explicit about the interests of his organisation, that is, to portray Australian higher education as a desirable option for students in Japan and hence the factors that he saw as essential are premised on these interests.

> in terms of the model of project I have five levels of resources that I need to think about. One of them obviously is financial, but more important resources considerations that need to be factored into any project situation are human resources, time resources, physical resources and information resources. Now, we also factor in something that we call representation resources. So there is a self-regression going on I agree but, how much of their time, energy, funding, people are to spend on doing the representation and the entertainment and the networking that's necessary to deliver the result that we want. The project has to be something that's delivered in partnership with certain target client groups. It can't be delivered in isolation and in that context one has to work hard to get the target group to agree that it needs it. In this country anyway particularly when your target group is the Japanese people you have to get their understanding of their need for the particular activity and then their support in delivering it.

Murray identified what he determined as the critical factors, or what I would call 'stakes', in the field: people, time, information, material goods and the way in which these resources convert into the economic resource of the field. Murray termed this latter resource as 'representation'. He later explained this resource as the cost of the impact of all of the resources on each other. The other critical factor that he named is the social capital in the field, that is, the way the agents establish connections between the 'right' people in the field, the type of connections which will further the interests of the provider and ensure that the project will be carried out. Of central interest to the main idea of this book, namely, problematising and questioning the assumed identity of the beneficiaries in the IELEP field, is the notion of legitimate expertise and knowledge and the processes by which this is recognised. In the case of the above project field the Japanese English language (EL) teachers and administrators were placed in a subordinate position in the field; the Australian universities were positioned as holding the cultural capital, the knowledge and expertise in ELT. However, in my analysis of the data the struggle was not primarily over cultural capital; it was over economic capital.

Murray continued to discuss the practices by which Australian institutions create a presence in the host country. He talked about Japan as being the largest market for English language in the world and also in market terms '... it is the largest market for a range of English language software in the world and [by] software I mean publishing, music, film, a whole range of other different things' (Murray). He gave the view that Australian institutions at times entered this market in a way that did not take account of the competition and the needs and wants of the consumers. In this sense, projects quickly became economically unviable. He raised the issue of quality and how this was a great determiner of whether the target group will take up the product:

> The reality is that most of this country's consumers can afford to pay for the best product in the world. . . . the perception of quality that permeates that whole demand equation in this country. So, in order for Australian institutions to be successful in offering certain products they require investment in infrastructures, whether that's physical infrastructure such as a number of institutions have done in partnership with other Australian institutions and Japanese institutions. Or whether that's by an information infrastructure and pipelines and things that they need and that's a decision for the relevant organisation to make.

Murray described a pivotal struggle in the work of this fee-based project which was around the accumulation of economic capital and this despite the fact that the raison d'etre for the project was the supposed superior cultural capital of the Australian agents. Chapter 2 illustrated that there is a homologous relationship between the two project fields and the multi-dimensional terrain of the two projects reflects similar relationships in the hierarchies of power and struggles over accumulation of capital. As outlined earlier, the project approach was derived from a particular context where for the dominant stakeholders, for example, the project management companies, everything about project work seems obvious and the question of knowing if the game is 'worth the candle'

(Bourdieu, 1998) will not even be asked. The term 'project' has become so embedded in the delivery of education services that it did not need a definition in the Project 1 proposal documents. It is stated in these documents that the planned establishment of a language centre will be *under a project approach*, whatever this may be. The documents also recommended *projectising* the English language training programme. There was no explanation of what this particular way of organising work implies or the struggles that emerge. Clearly in Project 2 (fee-based), the struggle was around the accumulation of economic capital. However, in Project 1 the struggle was also over economic capital although not explicitly stated as such. Lee illustrated how this dominant discourse of seeking economic gain surreptitiously worked to shape the field. In his faculty there were different views of what the project could mean, and different staff had different levels of experience with project work; he identified a prevalent dilemma in project work, that is, balancing management's pressure to make an economic profit with educational goals:

> Looking back, I think I'd absorbed these discourses, internalised them, the idea that I should be trying to not only develop a quality product but also to make some money for the faculty, because the faculty is always in crisis . . . it was more of a self-motivation than an imposed one, and it's one that I regret now because I can see now how much better a quality product we could have done, if I hadn't had that secondary motivation.

Here we can see that the interests of the stakeholders in the field or game are to 'be there' (Bourdieu, 1998), to participate – to believe that the game (of project work) is worth playing – that the stakes (those things that are determined to be valuable) created in and through the fact of playing are worth pursuing, to recognise the game and to recognise its stakes (Bourdieu, 1998). However, this game is not carried out on a 'level playing field' (an arena where all the players enter with the same amount of capital, and all are valued equally) since different stakeholders enter the game with different types and amounts of capital (the stakeholders' positions were clearly identified in Chapters 2 and 3). This equips the agents with different ways and approaches to carrying out the practices in the field – an unequal 'feel for the game' (Bourdieu, 1998). The result is that some stakeholders play the game better than others. This latter issue is highly significant in this story. Project work is not 'natural' to all stakeholders, and the fact that not everyone knows about the way projects operate is central to the ways in which work is deemed legitimate or not. Though shrouded by the rhetoric of quality, the fee-based project (Project 2) was as much beholden to the national interests of the provider as was the aid-funded project.

As discussed above, and in particular if we take the definitions offered by Smith (1998), it is obvious to say that many people from public sector education institutions do not have experience with short cycles or logical frameworks. This unfamiliarity does not neatly fall with one particular group of stakeholders, that is, the recipients of the project products. This raises the important question: who does know about project work? Lee, an Australian university lecturer, discussed his lack of experience in project work but this did not delegitimise him in taking on a role in project management as it may have done with the 'host-country stakeholders':

> I had no experience of project management, and there was nobody in the faculty who could help me. I didn't know what they were talking about with their spreadsheets and Gantt [see p. 104 below for definition] charts and ways of balancing projects. I mean, so, I was at a real disadvantage. And I learnt how to do some of it, but they [project management companies] run rings around you.

Lee pointed to lack of experience with the 'macro' organisation of the aid-funded project and how this places the university at a disadvantage vis-à-vis the project management company. Chris, an Australian university lecturer from Project 2, discussed how a lack of experience with the internal work of the project resulted in an inefficient use of time and this had implications for the faculty budget:

> Well, I know that at the time there were lots of rushed periods and lots of lulls when people's time wasn't being used as effectively. And there were lots of things that hadn't really presented themselves, the fact that maybe the writers needed to start before the translators needed to start, or that sort of thing. In hindsight we can say, well, people's time wasn't used efficiently, but on the other hand, you know, there wasn't anyone there at the time to, to bring that experience in.

This acknowledged lack of experience in what one could assume to be core work of a university still did not have an impact on whether the university was a legitimate player or not. The project documents referred to the host countries as needing capacity building and assistance in developing the skills and knowledge in the target language, yet a number of the project implementers did not necessarily have the skills, knowledge or experience in project management. This underscores struggle about legitimate work, knowledge and unfair or unequal positioning of legitimacy between donor and recipient players.

Discontent with the Project

IELEPs are not idyllic havens of 'good work'; in this story project participants concurred with the myriad of problems and dis-ease with international project work documented in numerous studies of international educational projects (Achren 2007; Appleby, R. *et al.*, 2002; Copely 1997). They identified common specific problems including: (1) short cycles of project life, (2) lack of continuity in host-country staff, (3) financial management and (4) difficulties in dealing with the host-country MOE.

Weng, a teacher trainer with the Lao MOE , expressed dissatisfaction with the short cycle of the project (as discussed earlier projects have a pre-determined end date and Project 1 was funded for a 4-year period). The education sector in the host country for Project 1 (see Chapter 2) is acutely under-developed and a 4-year project is unlikely to effect any change in the level of skill and service provision. Weng talked about how she believed the project should continue, that it was premature to stop after 4 years. She gave many reasons for why the project should continue but she stressed that the main rationale for a longer cycle was the training the project provided for 'counterpart' staff. Another aspect of discontent expressed by Weng was with the lack of continuity with the individual counterpart lecturers each year; this was due to the needs of their substantive institutions and the whims of the host-country MOE. And while this was a feature that the Australian management was not entirely in control of, it seemed obvious that this detracted from an effective model of staff development and one that the Australian management could negotiate with the host MOE. Weng believed that the counterpart personnel should have stayed the same each year since this continuity allowed them much more opportunity to fully develop their skills, 'strength and confidence in delivering the course'.

This short-term cycle is a feature of the project approach to aid-funded education; the very basis of the 'innovations' is, in the project world, short-term but is also expected to achieve a great degree of sustainability by the end of the project. This is in the face of comments such as those later in this chapter where the initial settling-in period for all staff took some time and the projects' frames were fairly fixed so there was little room to change the direction or activities.

The approach to the financial management of Project 1 was a source of much discontent among the host-country management team. The responses of a number of other Project 1 participants were that the project needed to have a more collaborative approach to planning, that their 'country's side' did not have access to certain management areas, in particular the financial management. Vong (P1LU1), from the project management committee and who was the head of a department at the local university, expressed disquiet with the way that the host-country managers were marginalised in the actual planning and implementation processes. She had had recent experience with another EL teacher training project funded by a foundation in South East Asia (referred to as Project X) and discussed the contrast between the two projects. She felt that Project 1 did not promote 'cooperation with the local people', that there was no space to work and plan together. This was, she thinks, a significant problem as the host-country team did not have experience with the particular approach to project work in Project 1 and the Lao participants would have benefited from gaining experience in this form of project management . But in saying this she also felt that there were people in the MOE and local university who did have the abilities required by the Australian project management team. This was a marked reference to the planning and implementation processes in the project work. Contrary to the donor's expectations there were host-country personnel available to do course and programme development. She offered a telling comment on the reasons why local team members were not centrally involved in developing the directions and infrastructure of the project: the project had already been designed and implemented and signed off before the local team members were brought on board and 'in that case it's really hard' to cooperate.

The project management companies inevitably require costs to be cut in the expenditure linked to project activities; what is curious for a number of interviewees from Project 1 is that this cost-cutting procedure seemed to begin before the project commenced its core activities. The 'implementation period', when a Project Implementation Document (PID) is submitted to the funding body for approval, outlines a number of areas where the projected expenditure is less than initially planned. Another intriguing aspect of the financial management of aid projects is a feature known as the 'team leader's budget'. There is a common practice among Australian aid projects that the team leader has his or her own project budget which is approximately 10% less than the project documents show (this is not a well-known feature but is common practice in private corporations). If the team leader is able to shave this percentage off the budget, he or she is rewarded by the project management company.

Project X, on the other hand, brought the host-country participants on board at the conception and planning stages and in this project Vong's team was provided with the management training the foundation thought necessary and which included financial management:

> In Project X we could manage the money ourselves, that was a good point. But in terms of your project, we didn't have the right to manage the money. (Vong)

Yvonne (P1AU1), an Australian university lecturer, discussed her discontent in carrying out negotiations with the host-country MOE. This is alluded to by other Australian team members and indicates the paucity of preparation and training undertaken by the Australian project management team. The MOE in the host country of Project 1 is centrally organised. It requested that changes to the project programmes or host-country staff must be channelled, top-down, through the appropriate ministry officials. This was an unfamiliar organisational model for the Australian university staff; they were inculcated into working within a more informal smaller type organisation indicative of many Australian universities. Yvonne (P1AU1) described her reactions and strategies to dealing with an unfamiliar context:

> I'd have to say there was degree of frustration on my part with how we engaged with, or interacted or made contact with the ministry of education officials and of not knowing the appropriate channels for how to talk with the upper levels of the MOE involved in the program, at the teacher training level. I recall there being frustration with, 'I don't know what the social mechanisms are', and it's not working and we wouldn't get certain things done, like the permissions for practical teaching in the schools. Eventually, at one point through having established a personal relationship with_____, an off the record relationship, if you like, with one of the people at the top, it became easier, I suppose.

Yvonne developed a personal friendship which circumvented the difficulties of finding the correct channels or appropriate person with whom to negotiate. She accumulated significant social capital which allowed her to move more freely within the official channels of the Lao MOE. It is evident in her that this friendship made negotiations easier for general requests in the teacher training component. However, the social capital accumulated by Yvonne could not necessarily be exchanged for economic capital within the field as a whole. The major players in the field, the donors and the Australian institutions did not view this accumulated capital as significant.

The host-country interviewees contested the view that only the donor or the provider enact the legitimate practices in project work. Son, a manager of the teacher training department in the MOE (Project 1), implied that the project management, as represented by the team leader, did not understand the way things work in his country (as represented by the MOE). He believed this lack of understanding jeopardised the success of the project. He touched on some tensions and conflict within the project and analysed these dynamics by differentiating between the work practices of the host-country project participants and those of the expatriates: '. . . maybe the procedure of working here is very different from Australian procedure.'

Son emphasised the differences in the approaches that the 'different sides' took and in his opinion there needed to be a greater focus on needs analysis and on giving priority to those teachers and students who have less resources and less access to training. He implied that there had been no study of needs that truly reflects the social, institutional and material conditions of his country's teachers. He made one telling remark about the expatriates' 'pessimistic approach' indicating that more optimism about the project's potential is warranted. The expatriates' pessimism was to do with a perceived reluctance of the Lao MOE to take up and run with the presented project plan. It is significant that Son did not point to any 'enduring cultural traits' to discuss problems he identified in the work of the projects but rather highlighted what he saw as problems with established project management practices.

He also pointed out that although this was an aid project there was nothing that he would recognise as the underlying care for the project participants, educational outcomes and adherence to the aid and development principles that he was aware of. Here I assume he meant that from his point of view the project management team did not embrace the rhetoric of the Australian aid agency which at that time foregrounded the concerns and interests of the aid recipients. He questioned whether the management had seriously taken on board the work to be undertaken for the teachers and students; he made the point that the choice was about 'work for humanity or just for work'. I understood him to question the motives of the Australian management team.

Son expressed concern that the Australian team had a problem with the way his department had handled their end of the project. In polite terms Son complained that the management followed the procedures according to the 'book' rather than organically responding to circumstances.

Son also raised the issue about how the project worked out after the funding had ended. The project document scheduled a handover of the project to the national university. The stages were worked out prior to the implementation of the project but seemingly not negotiated with the MOE. The Australian design team had assumed that the university should handle the project's work but this did not sit easily with the host-country MOE participants as the university and teacher training area were managed by two separate departments within the ministry.

Vong, a department head with the university, was concerned about how ready the host-country staff was to carry out the project's goal of sustainability (as it is defined by the donor). She did not feel that the local university staff had accumulated the relevant amount of cultural capital to conduct the programmes. She was concerned primarily with the new knowledge required to deliver the 'language teaching skills and techniques' that were taught within the project's courses.

Vong's (P1LU1) disquiet about the proposed transfer of the project illustrated the contradictions in the IELEP: aid-funded projects purportedly strive for sustainability but the aid industry needs to sustain its own economic viability. If the outcomes of aid-funded ELT projects are similar to those feared by Murray, there would be no need for Australian (or British or American etc.) EL teachers. The dominant values and beliefs of the field are conserved, the so-called 'native' English speaker teacher educators are the norm (and the best) and NABA (North American, British and Australian) teachers and projects maintain their desirability. Vong took on the doxa of the field, the imported teachers are best and she self-marginalisesd her own and other Lao teachers' skills.

Other participants feared that if the project was to move under the control of the host-country university it would create untold problems, not only administrative problems but also issues of protocol, for example, who would be managing what. The Australian presence in this area (over a period of some years) had unwittingly upset this protocol by deciding which institution should manage what, with little consultation with the relevant departments but resting only on what it thought should happen. From the Australian project design team's point of view it had probably seemed the most logical thing to do. Not only did the team not have the intimate knowledge of the host-country context but it was also operating from its (the design team's) dominant position in the field. After all, the Australian aid agency had the economic capital, the cultural capital in terms of qualifications and work experience in TESOL and higher education. The Australian presence in this host country had dominated the field in terms of how one should teach English; they have pushed and pulled until they have the best teachers from other subject areas to re-train as EL teachers, they have determined the procedures of the project-based funding and they have 'negotiated' all this in a newly imposed foreign language.

In this study, the donor, Australian universities, and government or corporate bodies as the dominant agents in the field determined how work was carried out in the project. They determine which practices were legitimate and who were legitimate project workers/team members. The criteria used in the projects replicate, in most cases, the way work was carried out in the Australian context. This was exemplified by the reporting mechanisms the funding bodies required, the style and content of reports and the way in which project activities were scheduled using the Gantt chart (this is a type of bar chart that sets out a project schedule. Gantt charts set out the organisational information about the project, for example, the start and finish dates of the project activities and it summarises all the project milestones and outcomes) and logical frame guidelines.

The logic of the field mystifies the practices of project management. This point was made several times by the recipient stakeholders and is well-exemplified by a 'research conversation' with Trong, a ministry official from the aid-funded project. He talked about the plan to decrease the presence of the Australian lecturers during the life of the project and production of a text book for secondary school students. Trong felt that the Australian project design team did not take into account the needs and desires of the local teacher training and education department experts, which was to first produce a text book and then to train teachers how to use it. Trong raised the problems with the Australian project management team but his concerns were sidelined when the management team responded that they had put the textbook in a package which included other teacher training activities. Trong, not familiar with the management and administrative side of aid projects and the funding criteria of the donor countries, assumed that there would be a second project to follow on from the work of the first project.

Trong discussed the project design period, that is, when the Australian team carried out what it assumed to be the necessary field work and consultation. This is most often a 2- to 3-week period of time. Trong relayed how he felt the design team ignored the MOE officials and other relevant Lao stakeholders. Although the project design can be adapted or changed during the implementation (usually a 3-month period), it is not usually changed through the evidence of ethnographic information; it is more likely to be on the grounds of budgetary concerns. Trong's concerns pointed to the lack of consultation and the resultant design that was controlled by the Australian project management team. Saying 'but we put it in a package for you already' was letting this participant, who was powerful in his own ministry, know that the Australian management will dominate how work will be organised in the project.

The discontent with the project covered a range of issues from inappropriate application of the project construct to notions of collaborative work and decision-making processes including negotiating unfamiliar contexts which was a highly significant issue for Australian project management teams (see Chapter 6 for this latter point). In summary data revealed that in many aspects of financial management and working relations between the host-country MOE and the Australian management there was wholesale rejection of legitimate knowledge and expertise of host-country agents and disregard for genuine collaboration as claimed in project goals. The reproduction of such patterns of domination and subordination brought into play the processes of marginalisation and practices of self-marginalisation; it did not recognise the capacity of the host-country staff and undermined any redistribution of resources in the field.

Distrust of Host-Country Experts

Sol, a university lecturer with Project 1, raised some interesting points around the issue of sustainability in the discussion about the end of the project. These were shared among the Lao stakeholders in Project 1. The discourse of sustainability in aid-funded projects, as constructed by the donors and funders, is not internalised by the host-country stakeholders in the same way as it is by the dominant agents. Sustainability from an aid and development view is where the project is no longer funded. In many ways the practices of self-marginalisation subvert the notion of sustainability; host-country participants glorify features of the imported project and stigmatise a host-country-run project believing that it would not contribute in the same way. Sol showed some disbelief that the budget would not continue. He raised some contentious points about sustainability and the possible problems if the project was run by host-country staff. He revealed significant positionings of participants in the field and even with the absence of foreigners the field would still be dominated by those players who have more valuable capital: 'I don't know why, maybe it is this country's style . . . we don't work completely 100 per cent, just only 80 or 90 per cent if we work with our Lao colleagues. If you work with the expatriate staff we work well. I don't know why it happens like this.'

He made a further point that his country's participants would not take the project seriously if it was run by Lao teacher trainers. He asked the question of 'who would teach the course in the host country?'. Sol was concerned about whether the host country's teacher educators or

Australian staff would run it; this was a significant issue for the participants. This was a point supported by the data from the other host-country
interviewees and indicated adherence to the discourse of the primacy
of the 'native speaker of English' (Phillipson, 1992b). The notion of the
native speaker of English here was extended to 'so-called' native-English-
speaking institutions and nations.

The host-country interviewees illustrated how deeply the discourses
of colonialism are internalised; a key discourse is that expatriate lecturers
(native speakers of English) are better and have accumulated more valuable stakes than local staff have. This is a key premise on which IELEPs are
predicated and explicates a powerful expression of the symbolic violence
of colonialism and aid, where the host-country experts are devalued and
marginalised in the unequal distribution of cultural capital. Host-country
experts, in conserving the relations in the field, self-marginalise, placing
their skills and expertise in a subordinate position. Drawing on Bourdieu's
multi-layered analysis we see how other interests of the dominant agents
work to distribute symbolic capital in their favour. The expatriate staff,
in fact, may not be as well-trained as the host-country staff are and they
have no real interest in the development of local teachers; their interests
may well lie with their own self-improvement and the accumulation of
economic capital.

The ELT Project: Teaching and Learning Practices

Symbolic violence runs through this whole discussion of the projects'
work and perhaps most strongly in discussing the core motive of the
projects, ELT. The foundation of both projects delegitimises (or invali-
dates) the host-country teaching practices. It is here that one is able to
see clearly the relations in the field as they pertain to ELT, in particular,
how one of the main goals of the projects, to replace existing behaviour
in the field, is realised. The projects were separated by time and geopolitical boundaries but once again I will demonstrate the homologies of the
projects in terms of the exportation of a particular approach to the teaching
of English and struggle over similar types of intellectual resources.

A highly contested area of the project field is where project participants are engaged in struggle over the scarce intellectual resources in
the field, that is, legitimacy in terms of voice and participation, intellectual and academic credibility, economic stakes and educational resources.
A key issue is that of the ways in which intellectual or knowledge
capital (or in Bourdieu's [1992] terms, symbolic capital) is accumulated.
Bourdieu argued that because legitimate knowledge in the different

fields is determined in relation to the dominant conception or ruling ideas/theories at any moment in a field (which is dominated by symbolic capital) on average it is unlikely that host-country (localised) knowledge or practices can change the structure of those dominant practices and legitimate knowledge (Bourdieu & Eagleton, 1992: 119). If we think about the nature of the symbolic capital (see Chapter 2 for a definition) in the fields, is it possible for a range of 'knowledges' to equally accumulate the relevant capital needed to create change or give recognition to indigenous practices? In his conversation with Terry Eagleton, Bourdieu was discussing the rise of 'rap' music and its impact on the field of popular culture and whether it would gain an orthodox position. This analysis is relevant to the dynamics of the project field and the ways in which legitimacy is bestowed on certain knowledge ('native speaker' of English) and practices (approaches to teaching, western corporate and aid organisation modes of work).

Australian universities' quest for economic capital, coupled with the increasing demand of English language on an international scale, provided fertile conditions for the conception of both projects. IELEP implementers are governed by the dominant ideas and theories of the time; these theories most often conserve, not challenge the current practices in the field. In both projects the design of teacher education programmes and courses emanated from the types of courses that were delivered by the Australian university. The projects were won because of the university's reputation in the field of TESOL and, as mentioned in Chapter 1, Australia's perceived national successful experience of teaching in linguistically and culturally diverse settings.

In both Project 1 and Project 2, the Ministries of Education desired that the English language communicative ability of the country's teachers and students be increased. In Laos (Project 1) English was a relatively recent foreign language and in Project 2 English has long history. The design documents of both projects foregrounded the implementation of the 'communicative approach to language teaching' – the dominant conception at the time.

ELT practices: Struggles around methodology in Project 1 and Project 2

The theory and practice of ELT has been largely produced in America and England (with a much smaller contribution from Australia and New Zealand) (Holliday, 1994; Liu, 1998; Pennycoook, 1998; Phillipson, 1992b). In recent decades, communicative language teaching (CLT) approaches have dominated ELT teacher training programmes, both in countries where English is the dominant language and in countries where English is used as a lingua franca (ELF), foreign language (EFL) or second language (ESL) (Phan Le Ha, 2008). CLT as an export commodity is critiqued and criticised as inappropriate to many contexts (Achren & Keolivay, 1998; Brown, 2000; Kubota, 2001b), as a 'colonising' force (Phan Le Ha, 2008: 88) and as an ineffective language teaching approach (Bax, 2003). In many cases the communicative approach is seen as having an emphasis on the production of oral language (Hird, 1995; Holliday, 2005). There are a multitude of reasons why the communicative approach is viewed in this way. One of the overriding ones is that the origin of this approach developed where English was taught in an English-dominated speaking environment to speakers of other languages (Hird, 1995). In this context there is unlimited supply of authentic oral interactions to use as models of language use in the classroom. This body of knowledge and practice espoused certain commonalties across the 'so-called' English-speaking cultures, for example, the role and status of the teacher; behaviour of students and teachers; expectations of how things are taught and learnt; and an understanding of the education system and how that relates to the wider society. This theory and practice of ELT has driven and guided the export of education of English teachers in countries where English is taught as an ELF or EFL; as methodologies have become outdated and replaced in English-speaking countries, these 'new' methodologies have been exported to the growing domain of EFL (Holliday, 1994; Pennycook, 1994, 1998). The ready exportation of a teaching methodology implies that the adoption of established NABA English language teaching methodologies is the ultimate aim for all classrooms (Holliday, 2005). In the case of these particular TESOL teacher education courses, the [university] staff had a genuine interest in designing and delivering a programme that would be of use to the Lao and Japanese English teachers. What is under consideration here is the issue of how transferable the methodology was to the host-country classrooms.

The host-country teachers in the countries of both projects were characterised, correctly or incorrectly, as having a reliance on the 'traditional' method of grammar translation. The way the project documents characterise methodology is another act of symbolic violence enacted by the dominant players in the projects. The dismissal and invalidation of the current teachers' teaching practices discounted any value and positive learning experiences in Lao and Japanese classrooms. The projects identified a most urgent pedagogical need: learning to use the (so-called) 'communicative approach'. All players in this game were complicit in the marginalisation and self-marginalisation of the host-country EL teacher. How is this compliance achieved? Bourdieu would say that all players have an interest in the game and they take on the dominant ideologies of the field. Another dimension, as Kumaravadivelu (2006: 12) explains, is that expatriate EL teachers use strategies to denigrate local knowledge, in particular by making local languages irrelevant to the learning and teaching of English.

English language proficiency was a powerful determiner of legitimacy and was seen as a concomitant need by the host-country participants; the teachers and MOE personnel in the host countries overwhelmingly felt that the EL teachers needed to increase their English proficiency. Target language proficiency is of course a common need of foreign language teachers in many countries; bilingual LOTE (languages other than English) teachers in Australia cite this as their overriding concern.

In both projects the host-country teachers spoke positively about their current approaches to ELT; many of the teachers named it as Grammar Translation and believed that this approach had an important role in their classes. In Project 2, the participant teachers were also involved in their own self-study groups (this was mentioned in Chapter 3) where they explored other approaches. In Project 1 several of the teachers had studied in Australia and were aware of the dominance of communicative type methodology in ELT teacher training. There were a range of responses to the CLT teaching approach. Min, a former EL teacher with Project 1, commented on how this methodology was preferred by Australians and was central to the Project 1 training course. From her point of view, Lao teachers found this method quite inconvenient because of the changes that they needed to make to their style of teaching and the type of resources they required. She wondered if there had been any research to see if this new method, communicative methodology, was more successful than the old methods. She also raised the point that this method was imposed on the teachers in the training programme.

The project's EL teaching approach was glorified and rationalised through the accumulation of culture capital afforded by a highly valued academic qualification. Weng (P1LM2) discussed some of the real issues that faced Lao EL teachers. In her comments below she described how CLT is not appropriate to her context and she questioned whether the teachers used this approach in the classroom.

> After the [course] they learn more about how to teach English in a communicative way, but due to the real situation in the school and other problems, as you know the teachers have to teach many hours

per week and other activities that they have to be responsible for, and with the communicative approach the teacher has to prepare a lot.... So,... I am not sure whether they follow what they have learned in the course here.

Weng's comments resonated with critics of the export of CLT such as Chowdhury (2003), Holliday (2005) and Phan Le Ha (2008) and call into question the continued legitimacy of this approach. She also questioned the overall teacher training approach and believed that teachers were abandoned after they finished the course. If teachers were trained to teach in an unfamiliar way, Weng would have liked to see the teacher receive support or mentoring:

> I felt abandoned myself after I came back from Australia in the early 1990s. At that time there were no resources at the school and I had 24 hours per week of teaching, it was very hard. I had energy, I had knowledge too, but the condition around me didn't allow me to teach in a new way. I am concerned about my colleagues who have recently graduated. they would have benefited from some follow up.

Sal (P2LT3), an EL teacher from Project 2, made a similar comment about the project's need to integrate and support its teacher training approach and resources with the Japanese EL teachers' context:

> The thing about teachers is they don't have much time, they're always pressed for time, they've got marking if they aren't preparing. So the project should know that context that the teachers are working in and provide them with a range of samples of teaching strategies, and materials that they can immediately apply and maybe adapt, for their own classroom. Together with some kind of theoretical framework, so they can see how it all fits in, but having the really practical things, and the kind of strategies that are going to work in a Japanese class-room are things that appeal to Japanese teenagers. There are masses of opportunities for learners in Japan to tap into English, so it shouldn't be hard to motivate them, but making that link between the outside world and the classroom, you know, providing strategies that teach-ers are going to be able to take in the next day, use, find it works, that's what's going to really make it a successful program.

Published CLT teaching materials and resources are commonly criticised for their strong British or American flavour. In the material English is not presented as an EIL (English as an international language) or ELF but rather glorified as belonging to English-speaking countries (Holliday,

2005; Phan Le Ha, 2008; Kubota, 1998; Phillipson & Karmani, 2005). This criticism of the approach in the teacher training programmes emerged in both projects. Tong (P1LU3) from Project 1 raised problems with the materials used for teacher training and a way to improve a course such as this would be to 'add some Lao context into the materials'. She also referred to the underlying theory of CLT as not appropriate to Laos:

> I mean some theory is really hard to adapt in our situation, because as you see we have large classes to compared to the number of students in other countries. For example, in Australia in language classes they might have only about 15 at most, but here we have 45–50.

Tong added to her point about large classes:

> ... So, another thing is we don't have enough facilities for our teachers to prepare lessons.... We do have the idea what we are going to do, but in this situation we cannot put what we have in our minds into practice.

So even if the teacher wished to create, for example, information-gap type activities that required photocopies of materials or give further reading activities, they were limited because of lack of the resources available to them. This questions the purpose of training in a teaching methodology which requires resources that are not available to the teacher.

The points about large classes and the teaching resources were also true for teachers in Project 2. Sal, a secondary school teacher from Project 2, drew particular attention to the larger class size and the extra duties that teachers have in his country.

> Usually the class size now is 40. This is designed or decided by the Board of Education and Minister of Education. So 40 is kind of a big number...I am afraid that most of the other schools they do the English conversation class with 40 students. Can you believe it? I personally very strongly disagree with this size because it's too large. That's why these other high schools they give up teaching the communicative way and do some writing and reading exercises.

Sal worked in an innovative school programme for school children who dropped out of the mainstream high schools. In the above quote he referred to how English was usually taught in secondary schools. Lin (P2LT1), also from Project 2, talked about the class size but she emphasised the burden of the extra duties that teachers in her country perform. These included coordinating and teaching the students' extracurricular activities during the 'holiday' periods. In one part of the interview she discussed the teachers' role and how it was 'very difficult for teachers to study only for themselves or for their career' and also that this was not counted as extra work:

> No, because we say summer vacation but there is no summer vacation as a system. We are paid during summer vacation so, we have to work for them.

Comments such as these led me to ask questions about the ways in which the projects were designed. How are these differences in professional work practices taken into account in the project design? Are the projects premised on the notion of teachers' work as it is in Australia?

As mentioned elsewhere in this book, the host-country Project 2 MOE committee was interested in what Australian universities had to offer because of the experience Australia had had with its immigration pro-gramme and the Adult Migrant Education Program. Ken, a university professor and member of the MOE committee for Project 2 (P2LU1), saw that Australia's experience was very different to, for example, British ELT institutions and universities where the majority of recent immigrants were from ex-colonies (where English is most often a lingua franca). However, while he acknowledged this experience and possible advantages, he was doubtful of what it means in practice:

> ... so I thought this experience would be an advantage but I don't see what sort of advantage you actually have, maybe the sensitivity to different cultures, different languages.

Discussions about methodology with participants in the projects led me to question the idea that there is a particular EL methodology that is relevant and useful for all and any situation. Kumaravadivelu's (2003b) 'postmethod pedagogy' dispenses with the idea that there is an EL teach-ing method that will suit all contexts at all times. His framework consists of pedagogic parameters: particularity, practicality and possibility. The parameter of particularity takes into account the needs and context of the particular learners when making decisions about how and what to teach. The parameter of practicality recognises and acknowledges the teachers' sense-making, the teacher-generated theory of practice which informs and is informed by teaching. This sense-making sees the classroom walls as permeable; the learners are situated within the context that exists out-side of the classroom. The third parameter of possibility takes account of the socio-political world and is the dimension which is concerned with identity and social transformation. Kumaravadivelu's parameters are interwoven and overlap; they each shape and are shaped by the other

(2003b: 34–36). It is clear in both projects' designs that these three dimensions of Kumaravadivelu's framework were not taken into account but rather a non-contextualised approach was favoured.

Legitimate work: Management practices

What has been argued above is that in serious structural ways the foundations of both projects work against interests of the purported beneficiaries. In this section I focus on how management practices entrench the same power relations in the field.

I continue the theme that work practices, the way things get done, in these projects seem natural for some of the project participants and that the struggle to produce and to control the dominant practices in the field helps to shape the power relations in the field. I discuss the way the struggle is borne out in implementation processes of Projects 1 and 2 and positions at work. To help understand the processes of domination and subordination I have integrated the analytical framework of glorification, stimagtisation and rationalisation (Skutnabb-Kangas, 1998). This phenomenon is a process by which the dominant ideas are legitimated in the field. Skutnabb-Kangas (1998) describes the three elements of the process: the non-material resources of the dominant group, including language and culture, are presented and glorified as modern, technologically developed and forward-looking whereas the host-country non-material resources are typified and stigmatised as being traditional, backward-looking and narrow. The latter are marginalised. The relationship between the dominant and subordinate players is rationalised so as to reproduce the unequal access to power and resources (pp. 17–18).

It is interesting to examine the processes by which an organisation or an institution can become 'legitimate' in the context of IELEP work. The most obvious path to legitimacy is to win the tenders of lucrative projects. Once the organisation or institution accumulates the scarce economic capital in the field, it is able to legitimise its ways of working, for example, the ways in which intellectual work is carried out. It can then claim academic superiority over the 'other' in the field.

An underlying assumption in the projects' field is that the Australian management teams model and bring legitimate work and management practices. Implicit in this, and as I demonstrate throughout this book, is the belief that the host-country or local teams do not have the required skills and abilities to take up the decision-making positions.

Lee outlined the procedures for designing, and perhaps winning, an aid-funded project. He described the composition of the project design team, that is, the group of people (business person, an aid agency representative and a technical expert in the field) who went to the country in which the project was to be located and who put together a document which outlined the objectives and activities of the project:

> ... And although they're briefed by the post in the host country, the characteristics of the cultural context are crucial to understand how a project could well develop the country's capability. I think it's also well known within the project management companies that if you can get yourself on the design team, that greatly helps your chances of securing the project when it goes to tender, which was in fact the case for us. So, the links within links ... networks.

The social capital embedded in this process is critical to the dynamics of the field. The project management companies who have accumulated large amounts of social capital are more likely to accumulate economic capital by winning project tenders. Symbolic capital is accrued through this process: the companies are recognised in the field as dominant agents and this delivers them a powerful position, since universities vie for a partnership with a successful company. The universities do not usually have the recognised management capacity to bid for projects alone. 'Successful' project management companies have such a powerful position in the field that they can approach tertiary institutions and choose with whom they form partnerships. Those very successful companies have the strength to bid for projects without partnering an educational institution because of their position in the field. An interesting feature of the field is that language education projects do not necessarily have to be developed or delivered by an educational institution. This latter point clearly has implications for the quality of the educational project products and delivery.

Legitimate knowledge

In the field of EL teacher training, one can easily find derogatory views of tertiary institutions in the target country. In a research conversation with the Australian project managers of the fee-based project (Project 2) the topic turned to the possible partnerships with a host-country university. The idea of a collaborative partnership was not taken serviously; the implementers did not view the host country's universities as real tertiary institutions. They went on to elaborate their views, that the students did not do any work and the university lecturers did not have any notion of scholarship. They also reflected a common view held in Australian universities that the methodology of teaching English in the host country's schools and universities was archaic. This view of the 'other' context is prevalent in much of the literature on the intellectual relationship between the donor and the recipient (Davis, 1991; Kubota, 1998; 1999, 2001a; Morris, 1996; Pennycook, 1994, 1995, 1998, 2000; Pottier, 1993); the goal of many projects has been to replace behaviours which are perceived by the donors as backward and inefficient with others designed to increase productivity and efficiency (Davis, 1991: 35).

The above discussion of legitimacy in management practices and intellectual resources would indicate that the Australian teams hold the legitimate knowledge, but this legitimacy can be brought into question when looking at some of the project documents concerning the ELT work. The documents (at the time they were written) did not reflect recent (last decade) developments in the field of ELT. At that time current developments around issues such as the role of the so-called native English speaker, the use of the first language in second (or additional) language classroom, management structures, recognition of indigenous knowledge and skills and recognition of the academic skills of the host-country teacher educators and classroom teachers are clearly absent in both projects. The stigmatisation of host-country teaching practices found in the documents allowed for Australian institutions to play out strategies of domination. The strategies undertaken to gain dominance glorified the donor and/or provider country's resources, employment of external agents, the technical or academic 'experts' who take control of the processes of the projects and determine how the objectives will be carried out. The external agents adopted the language and processes of being a manager and controller; the contributions of host-country staff, in terms of project management and holders of local expertise, are devalued (Medgyes' quote from Chapter 1 is pertinent here). Work can only be comprehended, rationalised and legitimated by those within the field (Bourdieu, 1986). Furthermore, it is those within the field that define the field, as the authority to legitimate is embedded in the power relations borne of the struggles within the field to position an agent as legitimately belonging to it. The subsequent world of the local project is then not only defined and brought into existence by the political, geographical and economic considerations of the dominant agent (in this case, the funding organisation/country) but also by the internal organisation of the project, that is, the hierarchies and privileges are a continuum of this international power play.

Aside from the accumulation of economic capital, what else legitimises Australian university work in international contexts? Murray from Project 2 acknowledged what Australian 'experts' are good at; the vast experience gained through teaching of English as a second (or additional) language is highly valuable to work in projects outside of Australia (ELT services funded through the Australian Adult Migrant Education Program). His view about what skills Australia brought is echoed by participants involved in the MOE Project 2 committee but Murray was concerned that the Australian project stakeholders did not recognise what he sees as the more important knowledge, skills and experiences for work in Project 2, namely, genuine collaboration and consultation in the design stage.

> Australia has got I think quite good at cross cultural interaction and biculturation and triculturation. But these skills are still not recognised as necessary, for example, in this particular project . . . My guess is that the qualification of the person heading the consortium . . . that judgement . . . would be made on their academic qualification. Not on their experience of delivering this sort of activity in a third country not on their ability to understand this country's culture or, this country's language, or this country's pedagogy or this country's social interaction. And, it's really interesting to see that those sort of skills are not often understood by service providers in Australia. On the contrary my organization recognises that we don't have the academic skills and abilities to deliver what we want to deliver in this country so we contract for it.

A common thread through the data in this story is that for a project to effectively deliver 'products' that are useful to the host-country teachers, the designers and implementers must embark on extensive collaborative, consultative preparation work before the project commences. Stories abound in the IELEP field that demonstrate how the lack of knowledge about the host country and a paucity of truly collaborative and consultative work are deemed responsible for the project's failure. These factors were sadly absent from the Australian project teams' priorities in both projects despite repeated references to collaboration in project documents.

Participants from Project 2 candidly discussed ways in which the needs of teachers and students can be effectively canvassed and ways that projects could work from a collaborative basis. Murray discussed this issue from a 'market-driven' point of view and although his approach is perhaps more mindful of the accumulation of economic capital, it also spoke of the imperative to deliver high-quality services which meet the needs of the 'clients', in this case, English language teachers and students. He believed that many education projects do not undertake effective 'market research', thus implying that the preliminary feasibility studies conducted by aid agencies and educational bodies do not suffice compared to the extensive research conducted by companies in search of new target audiences or the marketing of new products. He cited examples of how high-performing private sector companies effectively gather such information; in overtly economic terms he spoke of the university's obligation to the government and to its own academic capital and reputation.

Murray made a point that is highly relevant to both projects, that the project designers and implementers must seriously engage the host country's stakeholders and research needs and expectations. The main point here is that the Australian university consortium traded on its perceived dominance (economic and cultural capital) regardless of the reality on the ground. The consortium, in fact, did not have the expertise that it claimed. This point is further developed throughout the remainder of the book.

Ken, a university professor from Project 2 and a member of the MOE committee which liaised with the Australian project team, discussed an example of what he considered to be a successful procedure for establishing an effective teacher training project. He referred to an ongoing project within the MOE. The project was run by a British international organisation (referred to hereafter as the Learning Council) which facilitated student exchange, teacher exchange and EL teacher training. He described in detail the ways in which the Learning Council collected its 'ethnographic information' about the teaching and learning contexts in his country. The Learning Council held annual conferences where the governing body of the organisation invited speakers from the host country's MOE to discuss its ELT curriculum directions and related issues:

> they listen to the changes, for the developments, for the current situations of education in my country and . . . to . . . our expectations of those universities. This happens regularly once a year.

He described how the Learning Council questioned speakers about the current directions of the English language field and

> so I think that those people who are in charge of those programs are in a way more familiar about new directions shown in the course of study than are the actual participants in those programs. It's true, and they ask the participants to bring the MOE authorised text book to the universities where they are going to and show them to the teachers in charge of the programs. And also we ask them to take video recordings of the lessons they teach in the classrooms and ask directors or teachers to have the time for them to discuss their situations or the

problems in the actual lessons. And in this way I think the teaching staff at the universities who run those programs can know what sort of needs teachers have and what sort of real situations they are in the classrooms.

Ken continued to talk about the ways the MOE and the Learning Council project coordinators collected feedback from the host country's teachers and the participating universities. They held forums in the country where the teachers studied, for example, Scotland, England, and then back in the host country where the teacher or teachers worked. The teachers and participating universities evaluated the project's activities and this was fed back into the next year's programme. At no stage did the Australian consortium invest in this kind of time or collaboration.

Tan, a teacher educator from Project 2, gave some valuable information about the ways in which the project could be more relevant to the Japanese context. Firstly, he thought that the project should offer face-to-face courses within the host country; he gave examples of other foreign universities which had opened up offshore campuses. Secondly, he believed that teachers would want to study and work at the same time: 'most of them want to go there while they are working so the course should be given at night . . . as an evening course or a summer course or something like that . . .' Thirdly, he thought that Japanese universities and overseas ones prioritise research over teaching and he believed that the Australian course should value their work 'as educators not researchers'. Tan also spoke about the experiences of Japanese teachers studying in overseas universities: '. . . many of them think that there is a gap between study at university and what they teach at their school. That means their courses don't always reflect on the teaching in this country.'

Chris, a lecturer with an Australian university, raised the issue of how curriculum developed for an 'innovative' project should be informed by developments in other fields of language teaching. In particular, she referred to the way the EFL field could learn from developments in LOTE teaching in Australia. Chris was particularly knowledgeable about Japanese teaching and learning practices. She is bilingual, bicultural and an experienced LOTE and EFL teacher as well as an education manager. She was seconded to work on Project 2 because of her professional expertise. Throughout her interview she expressed disquiet about what she terms the 'misguided' focus of the curriculum and was doubtful of the way it would meet the needs of the target audience. During her involvement with the project she was particularly concerned about the suitability of the materials and she talks about how she continually sought ways to

offer her skills to the project. At one point she offered the Australian curriculum writers EFL teaching materials produced by bilingual Japanese
ELTs and expatriate ELTs in Japan and are freely available for teachers
to use. She explained how these resources were accessible, current, contextualised and interesting and reflected the sort of goals that the project
courses adhered to. Each initiative was rejected. She added the following
comment at the end of this discussion, 'it may not have had that international flavour then either, so it's hard to know,' but there is still a question
about the type of 'legitimate knowledge' that is allowed in project work.

The ELT field, dominated by 'so-called native speaking countries',
continues to think itself the leader in teaching English, that it has the
correct, appropriate and exportable approaches and methodology. In aid
or fee-based projects the implementers most usually seek to replace the
indigenous teaching methods with those from Britain, Australia or the
USA. An intriguing complexity of this field is that the host countries continue to seek the assistance of so-called native English speakers and organisations from English-speaking countries. The notion of 'native speaker'
legitimacy in knowledge and work practices is deeply embedded in ELT
projects. The processes of self-marginalisation work to ensure that the features of the IELEP field stay intact; the host-country teachers for many and
complex reasons do not claim a dominant position. Insider accounts from
projects, in addition to those gained from the participants for this story,
continue to demonstrate the power of those deemed to be legitimate.

Positions at work

The IELEP field sharply marks out the positions of expert and non-
expert. The following account of work practices in an aid-funded IELEP
in a South East Asian country by Appleby *et al.* (2002) outlines the way
positions of expertise and knowledge are delineated in the IELEP field.
Copley was a language education project adviser. In her recent writings
about project work in South East Asia she related a discussion with an
ex-colleague from that project. They occupied very different positions in
the field: she was engaged as an expatriate technical expert and he as
a 'counterpart' teacher as well as a respected member of the country's
MOE. They talked about the difficulties he was facing in the workplace,
inequity in remuneration, the expectation that local staff would work long
hours but earn their second income elsewhere, a lack of communication
and negotiation and unexplored assumptions on the part of many project
participants. His story concerned conflict over who would write an exam
for the local trainees. The local staff had all the relevant knowledge and

experience but expatriate staff decided that they would write the exam. It turned out that the exam was inappropriate for a number of reasons; the local staff had forewarned the expatriate staff but their advice was ignored. The result was that the majority of the students failed (Appleby *et al.*, 2002).

The Copley story of project work closely parallels the stories of inter-viewees from Project 1, particularly in terms of 'divisions of labour' and the positions of the 'counterpart'. It was clear from the start how the field would be differentiated; it was taken for granted that there would be 'counterparts' to the expatriate positions in the project, the counterparts shadow or are mentored in the work of that particular position, although at times these positions were ill-defined. However, there was no position for a 'counterpart team leader'. The counterparts were initially assigned to the expatriate teaching staff. In the third and fourth years of the project there were 'counterpart' course coordinators. There was a curious feature in this arrangement: the host-country 'counterpart' coordinators did not have a substantive non-counterpart (expatriate) member of staff, that is, there were no expatriate coordinator positions. In the case of Project 1, even though the local staff were eventually appointed to particular posi-tions in the project on their own merit, they were still called 'counterpart staff'. The term 'counterpart' is not neutral. It signifies that the staff mem-ber is not fully 'expert' or 'professional'. This naming of local staff as 'counterpart' contributes to the delineation of power in the field (Arnold & Sarhan, 1994; Murni & Susan, 1997).

An important factor concerning counterparts is that they do not have a singular role in the IELEP, and this is a complicating factor in the projects. For example, consider the position of a 'counterpart' lecturer on the 'university-run' course in Project 1; this person may have been the head of their department at the national university, a lecturer on the national university programmes, a lecturer on the private fee-based courses within their university and a member of the MOE project advi-sory committee, as well as a 'counterpart' lecturer, a 'counterpart' advisor on the project and may have taught on other English language courses in the project. The different roles occupied different positions in the project and were accorded (or not) differing accumulations of the capital in the field. The description of the above agent does not take into account other factors such as gender, age, ethnicity, political persuasion and activity, educational background or professional experiences which may also have had influence on practices pursued and subsequent positioning in the field.

Another controversial aspect of the organisation of staff in the project field and one which exacerbated the unequal power relations was around money. 'Counterparts' received a salary supplement, in addition to their local salary. This was another curious feature in that the 'counterpart' staff was a highly trained and qualified group (all had post-graduate qualifications from Australia and some had studied in Singapore and the USA as well). Yet they did not qualify for a full project adviser position and were not paid the equivalent rate. The expatriate staff group was paid a phenomenally high salary in spite of the host country's poverty and particularly low salaries were paid to host-country teachers. The economic disparity between the expatriates and host-country staff was a pre-eminent factor affecting the relations in the field. The counterpart salary question was a typical result of rationalisation of the glorification of the dominant player, the expatriate project worker and stigmatisation of the host-country staff. The dynamics of the IELEP field validate the knowledge, ethnicity and language nativeness of the Australian English speaking staff and invalidate all those attributes of the host-country participants.

Expatriate staff report how this factor hindered the development of collaborative relationships in the project. In general and as a feature of IELEPs, this is a critical issue in the running of aid projects but one that is least likely to be resolved. The expatriate staff is the beneficiary in a project's micro-economy. They are the dominant players in the struggle over economic capital within the project field and it is hard to imagine that they would relinquish this position. The counterpart staff, in Project 1, was apparently paid the equivalent of 10% to 12% of the average expatriate staff's wage. The 'counterpart' staff's bilingual and bicultural skills were not recognised by the project management; these staff were not employed as 'technical experts' unlike the sometimes less qualified technical expert Australian staff.

A common difficulty that all 'counterpart' participants raised was the problem of the 'double job'. The 'double job' they referred to was their IELEP position and their substantive position in the host-country institutions, not necessarily the other work these staff may be doing as their second or third jobs. The process by which they were seconded to the project was also problematic. Son, a university department head in Project 1, described how she managed her work life. Her substantive position was a department head in a university. During her secondment to the project she would finish her day as a 'counterpart' and then return to her substantive place of work to attend to her department duties. This was the case with all of the host-country participants. A common problem, it seems, was that they were inundated with problems and complaints from co-workers in their institutions or ministry departments. Their co-workers, the participants believed, feel that the 'counterparts' are shirking their substantive duties if they are not at their normal place of work when required.

The 'counterparts' in this story felt that they were constantly 'running to catch up on [their] work' (Tong P1LU3) and would have to regularly work a 7-day week. This was most often in stark contrast to the expatriate staff who were able to regulate their work and enjoy much more reasonable working hours.

From one perspective, it may seem that perhaps the 'counterparts' were well-off, for they were getting extra pay and the opportunity for professional development as well as being away from their regular place of work. However, the whole issue of 'counterpart' staff is vexed on all fronts. From the donor perspective, 'counterparts' are viewed as integral to fulfilling aid and development objectives, specifically those of 'sustainability' and 'capacity building'; also relevant to Project 1 was that of strengthening institutional links in the education sector. The host MOE, on the other hand, had the problem of scarce human resources, particularly in the educational leadership area, and these leaders were the staff the IELEP team wanted. The host-country participants were also concerned about working with the project for too long as then they would be in danger of losing their substantive positions with their institutions.

A central problem with the practices of the project management, as articulated by MOE teacher training staff from Project 1 (Son, Vong, Sol and Weng) and expatriate team members (Lee, Carla and Mel), was that the Australian project management did not recognise or did not acknowledge the complex internal relationships in the education field in the host country. The host-country MOE appeared to have complex, and at times tense, relations with the tertiary sector in the host country. Requests for project 'counterparts' needed to go through the MOE and, as Vong states, 'you can't jump across . . . it takes time, you know, too long.' This comment is in reference to the request procedure: first, the project management team writes to the MOE, the MOE then writes to the university management, who then writes to the relevant department of the university and then the head of department decides if it is possible to release the staff.

From Carla's view, the project management team put pressure on the MOE through the Teacher Training Department to release the counterpart staff. But the Australian team were not aware of the internal MOE machinations. The relations between the university management and the MOE were undergoing changes in terms of management responsibilities and the Australian project team was not cognisant of the particular interests of the host-country education institutions. What this all seemed to mean was a lack of clarity about when and who would be seconded to the project and really how willing the staff were to take up the 'counterpart' positions.

This examination of positions in project teams gives insight into the power relations in the field showing how strongly the power is invested in one side only in a supposedly collaborative venture.

Conflict within the Australian Teams

Counterpart positions and host-country partners in general are a site of struggle within the donor/Australian team. Right from the start in Project 1, Lee argued strongly that Lao staff should be placed in leadership positions or that at the very least there should be a Lao counterpart team leader. The Australian project management company was not in favour of placing host-country staff in leadership positions. In Project 2, Lee strongly advocated that the Australian university consortium establish a partnership with a Japanese university and collaborate on the development of the project programmes. This suggestion was not taken up by the Australian consortium. These struggles show that the dominant players are able to rationalise the relationships, the status and hierarchies in the field by claiming expertise and superior knowledge.

Conflict is a common thread in ethnographic studies of education projects. The issue of competing and conflicting interests is highlighted in Adrian Holliday's (1992, 1994, 1995, 2005) work on project life: 'conflict of interest is a recurring theme – between different professional groups, between curriculum developers and teachers, and between teachers and students, especially where there are cultural differences' (Holliday, 1994: 6).

There are many accounts in the literature of projects where the staff was left feeling personally devastated as a result of their work on international education projects (Brown, 2001; Goulet, 1995; Hall, 1997; Holliday, 1995, 1999; Murphy, 1999). The stories in this book resonate with the literature in the sense that many of the participants felt disenfranchised in the work of the project and felt that their objections about certain issues from the sideline were of no effect.

The relations in the field are hierarchical; the project management company in Project 1 occupied a much more dominant role than that of its partner, the Australian university. Lee from the university talked about his experience of conflict within the project: the 'playing field' was far from 'level'. He was employed as the project team leader by the company and was therefore its representative in the field. He described the relationships in the field in terms of levels of expertise, authority and responsibility. Clearly the project management company did not have the cultural capital (knowledge or qualifications) but it did take up an authoritative role if any dispute arose. The university was complicit in this power arrangement and left its own staff, who took responsibility for the quality and delivery of programmes, to fend for themselves if there was any conflict, for example, over work practices or budget. Lee described the difficulties and tensions within the project management 'team' as a gap between the vision he and other teachers held and that of the team leader and the project management company. There were great differences between ways of looking at culture, language, teaching and the whole notion of development projects, and the gap had widened considerably during the first year of the project. He had worked with ELT professionals in the host country for a number of years and had bilingual language skills as well as his own status within the academy and while he was seen as a valued partner in the project, he did not feel that he held any real authority in the field. As I have demonstrated in the preceding chapters, the IELEP is complicated and while the expatriate group is the dominant player, individuals within this group hold dissimilar views about the role and work of the project. Lee made a point of emphasising a positive aspect of the work in Project 1, the strong and constructive relationships that developed between the Australian TESOL professionals and the host-country TESOL professionals. He used the term 'fantastic' to describe the collaborative work efforts that were achieved in the university study programmes conducted under the project.

A dominant notion of teaching, work organisation and work practices emerged from the participants' stories; this notion reflects the economic rationalist model of the project. The behaviours inculcated by the field reproduced the 'institutional practice' (Fairclough 1989: 33) from the donor's or provider's context. Bourdieu offers a description of this inculcated habitus:

> (The) habitus, the product of history, produces individual and collective practices ... [in accordance with a] .... principle of continuity and regularity ... [seemingly] without a rational basis. (Bourdieu & Passeron, 1977: 82)

This notion of practices as a realisation of the dynamics of a field which have largely been derived from events and organisations that have gone before allows me to understand the seeming reappearance of international relations predicated on those established during the colonial era

(Phillipson, 2008). The dynamics of the field, that is, where revenue-hungry organisations from nations holding the most valued capital such as universities, project management companies and other related institutions search the globe for opportunities to maximise profits, are not unfamiliar territory. The international and national funding bodies, often in collaboration with transnational companies and/or the private wings of universities, determine the priorities and focuses of future funding grants. Negotiation and collaboration, supposedly the guiding concepts of the establishment of genuinely international projects, take place only within the inner sanctums of the above organisations and only among the key stakeholders with capital recognised and valued in the field.

The regularities of the field embed the uneven distribution of resources. One of my goals in writing this book is to find ways to disrupt the field and transform relations in the IELEP. A way to do this is to increase local participation in project design and implementation. A curious element in this story is to uncover why this simple remedy to the ongoing problem of the failure of international language education projects has not been taken up. The participation of host-country staff in the development of projects is a strategy recommended by others in the field of project implementation and development (Abdul-Raheem, 2000; Phelan & Hill, 1998).

Chapter 5
Talk in the Field: The 'English Only' IELEP

Language is a pivotal factor and a constant point of reference in both of the projects as their very existence is predicated on promoting and supporting the teaching of English. The project goals are to train English language teachers and to offer a range of English language courses, for example, English for academic and teaching purposes and English for specific purposes. This chapter explores the role of English, linguistic practices and the discourses in project work through the perceptions of the participants in this study. It also illustrates how the roles of languages and linguistic practices are used to delineate positions in the field. In Chapter 4 I introduced the processes of glorification, stigmatisation and rationalisation as named by Skutnabb-Kangas (1998); these processes are highly relevant to the analysis of linguistic practices in the IELEPs and I draw on them to examine how domination and subordination take place. The linguistic practices of a project are sites of struggle and an analysis of the role of English and project talk offers significant insights for the running of international IELEPs. Additionally, this chapter explores the positioning of the national languages of the projects' host countries and what is considered to be 'normal' project talk.

In particular I look at discourses at work in the projects from a number of different levels: the talk that happens within project work; those discourses that inform the ways projects work, including the project documents and; and those discourses that emerge from the relations within the project. I aim to reveal what underlies the linguistic terms such as bilateral aid, collaborative work practices, cooperation and, significantly, 'internationalisation'. My analysis shows that everything is not as it seems. The discourses of the aid project world assume a lack of pecuniary interest. Other discourses which help to shape project work signal ways of operating and/or working that appears on the surface as 'fair' or 'on behalf of others'.

I seek to understand the way that, within the discourses, positions are taken up or designated in IELEPs. What are the discourses that help to delineate the power relationships in the field? On an initial reading, the data (which include analyses of project implementation documents and interview material) seem to add substance to the view that there is a binary relationship between the recipients and donors or providers of language education and that this relationship is the sole site of contesting and competing discourses. However, as I have shown in previous chapters, the story is far more multi-layered and complicated than a straightforward two-party relationship.

This chapter draws on the concepts of 'discourse' as discussed by Chiapello and Fairclough (2002), Gee (1996, 1999, 2000) and Fairclough (1989, 1992, 2001). I also draw on Bourdieu's notions of linguistic capital and legitimate voice, which are embedded within his relational concepts of field, habitus and capital. A significant question for this research is: 'who has the "legitimate voice" and the "legitimate language" and subsequently is able to best negotiate their interests?' Whose voice is heard in language education projects?

The project documents reveal much about the power relations in the field and the ways in which project practices are conceptualised. This chapter examines the way that English is represented in the documents and by the project participants. What is its role and importance in the host countries? I illustrate the arguments in this chapter with an in-depth analysis of two examples where the power relations of the field are revealed in the experiences of project practices. These examples are based on the interviewees' experiences of differing understandings of the dynamics of the field.

Talking Up the Project: Project Documents

The project documents offer a fertile pool of data for this study. The documents for the two IELEPs in this study are not unique; there are regularities and homologies in how international/multinational/transnational project management companies tender for project funding, whether in the aid or in the private sector. The particular documents examined here reveal some key issues that frame the way projects are constructed; these issues include donor (or provider) perspectives of the recipient country, perceptions of the recipient's education system, the relations in the field, goals of the project, inputs, the anticipated outcomes, staff profiles, ways of working (this is termed 'methodology') and budgetary information. What is also important is what the documents did not address: for example, the role of the host-country language, the position or role of host-country technical experts and how the host-country project participants defined the 'problem', that is, the gap the project will fill.

In this particular study the documents are a source of information through which I can make some comments about the two projects as whole entities and the field in general. The document extracts discussed below are prime examples of the types of texts which contribute to the construction of project work and inculcate project participants with the types of behaviour (linguistic and otherwise) that allow them to 'play the game' successfully. One question for this study is to investigate how accessible, in terms of both physical and linguistic access, these documents are to all the project participants.

The project design documents appear to foreground good communication and the fostering of equal working relationships between project partners. Participants in aid projects (and in the fee-based project) are typically described as *partners, stakeholders* and *counterparts*. Notions such as *partnership, bilateral relations* and *collaboration*, for example, suggest equality. Partners are assumed to have equal rights in the decision-making process and access to the relevant institutions and individuals with whom decisions lay. What possibilities were there for the host country to have genuine partnerships? For example, in Project 1, as *partners* in the host country's language education what access might the host country's ministry officials and project committee members have had in the decision-making processes by which policy and project initiatives are prioritised? How can these *partners* have had a voice in negotiations and consultations with such monolithic systems as the foreign-based donor agencies or their own ministry of education (MOE)?

The goals of the project are at first glance commendable and achievable. They aimed to fulfill the oft-repeated discourses of social good and justice in the field, phrases such as the following: the project will *empower* the participants, the outcome will be a *sustainable* language education service, the host partners will have *ownership* of the endeavour, the activities of the project will build the country's *capacity* and access will be improved. The processes by which these outcomes were supposed to be achieved are described as *regular communication, partnership development, participative approach* and processes of *collaboration*. These processes expressed the underlying dominant discourses of aid, that is, the donors' or organisations' interests are in the public 'good'.

The outcomes for Project 1 related to the development and production of an English language syllabus for secondary school students, English language teacher training, establishment of a network of resource centres for teachers and English language training for ministry officials. The project objectives were ambitious and the documents acknowledged this: *achieving the major objectives of the project will be a challenge within the time frames nominated*. This was a worthy admission but what I found interesting in the written discussion about the project's objectives is that it did not set any mechanisms in place to relate the outcomes to baseline data the project proposal team had collected. The objectives were clearly driven by what the funding body saw as the gap in the host country's education system.

The documents for the fee-based project (Project 2) put forward outcomes in a slightly different way; the Australian educational providers had the expectation that the project itself would generate sufficient income to support itself. The outcomes were therefore expressed in terms which described the way that the project's programmes would attract and retain English language teachers. This aspect of Project 2 differentiated it from Project 1. Project 2 documents did not mention *capacity building* and again in contrast the Project 1 documents put the onus on the MOE to pursue a *sustainable* outcome. In Project 2 the onus was on the Australian providers to supply a desirable product to English language teachers in a country which abounded with similar courses.

The project documents described the framework from which the projects would carry out their activities. In Project 1 these were encapsulated in the *Principles* section. The notions which underlie the operation of the project were: *collaboration, liaison* and *exchange*. This paragraph went on to describe how this would be carried out: in the description of collaboration *this participatory approach offers rewards for all participants* and at the micro level, that is, among local and expatriate staff, this collaboration *will be mutually enriching*. In the explanation of liaison, the document described how in the relations to be established with other donors and providers, *we will strive to foster personal relationships as vigorously as we promote institutional links*.

The notion of *flexibility* is foregrounded in both proposal documents. The issue of flexibility arose in interviewee discussions about project work practices. Here I wish to focus on how the project documents represented their approach to the organisation of work and to relations between the project participants. *Flexibility* is used to naturally collocate with the methodology of the projects' organisational and educational work (specifically the one that is being exported from Australia). For example, in Project 1 the management of the project would *remain flexible in approach* and in its education work *the project's flexibility will facilitate creative and speedy responses* to emerging training needs. In Project 2 the *flexibility of the programme* allowed the students to choose the best option for their *professional* needs. The documents from Project 1 foregrounded flexibility as one of the key attributes of the approach of the *consultant*. The documents raised the issue of flexibility as an attribute that was particularly appropriate for what seemed to be the *overseas* context; for example, the *degree of certainty* was less in those countries outside of Australia. While there may have been some history of social or political upheaval, and this was a realistic concern, the documents produced a picture of a country that has little economic resources, undeveloped public infrastructure and a dependence on external funding. This description signalled a need of much more than a simple ELT training programme. Australia, on the other hand, was depicted as the supplier of stability. While not overtly spoken about in this way, the genre of the proposal document was one which required the tenderer to be a dependable provider. The implication was that the recipient countries (both the aid-dependent and the economically independent) were prone to unpredictable, and perhaps volatile, changes.

The project proposal and implementation documents created an understanding of the ways the projects work. The documents glorified the donor's or provider's approach to work, the host-country practices were stigmatised and they needed to be replaced and the imposition of the dominant players' approaches to work and teaching were rationalised in this process. The host countries lacked capacity; again they were stigmatised. The documents guided the projects in building (inculcating) an idealised project habitus. The documents acknowledged that some of the project participants were more easily inculcated into the behaviours suited to the project field. The following sections amplify this notion with examples from instances of project work.

Role and position of English

The role of English in the IELEP field is a contested one. The goals of both projects were primarily about improving teachers' proficiency in the teaching and use of English. The goals also implied that the types of professional development offered by the project were not available in the host countries. This was partially the case with Project 1, although there were programmes available within the host country's region that might have been more accessible and more relevant. As for Project 2, the ELT marketplace was highly competitive. Underlying the goals of both projects was the glorification of the projects' English teaching programmes and the stigmatisation of the host countries' programmes.

The goals of Project 1 were also to improve the regional provision of English and to organise English language courses for government officials. Underlying the goals for targeting the teachers' professional development was concern for the ministry staff (Project 1) and tertiary and school students' learning of English. Consequently, the way the research participants represented 'English' is of great significance here.

The interviewees were asked about the role of English in their country and its importance within the school curriculum. There was a great range of comments in the answer to these questions, not so much as a source of difference or sense of contest but rather, in the scope. Some interviewees gave answers which drew on issues of historical relevancy, for example, how English was introduced or imposed on their nation. Lan (P2LT4) described how English was introduced to her country 200 years ago in response to an invasion and English was viewed as a means by which the country could 'introduce the knowledge and information and technology from the outside world . . . So English was a tool . . .' Song (P1LU2) gave a trajectory of the roles of foreign languages in his country; he has studied a range of languages which includes English, French and Russian (see Chapter 2 for further details on the historical aspects of English in Projects 1 and 2).

English was a compulsory subject in the secondary schools of both of the project host countries. In Laos (Project 1) English was a recent introduction into the school curriculum and at the time of the project there was a dearth of teachers with high-level English language skills. In Japan (Project 2) English has had a much longer presence in the school curriculum and it was essential for students to do well in English to pass the university entrance examination. There was a lot of ambivalence (in Project 2) among the teachers about the position of English as a compulsory subject. In a discussion about this topic, Lan (P2LT4) thought that many of the students in Japan do not see a reason for studying English and for this reason some teachers think it should not be compulsory:

> . . . a lot of English teachers say that English should be an elective. Not all students . . . have to learn English so that the students who are really interested in or motivated in learning English should take English classes.

Sal (P2LT3) agreed with the sentiments of the above quote. He saw English as an important subject of study but felt that students would take more responsibility for their learning if they elected to do it:

I think an elective subject always requires students to have a kind of sense of responsibility. But if it's compulsory then it's kind of being forced to learn, and actually English is important, it is the major language all over the world in the modern age.... in terms of the diplomatic relations ... business associations ... it's a big advantage for them to learn English but still I think to give them a choice is important.

In spite of these views all of the Lao and Japanese interviewees agreed that English language education was high in the national priorities for their countries. There were many reasons given as to why English was important and interestingly almost all of the interviewees, both host-country and foreign project interviewees, expressed the importance in terms of the 'national interest' of the particular country. Weng (P1LM2) talked about how English would improve her country's status within the region and identified the (hoped for) linguistic capital that English brings:

like the other countries nowadays English is very important especially in south east Asia. Our government has opened up the country and we know that English is a key.

Whether English does bring this desired status or not is a future chapter in this story. The glorification of English and the stigmatisation of Lao and Japanese result in the rationalisation of the project model and support the delineations within the IELEP field. The participants seem to have internalised the discourses about the power of English and the linguistic capital English language holds is unquestioned.

English as an International Language/Lingua Franca

Host-country participants from both projects talked about the importance of English as a 'bridging' language, to speak with people from surrounding countries, and as Sen (P2LM2) explained, it would not be possible to choose one of the languages of the surrounding countries as this would place that particular country in a dominant position.

Mak (P2LT2) from Project 2 raised the role of English as a lingua franca (ELF). He talked about a visit he made to Australia, and how English was an important tool for him to communicate with students from different Asian countries:

... we live in Asia and we need to communicate with other Asian people ... and the language that we can communicate with them is mainly English. When I was in Australia I can communicate with many students who came from many different Asian countries through English. It is necessary for us to understand their English and it's hard for us people here to learn other Asian languages . . . when we want to communicate English is already the international language or tool to communicate.

Son (P1LU1) below postulated the view of English as an escape route out of an 'economically desperate' situation and while she differentiated between the different motivations and desires between the 'ordinary person' and that of the 'national interest', it is still with the sense that the country would be able to 'better itself'. She saw English as the natural, neutral choice for Lao people, 'English does not belong to one group of people', and because Laos is a small country with no political or economic power then English is the right choice.

Son from Project 1, in discussing her country's 'national interest', joins other Lao participants in supporting the need for English since Laos separated from the former Soviet Union and has adopted a more market-oriented economy. English was seen as a necessary skill to have a more active involvement in international affairs. Son identified how English language is the dominant language of the communication activities within the government arena:

since the opening of our country to the outside world . . . English is very important for every ministry. All the documents we receive right now are mostly in English . . . also in the government, also any position with companies or organisations they need people who can speak English.

It is intriguing that the interviewee constructed an equivalence between the experience of the individual and that of the nation-state. Most of the population of Laos (Project 1) were and still are among the poorest people of the world and the government's gross domestic product was largely funded (70%) by aid monies. The hope that the development of English language skills would lead to accumulation of wealth (economic capital) clearly demonstrated how the discourses of English language study as 'empowerment' and 'capacity building' are internalised in the hearts and minds of the individuals and institutions as represented by the host-country interviewees above. Son, from Project 1, continued to talk about the dominance of English and how her university department (English) had double the number of students of any other department in the university. She saw this as indicative of the importance of English in her country. She also mentioned that each ministry office had a special English course.

It is highly significant that in a country where there are inadequate health services and provision of elementary education, the department with the most students is the English department. This speaks clearly of the linguistic capital English embodies and consequently aid and fee-based projects feed off the demand that is created by the role of English in the international context. The questionable benefits of English language teaching and teacher training have been raised in previous chapters in this book and it is important to recognise how the role of these projects masks the inequitable distribution of global resources (see Bruthiaux, 2002, cited on p. 19); also critical to the dynamic of the IELEP field is the denial of linguistic rights and diversity. These issues are taken up later in this chapter.

The overall goal, as expressed in the proposal for Project 1, is an excellent example of how successfully the notion of English was glorified; it was a key to economic success and has embedded itself into the minds of those concerned with winning bids for aid projects. The project proposal confidently outlined how the programmes it proposed to implement would *assist the country to build a critical mass of EL capabilities, leading to enhanced social and economic development.* One wonders how in a very poor country where access to basic L1 education is severely limited, a project constrained by its own internal mechanisms would impact on the economic development of the country. My musings on the self-serving interests of the document resonate with the work of Bruthiaux (2002) (see Chapter 1) where he revealed English to have no influence in the lives of the very poor. In fact his work revealed that the influence of English in the world is not growing and the total use of English by mother tongue speakers and those highly proficient bilingual speakers comes to about 10% of the world's population (approximately 600 million).

In contrast to this, Song from Project 1 testified to the positive linguistic capital that English language holds and vividly described how individuals can convert their linguistic capital to economic capital. As a teacher he was in high demand and could not meet the numerous requests for English lessons:

> According to my point of view I can say that the majority of students in the capital city and the provinces want to study English. You know why they want to study English? ... if you can speak English, if you can write English, you can find a job now, an important one.

The Japanese participants from Project 2 described the importance of English in ways that differ by only a matter of degree. The interviewees take Japan's role in the international arena for granted, since their country is highly industrialised and economically successful and, as Murray

(P2AM1) stated in Chapter 4, it represents potentially one of the biggest English language consumer markets in the world. English was portrayed as the means by which the professional sector of this country could participate in international affairs; for example, '... for businessmen [*sic*], for engineers and for researchers to give lectures at conventions. They have to write in English for publication in major journals. So especially in business and science they need English...' (Lan, P2LT4). Vong (P1LU1) from Project 1 concurred with this view. He talked about this particular aspect of English as an international tool in the light of the national government's change in economic policy; he emphasised how a good knowledge of English would allow Lao specialists to participate in international conferences and negotiate economic deals with foreign investors. He was also concerned that Lao people would not 'catch up with new technological developments' if English language skills were not developed.

In Japan it was also seen as the tool for communication in a 'worldly' sense: '... and these days in Japan the board of education says that students must communicate with others internationally in English...' (Lin P2LT1). The view of English as a lingua franca is also reflected in interviews with other Lao and Japanese participants. In other interviews English was also seen as providing access to areas of work that were previously barred (Weng P1LM2). The following are some other samples of what different interviewees said about the role of English as an international language (EIL). Ken from Project 2 below referred to the ambivalence about the study of English (mentioned earlier in this chapter) but believed that English would prove to be highly significant to school and university students in his country:

> As I said before teachers and students in this country do not actually feel the necessity of actually using English here. But at the same time the students who live in the 21st century will have greater opportunities to be exposed to English as an international language and we have to prepare our students. So, even though we know that at the moment we don't have so many opportunities to use English outside the classrooms but sooner or later people in the 21st century will probably use English as a means of communication and we have to prepare for that.

Ken's view is supported by Mak (P2LT2) who described the capital city as a linguistically diverse environment and that it was important for the host country's people to use English as a communication tool.

As mentioned earlier in this section, English was a compulsory subject in Japan and it had a particular function in its prominence in the university entrance examinations. Lan (P2LT4) was a secondary school teacher and was quite candid about the role of English: 'these days for high school students it is a tool to get into university.' She felt similarly to other Japanese teachers that many students were not highly motivated to study English as the students did not see its relevance to their lives.

Teaching English: EIL/ESL/EFL/ELF?

For many in the ELT field the delineations between the English as a second language (ESL) and English as a foreign language (EFL) are not useful; the terms come from a particular history of colonisation and demography and are not related to any language or linguistic reality (Nayar, 1997). As discussed earlier, the historical terms of 'native speaker' and 'non-native speaker' are ideological constructs which represent and validate an idealised 'western' teacher using a superior teaching methodology; Holliday (2006) calls this native-speakerism. The latter term, the 'non-native speaker' of English, is stigmatised and invalidated by being defined in essentialist cultural terms (see Chapter 6 for a discussion of this issue). Rampton (1990) believes that these two terms should be replaced by ideas such as language expertise, language inheritance and language affiliation. Questions can then be asked about the teacher or learner's linguistic repertoire and their relationship to certain languages based on Rampton's ideas of expertise, inheritance and affiliation. Dispelling with the binary of the ESL/EFL allows for a more fruitful discussion of ELT where bilingual skills are rightfully recognised and validated and the learners' linguistic needs are central.

Speakers in Kachru's expanding circle of users of English (definition in Chapter 1) do not use English for extra-community relations alone. For countries in East Asia, South America and Europe, English also performs important functions within their own borders (see Jenkins, 2006). This development again calls into question the ESL/EFL distinction and demands that we take account of the increasing intranational use of English in expanding circle of countries (Canagarajah, 2006).

Acknowledgement of the differences between teaching ELT in Japan and Laos and teaching in Australia was a strong source of tension within both projects. Within the Australian project staff some members felt that the teams needed to spend more time understanding the teaching of English in the particular project sites but they also felt pushed by the economic imperatives driving the universities' involvement in the projects. As mentioned in previous chapters, the project model is tied to timelines and outcomes and there is little flexibility to undertake ethnographic research. Murray (P2AM1) was the only one of the donor/provider management group that was concerned about the way that the universities were rushing to produce materials without fully understanding the local context.

Further evidence of the dominant role the accumulation of economic capital plays is found in the data for Project 2, where one of the writers of the original proposal for the project highlighted the need to work from within a framework of knowledge and understanding of the diverse needs of the English language teacher. However, in the interview, she told how this was in a sense hijacked by the demands of expediency due to budget constraints. It is important to consider how agents are positioned in the field. The so-called native speaker teacher of English and so-called native speaking tertiary institutions hold a dominant position in the broad field of ELT. The Australian 'institutional practice' embodies the rhetoric of the field in terms of dominant and subordinate positions and promotes dominant notions about the expert position of the 'native' English speaker teacher. Knowledge of the host-country context and legitimate forms of knowledge are contested notions and a struggle in the field is around recognition of these factors.

The Japanese and Australian participants in Project 2 discussed the importance of recognising the differences between teaching what was traditionally known as ESL and EFL and the different ways English was positioned in the host countries. Lee and teacher participants from Project 2 typified EFL as '... teaching EFL was like teaching any other school subject. The students probably had 2 or 3 classes a week of English.' In this context the teacher is often the sole source of target language knowledge and language use. The teacher and students may attempt ways of constructing an EL speaking environment but the success of such ventures depends upon the economic and social resources available (Kamhi-Stein, 1999; Medgyes, 1994). In Laos (Project 1) the teacher and students had very little access to resources which gave useful examples of English language in that particular international context.

The Project 2 teachers strongly felt that their teaching situation was very different from teaching English in an English-speaking country where the target language is readily available outside of the classroom. These interviewees were keen that the Australian project team be made aware of these differences and develop materials accordingly. Lee (P1/2AU2) discussed the priorities in the teacher education programmes and concluded that the teachers, in short, needed assistance in teaching English with either the limited number of textbooks available or nothing at all and to improve their English language skills and abilities.

The ELT sector in Australia is traditionally described as ESL where English language courses are provided for adults in public and private sector institutions and for school children in intensive English language schools. In the Australian context the teacher, most usually a monolingual speaker of English (although at the time of writing this book a greater number of bilingual EL teachers are being employed in the public sector), knows that the student has an authentic language environment available in which to practise and produce language gained from the classroom. This issue caused concern to some Australian project participants in the sense that many of the Australian project team lecturers have only had experience with Australian ESL programmes and have not taken account of the particularities of teaching and learning in more bilingual contexts.

The monolingual project

One of the critical themes of work in IELEPs is the respective roles of English and the host-country national language(s). It appeared that English was used as the dominant language of project work (in all international contexts), that is, all project documentation was in English and English was the language of meetings, appraisal work and teacher training. The course materials had minimal bilingual course notes, and the Japanese translations of key terms and concepts were in the margins of the pages of the learning guides. The explicit role of English in this capacity was not addressed by the project proposals, but it was addressed by a number of interviewees. While some project team members saw the dominance of English as its natural position, others contested this continuing dominance. The language(s) of the host countries was not mentioned in the documentation except as an aid in teaching low-level English language learners. To give further detail on this, in the Project 1 documents, the host-country national language(s) was only mentioned once: a *bilingual in-service*. This is in a country where English was a recently introduced foreign language and where the Lao project stakeholders (as described below) worked overtime to become adequately proficient in English so as to be able to participate in the project processes.

The documents for Project 2 were written sometime after those for Project 1 and they reflected a slightly more inclusive attitude towards the host-country language. This paralleled a change in the NABA (North American, British and Australian) TESOL field. Japanese was included in the key features of the project but relegated to 'bilingual support' for the lower-level courses within the project. Japanese was excluded from discussions about the management of the project in spite of the fact that there were Australian stakeholders fluent in Japanese.

The issue of which language was used in project work was a particular point of tension, a struggle, for a number of the expatriate staff in Project 1. Lee, an Australian project advisor, suggested to the Australian team that every second committee meeting be run in Lao. English was a relatively new foreign language in this particular context. Lee recognised difficulties in carrying out any truly collaborative work when English was used as the sole language of communication and negotiation in project management. However, the other members of the Australian team thought that this was an absurd idea and Lee described how the Australian project director laughed out loud when this was raised at a Project Coordinating Committee meeting. Lee described how members of the host country's team were obviously struggling with English and how their roles as project coordinating committee members and project collaborators were constrained by having to communicate in a new language. Peter Medgyes raised this specific issue when describing the dynamics between Hungarian and British Council staff in an IELEP in Hungary (see Chapter 1). The Hungarian staff were at a constant disadvantage in discussions about how the project work was to be carried out.

In Project 1 a number of the Lao team members were fluent speakers of European languages such as French, Czechoslovakian and Russian but this did not give them any linguistic capital in this particular project field. The reaction to a possible rearranging of the subordinate and dominant positions by simply allocating space for the meetings to be run in the national language of the host country explicated the power relations in the field. The expatriate advisers would be in the position of having to have the meetings interpreted and would lose the ability to control the process as well as the content.

Con (P1AM1), an Australian official who worked with the in-country office of the funding body, endorsed the view that English is the 'natural' project language. He dismissed the need for expatriate staff to develop local language skills. He extended the role of English; he believed that it was not 'functional' to learn Lao, and it did not help the intended practices of the project because 'We're headed for English.' He stigmatised Lao and relegated it to a subordinate position in the field and advised expatriate staff to get assistance from one of the host-country staff if they needed to use the 'local language'. He had a particularly interesting attitude to the affective factors embedded in the language learning: 'Some of the Australian teachers have learnt a bit of the local language. I've heard a few words dropped around the place and that keeps everybody happy . . .'

Con expressed perhaps, from one point of view, what was realistic in terms of language learning. However, the point about 'which language?' in an IELEP is not a neutral question. A number of issues emerge about the respective roles of the host-country language and English in a project. Lee (P1/2AU2), in the first part of this extract below, encapsulated what I believe is a central dynamic of the field of aid projects:

> I mean, when people from a rich country like the one we live in are working with people from a very poor country, and we're communicating almost only in the language of the rich country, never in the language of the poor country, we have so much power. There's a power imbalance that's so enormous there, we can hardly conceive of it, and that power gives us certain strengths and also certain limitations.

Con might be seen as representing the practicalities of the situation but in doing so he ignored the particular dynamics and relations in the field as identified by Lee. The initial project proposals were responsible for the way the host language was positioned but Con was one of the aid agency project implementers and hence connected with the ongoing development of the project as was Lee. My analysis of these different views of the power of 'which language?' is not simply a matter of practicalities. Certainly the Japanese teachers in Project 2 and similarly the Lao participants in Project 1 and other host-country project participants in both projects think that Australian project team members should develop at least an elementary proficiency in the local language. Sal, a teacher from Project 2, felt strongly that the English-speaking Assistant Language Teachers (ALT) should have some knowledge of Japanese; he believed that it would help the ALTs to understand the relationship between the mother tongue and English.

> I've worked with more than 20 different language assistant English teachers and mostly they just speak English, and he or she doesn't have any knowledge of Japanese. I ask them many times, speak more slowly or use simple instructions and easy vocabulary. But the point is that it is very hard to judge what is easy for the Japanese student to learn. As you already know over here we have authorised English textbooks and so in order to be a teacher here in Japan, the key is, take a look at the junior high school level English text books. That will give you some overview of the level of vocabulary or structure and that is closely connected with the textbooks in senior high schools. Some knowledge on the Japanese language and authorised textbooks are important here in Japan and the ALTs need to control their speaking speed, slow down.

While Con's belief that there was little need for learning the national language of the country where one works is prevalent within the expatriate communities, the host-country teachers, teacher trainers and ministry officials did not concur with the 'English only' view. In terms of the process of 'internationalisation' as represented by the learning of English, the above examples, firstly of the role of English in Project 1 committee meetings and secondly the view of the Australian aid official, explicitly support what has been argued critically elsewhere in this book, that this process is one-way. The host-country ministry officials, teachers, teacher trainers and students are engaged in the process of learning English, and working in English, but there was very little engagement in the learning or use of the host-country national language(s). The majority of project participants (including the 'counterpart' staff) were native speakers of the host-country languages. The positions of the local languages and native speakers of these languages were revealing and a telling feature of the project field. Masaki Oda (1999), in his article about how the use of English can disenfranchise some parties in EFL organisations, identifies a number of ways that native speakers of English marginalise the bilingual host-country teachers. He draws on his and other bilingual teachers' experience in JALT, an organisation for language teachers in Japan. This organisation was originally formed by English language teachers but is now no longer exclusively for ELT. Oda points out that although there may be teachers of French, Thai and so on:

> non-native speakers of English members, most of who are native speakers of Japanese, have had to be competent in English to fully participate in the organisation's activities. (Oda, 1999: 106–107)

He also describes the power plays of English native speaking officers as against non-native speaking ones:

> English native speaking teachers, including those who are monolinguals, appear to be given a privileged status in the profession. Many TESOL affiliates are controlled by English native speaking professionals who are not necessarily more qualified as language teaching professionals than their non-native speaking counterparts. (Oda, 1999: 119)

The above brief descriptions of the relations in the field of an EFL organisation explicate the ways that (I contend) the general field of English language education plays itself out. The linguistic relations of power, as previously stated by Lee, dominated in Project 1 and for Project 2, while in a completely different context, the host-country languages are relegated to the margins (quite literally in the course materials). The matter of learning the host-country language(s) was not to necessarily expect that the expatriate staff will become proficient enough to engage in high-level discussions, though this was expected of the host-country staff. The learning of the host-country language(s) would simply place that language in a different position to that where it currently was, invisible. There are many examples of non-government organisations (NGOs) who give priority to the learning of host-country languages, for example, the volunteer community workers, educators and other smaller project-type ventures. These organisations arrange for staff to undertake language study as part of their induction to work in the new context and clearly see the learning of the host-country language as a significant attribute of project work.

Rights of bilingual teachers

Bilingual (or multilingual) language teachers are the norm in most countries in the world. The rights of bilingual teachers are invalidated by the IELEPs even though in its recommendations the Hague Convention (1996) enshrines the right to a bilingual education. The right to bilingual education is strongly advocated by Skutnabb-Kangas (2008); she has committed decades of work to demonstrate how bilingual education improves broader educational outcomes for linguistic minority communities (Skutnabb-Kangas in Cummins and Hornberger, 2008). English can be taught additively, to supplement the learner's mother tongue, and in this respect the outcome is successful. Skutnabb-Kangas cites successful bilingual education in countries such the Netherlands, Norway and Denmark as examples of how the mother tongue is validated during the process of bilingually learning English.

The IELEPs in this study were described as being based in the current body of (Australian) language education theory and practice. Current literature in TESOL and Teaching English as a Foreign Language (TEFL) (e.g. Kumaravadivelu, 2008; Pennycook, 1999, 2000; Phillipson & Skutnabb-Kangas, 1996; Skutnabb-Kangas & Phillipson, 2001) espouses the critical questions of the relationship of identity and language and is mindful of ways in which the home or mother tongue must be given its rightful place. This framework for current practice is espoused and adopted unless, I imagine, you are in an IELEP. Here, the first language of the host country is rarely mentioned; project proposal documents carefully step around the issue and certainly in the language teaching approaches most common in English language projects, the first language is viewed (e.g. by the majority of Australian project staff and officials) as a barrier to English language development. Carla, an expatriate teacher from Project 1, recounts how the team leader of Project 1 did not want to allow any of the counterpart teaching staff (Lao English teachers) to use their first language in the courses run by the project. She recalled him as saying '… they (the students) will not learn anything if the teachers use their own language. They must only use English.'

The rights of bilingual Lao and Japanese teachers are denied. The bilingual teacher brings more skills and knowledge to the project and the classroom than the monolingual English teacher does. It is axiomatic to say that a monolingual teacher is a bad role model for bilingual-to-be learners; it is also the case that a monolingual teacher educator is a bad role model for bilingual EL teachers. Students must have a language right to bilingual teaching, teacher training and material writers who know the target languages and the students' mother tongue. In many people's views (Skutnabb-Kangas, 2008), you cannot write effective EFL materials for a specific group unless you know their mother tongue. Think of the iceberg metaphor. If the material writers only know the Basic Interpersonal Communication Skills (BICS) and Cognitive Academic Language Proficiency (CALP) of the target language (in this case English) but do not know the CALP specificities of each host-country language and what is common English for each of them, they are wasting the students' time.

Song (P1LU2), a 'counterpart' lecturer, expressed the thoughts of many of the other host-country interviewees in Project 1, that although Australian presenters should use as much L2 (English) as possible there is an important role for Lao in explanation. He also thinks that the Australian presenters should learn the country's language and something of the country's culture:

> … if Australian teachers can speak our language, understand our language I think this would be easier to present lessons. More or less this can save the time and is also fun when foreigners speak Lao – they understand now.

Interviewees in Project 2 supported this view. Sal (P2LT3) called for Australian lecturers to 'have some knowledge of his country's language'. He believed that this would assist the lecturers in teaching the country's learners. Knowledge of the host country's language would give insight into the problems that the students have in learning English.

Murray (P2AM1) raised the issue of bilingual skills. He believed that it was highly desirable that Australian IELEP team members were bilingual. This important attribute was also talked about by other interviewees in both projects. The Project 2 host-country teachers, and similarly in

Project 1, all expressed the view that bilingual skills were integral to the 'success' or not of the project. For example, Sal (P2LT3) acknowledged how this would be difficult but it still was important for the lecturers and reiterated the view that the expatriate lecturers did not have to 'master Japanese as the structure is completely different to English'. He would have liked the lecturers to have some knowledge of the language.

Some of the above interviewees from Project 2 gave examples of a number of successful foreign university programmes delivering courses to Japanese teachers and thought that foreign educators' skill in Japanese and knowledge of the context contributed greatly to their success, that is, the number of project participants they attracted. On the other hand, when this issue was raised with the Australian stakeholders, most expressed the view that generic experience of work in offshore projects (and perhaps another language skill) was adequate. I must point out that this was not the view of all Australian stakeholders, but what is interesting is the absence of the host country's language speakers, either native or non-native, as key stakeholders in Project 2.

In Bourdieu's terms the dominant players' lack of skill in and acknowledgement of the role of the host-country language is a way of conserving the dominant positions in the IELEP. This lack of recognition is characteristic of the teaching and academic world; it is a way of stigmatising, of placing particular players in a subordinate position. Another characteristic of the field is that the boundaries are constantly shifting and the dominant players are challenged by potential successors who may possess more valuable forms of capital. The players engage in struggles around the legitimation of ideas and academic creditability. However, the successful contender will most likely conserve the values and behaviour of the previous dominant player. In the project fields English maintains its ascendancy.

Varieties of English

Participants in Project 2 raised the issue of the different varieties of English and the status of those varieties vis-à-vis what is considered the 'true' native speaker forms:

> in the revised course of study especially at senior high level we have included one sentence, a sentence that says that since English is used as a means of international communication teachers should be sensitive to the fact that there are different kinds of English in the world, so this is very short sentence but the existence of this sentence in the course of studies is very significant. (Ken P2LU1)

Ken recounted an experience of a group of teachers who participated in an English language teacher training programme in a Scottish city some years ago. This was part of a larger teacher training project. The teachers' feedback indicated that the type of English they were exposed to would not provide them with the 'good samples of English' that they would need when they returned to their country to teach. However, a recent group of teachers who trained in the same city did not raise the issue of varieties of English. Ken (P2LU1), a ministry official responsible for English language teacher training, used this example to explain how attitudes towards the notion of the 'true native speaker' have shifted. He continued to discuss this 'opening up' of the MOE to English speakers from Kachru's (1986) 'the outer circle' (see Chapter 1). At the time of the interview the MOE was actively seeking English language teachers from a broader range of countries where English is spoken as a first language and is hoping to include teachers from the Philippines and Singapore in the near future:

> In this country nowadays, the Ministry of Education is not so worried about the different types of English, it is thinking of including assistant language teachers from Singapore and Philippines. In the revised course of study at senior level, teachers should be sensitive to the fact that there are different kinds of English [this is in reference to English as a means of international communication].

It is interesting in this discussion that forms of English, such as Australian and New Zealand, were considered 'kinds of English' rather than 'proper English'. Ken pointed out, in another part of his interview, that it was not too long ago that Australian English was considered an inferior form of English, a 'dirty accent', and Australia was not a popular destination choice for those wishing to study English.

The view of Australian English, once seen as the poor cousin to US or British English, was changing as discussed by Tan (P2LM1) from the ministry:

> OK, honestly speaking you know there is a kind of image to us 'cause you know Australian English has some kind of dialects, such as especially in terms of colonisation so (i) sound for (a) right? So 'to die' for 'today' or something like that. But you know things are changing, . . . because English is not the property of the United States obviously so it's a world wide international language. So naturally we should have a kind of our own style of English even we have some kind of dialect . . . So, you know of course Australia is a native speaking country of English so I don't think Australia is inferior or worse than other English-speaking countries.

Tan represented what has been perceived to be a particular dynamic of the ELT field and one that has been significant in helping to determine where teachers from the host country of Project 2 choose to study TESOL. Discussion of challenges to the notion of a 'true native speaker' gives room for Rampton's idea of a speaker's language expertise to be utilised in the IELEP. Teaching and teacher education work in an IELEP require a high degree of linguistic expertise and capability. The ideological constructs of the EL 'native-speaker' and 'non-native speaker' are sites of struggle, the monolingual English speaker is under threat and perhaps, as Graddol (2006) predicts, will become obsolete.

Language in the project: Whose voice is legitimate?

Competency in English is a sought-after skill, and one that is often a pre-requisite to gaining work; secondment from government posts into projects; or inclusion in the management of language education projects. In practice, however (as mentioned earlier), often insurmountable barriers prevent host-country project team members from participating fully and equally in the decision-making processes of the project, to have what Bourdieu would term a 'legitimate' voice in the project practices (Copley & Widin, 2001).

Two issues emerged from the data of interviewees from the host countries that spoke of the issue of 'legitimate voice'. One was the issue of the decision to change the study arrangements in Project 1 and the other issue was the type and nomenclature of the initial TESOL qualification that was offered in both Project 1 and Project 2. These issues were seen as worthy of comment by the host participants in both projects and ones where they perceived that their voice was not legitimate. The interviewees went on to offer stories of how their voices had been delegitimised in these two particular instances.

Whose voice legitimates change: Study arrangements

The first issue, as described by Lao ministry officials and teacher participants, was the change of study arrangements for one of the degree programmes which had previously been undertaken wholly in Australia. The discussion about the change of study arrangements occurred during the later stages of Project 1. The suggestion to shorten the time candidates spent studying in Australia came from the Australian manager. The previous intakes of students spent six months full-time study in Australia. The new arrangements would see more students study for less time in Australia and the remaining subjects to be taught by the Australian lecturers in the host country. This proposal went to the host-country MOE for approval and it generated a range of responses from the host country's stakeholders, mostly dismay at the shortening of the students' time in Australia.

According to the interviewees mentioned above, the Australian manager, in correspondence with the in-country project manager, reported on a mini-survey on this issue conducted with host-country stakeholders. The host-country project participants were overwhelmingly in favour of maintaining the original arrangements, that is, of a smaller number of students staying for the full six months in Australia. The report detailing the responses was circulated to the key stakeholders.

As mentioned earlier, Project 1 was described in the project documents as employing a 'participatory approach' to project management. This suggests that the Australian project management team would openly welcome and encourage the contributions and the active participation of local project partners. This did happen on occasions as reported in other parts of this book, but the way the opinion of the host-country interviewees was dealt with on this occasion suggests that in fact, at least in their perception, their contribution was given very little or no weight. They feel that their words were not considered. Despite the rhetoric about participation and the centrality of local stakeholders' voices in the decision-making process, there was no space for host-country participant to air their views, their expertise and experience.

The Lao participants explained the value of spending the longer time in Australia: Firstly, there was obviously more opportunities for English language development, as the students (as teachers) in their home environment very rarely interacted with speakers of English or had access to English in the media. Secondly, there was the concurrent incidental learning which occurs when living in another cultural context. Thirdly, there was the opportunity to have extended study time where the students did not have to contend with their domestic demands. Other reasons cited in the report were, *the creation of a post-graduate study path, incentive factor, and the special value of overseas study.*

The host-country participants initially believed that their opinions did count; they assumed that the Australian management group in the IELEP communicated, listened and are open to being influenced by one another. The interviewees recounted how they questioned the decision-making process and underlying relations of power of the purportedly collaborative practices. Instances such as these contradicted notions of trust which were often assumed or stated by the donor. Later on I refer to an instance of project talk where the project manager demanded that the host stakeholders must 'trust' the expatriate management. In the decision about the study arrangements, the host-country interviewees explained that they were not able to 'trust' that their interests would be looked after. The Australian manager believed that the value of giving more students access to further post-graduate study was for the greater good and went ahead with planning for the new arrangements. What was unstated but certainly visible was that the Australian university profited from this decision; the increase in the number of students in Australia was an increase in fee income and the pecuniary interest prevailed.

This instance of project talk is illuminating, because it foregrounds the frustration that is felt by many host-country participants on aid-funded projects (and I would contend, fee-based projects) about the amount of regard paid to the opinions of the host-country partners. In their recounts the interviewees felt that even though they made several seemingly valid points in their support of the original option, their comments, while based on their experience and expertise as teachers, teacher trainers and having studied in another country, were not authoritative enough to affect the decision. In addition, this example revealed the limitations that host-country participants worked within in terms of how far they could actually influence the direction the project took.

The above example raises issues both of language and of discourses: the importance of language in the bilateral project process, how it is used as a tool to gain and consolidate positions of advantage within the IELEP field and the way the projects work for the 'good' of the recipients. Within the context of the aid-funded project (Project 1), the competing discourses of aid and development are identified according to the groups and individuals participating in them: host-country stakeholders, project implementation personnel, project implementation administration and management staff and donor personnel. These discourses reflect the relations in the field, that is, the way that the field is delineated by uneven positions of power constructed by the relative distribution of the valued resources. In this context, the dominant discourses are generally those within which the donor and provider groups operate. These depict particular views of the world which demand economic accountability and transparency, supported by empirically identifiable evidence and rational investigation.

A particularly powerful differentiation is the symbolic violence afforded by a particular representation of host-country stakeholders. The donor (dominant) stakeholders are most usually represented as the rationale, objective and stable agents in the field. As stated earlier in this chapter, project proposal documents very often represent the host-country stakeholders/participants (particularly in aid-funded projects) as less objective, less stable and more untenable, and are relegated to a subordinate position in the field. This representation sets up the dynamics of the relationships in the field. The host-country participants in the IELEPs held professional positions within their areas of work and these positions often required competence in English language. These project participants were highly skilled in their profession. They were articulate in their ability to express themselves in English and they presented as confident and authoritative. Yet, their comments on the study arrangements were discounted and they failed in their endeavours to provide what they viewed as the best option for the English language teachers. Thus, while English is seen as a skill which enables the active participation of host-country participants, and indeed can be seen as a gatekeeper into the IELEP workplace, competency in English (in addition to the professional skills/expertise in their field) is not enough to give authority to the host-country stakeholders' contributions.

In exploring this example further, Bourdieu's (1991) work on the dynamics of participant relations is useful. The context of instances such as discussions over arrangements of study plans would, on first glance, seem to be one where the relations of agents in the field are made explicit and the views of the host participants would be given significant weight. While in the end, the relations of the agents are made explicit in terms of dominance and subordination, further investigation of the question of what it takes for an utterance to be effective reveals deeper information about the dynamics of the field. Of interest here is Bourdieu's arguments that authority does not stem from words alone, but that 'the authority that utterances have is an authority bestowed upon language by factors external to it' (1989: 9). This may seem obvious, particularly if one draws on an example of institutional authority such as a judge's verdict, but what I am talking about here is a project which is purportedly based on *partnership* and *collaboration* and one where the host-country participants could be assumed to hold *insider* information.

The linguistic practices within the project reflect and reinforce the habitus of the agents in the field. The practices highlight the differences and/or equivalences between the social groups in the field (Grenfell, 1998). The host-country interviewees spoke of how the original study arrangements benefited the post-graduate students, and it was expected that these arrangements would continue. However, the host-country interviewees were not fully cognisant of the 'characteristics of the game', and while their linguistic performance was evidence that they had seemingly appropriated what the discursive field offers, they had not accumulated the linguistic (and other) capital to speak with authority and even if they had their discourses may have been invalidated by the field.

The IELEP field (Project 1) is discursively constructed by discourses of aid and development, language, education and international relations, to name the most obvious (similar to how the field is described in Copley, 1997). The features which denote legitimacy (and consequently authority) in this field might be status or position within the project management or the host-country MOE, educational qualifications, nationality, ethnicity and language background. The power relations within the project may not be quite so obvious and may be masked by the rhetoric of collaboration and partnership. But at the bottom line the funding power lies with the donor, the Australian aid agency. An underlying fear or threat for the host stakeholders is that funding may be withdrawn if there are any serious problems. There is no doubt about the ultimate power relations in the field. The project management team (comprising the project management company and the university) holds the greatest amount of economic capital in the field and in terms of the objectives of the project, the cultural capital, that is, the desired professional qualifications.

In this discursive incident, the project participants may have been disadvantaged by a limited understanding of the discourses operating within this field. The implicit markers of the power relations are implanted in the discourses at work in the field and are realised by language. Thus, not only may they be disadvantaged by their so-called 'non-native' or non-expert speaker of English status, they might be further disadvantaged by their lack of familiarity with the legitimate instruments of expression of the discourses which operate within IELEPs and therefore blocked from any authoritative participation in the institution.

Whose voice legitimates project programmes?

The second example further illuminates the question of legitimate and authoritative speakers in the work of the projects. Host-country interviewees from both projects and Chris, an Australian academic (Project 2), raised the name and status of a particular degree course in the project. A number of the participants expressed confusion about the name and meaning of degree programmes and articulated pathways. The participants from the respective MOEs from both countries believed that they brought up this issue with the respective project management but had no response. Weng, from Project 1, a teacher training official who had worked with the aid-funded project for two years, was still left unclear about the status of a particular course offered within the project:

> people don't understand this certificate, you know … They are not sure whether this certificate must come after a bachelor's degree or if it is an undergraduate program.

She was concerned that this qualification would not be recognised by institutions in other countries: 'I mean if these people go to other parts of … Australia … or if they are sent to other institutions, do these institutions accept this kind of course?' She expressed a concern about the status of a graduate certificate, is the qualification valuable? The graduate certificate it appears, both in its nomenclature and in its status, was not part of the articulated degree programmes in both of these countries. Weng expanded on this point by explaining that the normal pathway in Laos was that students undertake a diploma after their undergraduate studies. When they then come to study in the project courses years after getting the diploma they are awarded a graduate certificate. Her query was whether the project's qualification is lower than their first university award.

As it happens, this same type of course was the core teacher education programme within Project 2. It now appears that there may have been a mismatch between what the MOE desired for the teachers and what the Australian university wanted to offer. Ken (P2LU1) and Lan (P2LT4) from Project 2 expressed concern about the naming and status of the course:

> I have raised this before with the director of the [Australian government agency], you should not have too much focus on the pre-masters qualification. This country's teachers will not understand about this course, the most important aim is to get a masters qualification. (Lan P2LT4)

This view is reinforced by Ken (P2LU1), a host-country university professor, and the concern was with how the teachers will proceed onto a master's degree. The general unfamiliarity with the graduate certificate level caused Ken and Lan some disquiet about the responsiveness of the project managers to the local context:

> And as I said – and this is what we have perceived during your visit to senior high schools – there are lots of teachers who need training at the MA level. … since most of this country's teachers these days are interested in qualifications, so, you have to offer the way closest to MA. That is what I expect you to do.

The MOE and other project participants were unsure about the particular university qualification on offer as it was not a qualification familiar to this country's students, but the Australian universities felt sure that this qualification was suitable for this country's teachers and wished to promote it.

The universities had ethnographic advice from a bilingual member of staff, with extensive experience of working in the education sector of the host country, that this qualification was not recognised in the host country of Project 2. In spite of this advice the project management went ahead with the development of the unfamiliar programme.

The struggle about the courses offered in the projects was over the accumulation of cultural capital. The host-country participants in both projects expected to have access to the valuable resources in the field and in this instance it was hoped to be in the form of a higher degree. The degree offered by the dominant stakeholders was not recognised as valuable in the host countries but the host country participants' concerns about their teachers' qualifications were not legitimated; they did not hold the authority in the field to change what was on offer.

Legitimate Voice: Who Is In Charge?

The IELEP field is one where the dominant stakeholders consider there is 'normal' project talk and that talk is conducted in English. I have shown that competency in English and professional expertise do not guarantee legitimacy in the field. Son (P1LU1) from Project 1 believed that even when host-country participants are skilled in terms of English language and the management area of the project work they are still excluded from management decision making. So what is going on in these situations? What other skills are needed and what other interests are at stake?

A number of the project participants recalled a formal regular meeting between the key stakeholders that occurred mid-way through the project. The purpose was to discuss the direction and activities of the project using the logical framework methodology. The logical frame (log frame) process involved a methodology of analysis and participation: brainstorming of problems and group discussion. The system aimed to ensure specific outcomes and indicators for outcomes that were quantifiable by the donor and thus the donor could be accountable. The difficulty with using such an approach was that, certainly in a MOE's meeting session, the host country's representatives typically have a different 'institutional practice' (Fairclough, 1989: 33). An assumption underlying the use of such procedures is that the expatriate or the donor's 'institutional practice' is democratic and reflects the rhetoric and ideals held by the log frame approach. The expatriate participants may well begin to believe in the idealisation of their work practices and use this sense of more highly developed ways of operating to further dominate the field.

The meeting group was diverse: representatives of the host MOE, officials who had very different levels of experience with both this particular conceptualisation of project work and the ELT field; representatives from the participating local university; project staff, both local and expatriate; and Australian project management staff. The group was also diverse according to gender, age, beliefs and values about education, professional experience, language skills (in a range of languages) and status. Many of the interviewees felt that the logical framework methodology of the workshop did not account for the group's diversity. The Australian project management introduced this procedure as a 'normal' regular activity within 'bilateral, collaborative work' with which the project is (supposedly) engaged. The procedure relied on the participants being able to interact with each other on an equal basis. This was taken for granted. And the management team assumed that the meeting would be conducted in English. The Australian project management team also seemed to assume that this *collaborative and cooperative* organisational practice would sit equally well with all participants.

But all participating stakeholders work with institutions that were not particularly democratic. The donor/aid agency is a bureaucratic organisation that had a linear chain of command and outside of a few NGOs had a very traditional hierarchical structure. The Australian university partner also operated under a very traditional, hierarchical type of work organisation where input to discussion is filtered through status channels and line management. The institutional practices of the host-country MOE are predicated on strict hierarchies (similar to Australia's) which operated in overt ways, so that from one participant's perspective, project participants in the lower echelons of the MOE were reluctant to offer an opinion in front of someone higher up in the ministry. This was particularly the case if the participant wanted to make an adverse comment.

From the participants' accounts of this meeting, or rather workshop, it appeared that the production of a logical framework was introduced as a 'normal and natural' way of proceeding in the work of this project. It was not framed as a procedure that the donor/provider was familiar with and those from other institutions may not be. It was an integral part of how the project was set up to operate and the procedures that would be followed. It was in fact quite new and foreign to a range of participants in the workshop; the university representatives and the first-time expatriate project workers were as unfamiliar with the intricacies of the procedure as were the host participants. But the seemingly major difference was that the expatriate staff were able to participate in the dominant discourse of the meeting; they were able to act familiar enough with the terms to take them on 'as natural and legitimate because it is simply the way of conducting oneself' (Fairclough, 1989: 91).

The participants recalled a particularly disturbing event: at one stage of the workshop the host-country members of the project coordinating committee requested that they receive the project's budgets, that is, how much funding the project receives, how much was allocated to each component and so on. The request came, I imagine, because the host-country participants assumed that the bilateral project, the partnership, collaboration and cooperation applied equally to both parties. The response by the team leader to this request was 'this is a bilateral project, we have to operate on trust and they (the MOE) would not understand the movement of money . . . .' Before analysing this comment it is also worth noting a comment from an interviewee – the project management had offered to run a management training workshop for the host country's 'counterpart' management staff. The management team has had experience in running one with another project in another country and seemed to think this a positive idea; however, the workshop never eventuated.

The use of the phrase 'we have to operate on trust' indicated that the team leader asked the host-country stakeholders to believe that the Australian management team was working in their interests. His following comments alluded to the host-country stakeholders' lack of knowledge about project management. In looking at the comments more closely, the idea that the host-country stakeholders 'would not understand about the movement of money' indicated that the project budgets did not reveal the money that was truly available for the projects' activity. The money must have been used somewhat differently to the original agreement and the books did not faithfully indicate what was available for use in the host country. It is enlightening to understand that the donor's funding was perhaps used creatively by the project management and obviously it was the team leader's role to not disclose the 'books' to those who may question the way that money is spent. The underlying issue is that the team leader did not want to hand over this financial knowledge regardless of what the 'books' said. The symbolic violence enacted by the team leader exposed the relations in the field: the dominant players can invalidate a player's participation at will and, in this case, the authority of the Lao MOE was utterly invalidated.

In a conversation about international language education projects in Hungary (Bolitho & Medgyes, 2000), Medgyes refers to the opaqueness of the terminology of project work. The opaqueness can function in favour of certain individuals and organisations as they claim ownership of the project jargon without having to explain it. But for the power relations to function effectively the group that claims ownership must conform to those behaviours inculcated by the project documents and expected by the top-level management. The Australian teams must conform to the demands of the management companies in order to retain their positions in the project.

Talk about the project also raises complex issues around how to work out shared understandings. This does not mean that the expatriate stake-holders hold knowledge about how best to manage the meanings behind the terms but they clearly own them; in Bourdieu's framework, they are the legitimate speakers about project work. What is extraordinary about the positioning of agents in the project field is that one can know so lit-tle and yet be elevated to a dominant position in the field. It is not only English language skills that positions the agents in this way as we've seen – many host-country project team members are sophisticated speak-ers of English and have higher educational qualifications than that of the expatriate staff – so what is going on? What discourses are in play to bring about this positioning? Is there any way that the host-country project team members can become legitimate voices in project work?

The design and proposal documents set the projects up as entities which embrace the goals of bilateral partnerships and will form truly collaborative endeavours. However, if we look beneath the surface to investigate how these goals will be achieved, we hear stories about lack of communication and competing interests. We also hear that the projects are not established on mutual understandings of how 'the game is played'; there is not consensus about the process and content of the project activi-ties. The influential discourses in the field are the dominant ones about the role of English and the 'native' speaker, about work practices and power relations. Bourdieu's concepts of linguistic capital and legitimate voice have allowed us to identify the ways in which some agents have domi-nant positions in the field of project work and how the accumulation of capital in terms of language and speaking rights perpetuates a particular set of power relations in whose interests they work.

The role of English is a key factor in the work of the projects and hence an area that project managers need to resolve with regard to the power relations within a project. This is a very complex issue as English is 'the language of international communication', but it does seem that those that advocate the programmatic value of English as an international language tend not to problematise the ideological power of English. These two accounts of English as a benign communication tool and as a means of domination (as Kubota [1998] suggests) do not have to be mutually exclusive. In developing a critical pedagogy of ELT, as is essential for work in IELEPs, one needs to take account of how to develop students' communicative skills and awareness of the ideological role of English as a language of power, how it oppresses other languages, cultures and societies and how these roles can further increase global inequality and a 'biased view of language, culture and race' (Kubota, 1998: 304). This chapter suggests the need for an investigation into what constitutes relevant and meaningful language use in local contexts and the development of more productive and equitable relationships between stakeholders. Chapter 6 continues this theme of critical examination as another key area of struggle, culture, is investigated.

Chapter 6
Cultural Practices: The Project Field

A Personal Mis-construction of Culture

I start this chapter with a personal (short) story about work in an IELEP. I was working with a university English language teacher training project in North Vietnam over two decades ago. At the end of my first workshop session I asked my Vietnamese counterpart, Ha, for her comments about the success of the session which I had just co-delivered with an Australian colleague. She responded, 'Jacquie, it was a shame to see you work so hard for nothing....' The TESOL workshop my colleague and I delivered was prepared in Australia with little knowledge of ELT in North Vietnam. We expected that our work would be relevant and of interest to Vietnamese teachers of English. Ha's comment revealed the lack of connection our Australian-based paper had with the conditions and needs of the Vietnamese teachers in the workshop. While I was initially taken aback, further discussions with Ha allowed us to jointly develop more relevant and useful training workshops.

I tell this story to draw attention to the significance of understanding the local context in which one works. I believed that I had prepared for this particular task both in an academic and in a cultural sense, but my preparation was obviously inadequate. The vignette above sheds light on one understanding that I had had of 'culture'; however, this understanding was based on the unequal power relations between the ELT field in Vietnam and the one in Australia. The Australian university lecturers were exporting their knowledge products to the EL teachers in Vietnam and expected that these products would be unconditionally accepted.

In the opening plenary of the project workshop mentioned above, an official from the Vietnamese Ministry of Education (MOE) described the ELT field in North Vietnam as one that is 'chasing English'. He was referring to Vietnam's position in relation to the dominant 'international' languages. He made the comment that Vietnam is 'always running after languages: in this last century we have run after French, then we

157

ran after Russian and now English.' I had assumed that as native EL speakers of the desired product whatever we had to offer would be appropriate.

The project participants' stories contain rich material about the differing ways that culture was referred to and the many meanings it carried in the broad field of project work and the social relations within the project. 'Culture' is recognised as a difficult concept to define; Raymond Williams (1983) in *Keywords* writes that the word 'culture' is one of the two or three most complicated words in the English language. Notions of 'culture' are revealed in both the ways in which the projects are constructed through project documentation and the official institutions of both the donor/provider country and the host countries. Concepts of culture are a recurrent theme in the empirical data, voiced by interviewees, researcher observations and anecdotal evidence.

The stories about culture and habitus in project life are necessarily partial; the data speak of the individual's experience and views and can only offer glimpses into the way that the constructions of meanings of these concepts shaped the practices of the IELEPs. The notions held by the interviewees and those reflected in the practices of the project shed light on the ways that enduring relations of power established under the rubric of colonial rule are sustained under different guises.

Introduction to Culture and Habitus

This chapter analyses competing notions of culture as represented in documents and by the project participants of both projects. It also shows how the diversity of the constructions of culture and the relationship of language and culture impact on the work of the projects. In Chapter 1 (page 24) I explained how the term 'culture' is somewhat contaminated, it is as complicated as Raymond Williams (1983) so powerfully describes and delineates the field. The repeated references to 'culture' in the data conveys its currency in the project field, the comfort participants feel with it and the assumed shared understandings. However the term has too many limitations to productively describe the relations in the field. My preference (as set out in Chapter 1) is to use Bourdieu's notion of habitus to discuss the way participants do project work.

I also draw on tools from linguistic analysis to show how donor or provider notions of culture are assumed the norm 'unmarked' (or dominant) while those of host country are different, 'marked' (or subordinate) (Halliday, 1978). The cultures and languages of Laos and Japan are 'marked' in that they are named and defined. The marked is often stigmatised. By making something 'unmarked' and constructing it as the norm, one implicitly glorifies it and helps to rationalise the dominant and subordinate relationships in the field. The participants speak of their practice in ways that exemplify habitus. Their descriptions and recounts encapsulate ways in which a person's dispositions are partly individually subjective but also influenced by the objective positions and social, material and historical traditions in which that person lives.

I critique the notion of the IELEP as a small site of culture which is different from the culture outside of the project and different to the culture of the donor or provider countries. I contend that the projects are not unique entities of culturally appropriate practice; rather they embody symbolic violence in their constructions of culture and national characteristics (Morris, 1991; Murphy, 1999; Swales, 1980). The issues of culture and language are paramount in the work of IELEPs but as revealed here there are many dynamics at work in the 'complex and unpredictable' (Coleman, 1995) life of projects.

The project documents reveal the ways in which culture is constructed in the design and implementation of the projects. I put forward the idea of project habitus, the ways the participants speak of culture and the understandings that are attributed to the way culture positions agents in the field. Teaching and learning are examined as a cultural practice and I then look at the vexed notions of the relevance of knowledge of the host countries' local context; what expatriate project staff need to know about the local context and the perceived impact of lack of knowledge about the local context of the project.

Constructions of culture in the project documents

How did the project proposals construct and position 'culture'? An Australian-based team wrote the proposal documents. The notion 'culture' was foregrounded in project documentation and the work of the project. The work was written about as being either *intercultural, cross-cultural, culturally sensitive, working with cultural difference, working in a different cultural context* or *working with people from another culture*. The project proposals/submissions/tender documents all prioritised the 'culture' aspect of their work. The documents for both projects described the host countries as having a 'culture' that donors must take notice of and account for in their work. This occurred in different ways in different documents, implicit in some instances and explicit in others. For example, the host country's 'culture of work' in Project 1 was described as *hierarchical, conservative,* implying that the practices of work stem from a society governed by outdated traditions.

The host countries were depicted as unitary geopolitical formations, not as countries which contain social, material and linguistic diversity (other than noting the differences between city and country in Project 1). The representation of a single cultural entity was much simpler for the project tenderers to deal with making it more possible to 'know' the 'culture' of the country.

The documents did not correspondingly attempt to describe or have a role for 'Australian culture'; it is an unmarked invisible culture. In this act the project documents were taking the stance that the Australian 'why and how we do what we do' is the norm. The project documents writers evidently felt there was no need to be explicit about what informs the expectations of how the practices of the IELEP will be carried out, even at the level of classroom teaching. The apparent rationale was that the practices developed in the dominant context would be the norm to another.

The host countries were perceived to be almost burdened by their *problem of culture;* the ways people go about doing what they do were, to a greater or lesser degree, the root causes of the problems in the teaching of English. The host-country approaches to teaching were talked, by the documents and by Australian aid officials, about as being rooted in the traditions/cultures of the country. By the very definition of project goals, the teaching approaches in both projects were placed in a subordinate position: a key strategy used to position the foreign language teaching practices as such is to describe them as based on the grammar-translation approach. This approach is often characterised as out-of-date or traditional by Australian TESOL training institutions.

The proposal documents for both projects emphasised the Australian institutional and personal connections (social capital) and familiarity with the host countries and, implicitly, the cultures of these countries. For Project 1, the familiarity was represented by professional links; at the time of writing the proposal, the current ELT adviser in-country was to become a technical adviser for the team. The Australian university partner for the bid had staff who had worked on short in-country courses in the host country. For Project 2, the familiarity was represented by a vast number of professional links the consortium members had with universities in the host country, ranging from individual to faculty or university-based.

The project documents also listed individual or faculty general international experience and anything else that specifically or vaguely connected the Australian team with the education sector in the host country. The links and familiarity emphasised in the proposals were one way that the bidders highlighted the amount of social capital they had accumulated in this field. The institution with the greater number of international connections could claim a dominant position in a bidding arena where this form of capital was recognised. The academic field puts great store on the connections between 'significant' individuals and institutions and this capital, while varyingly important in the entrepreneurial arena, was of great significance inside the academic institutions.

By contrast, a noted absence in the documents is that of host-country technical experts on either project team. In the project world the advisers or other key staff were often referred to as technical experts and these positions are most often filled by expatriate staff. The project proposal writers detailed their accumulated significant social capital (represented by professional links), but evidently the inclusion of host-country technical experts as key team members did not increase the social or cultural capital of the proposal.

The notions of culture held in the documents gave a sense that there was something whole and definable about the social relations in the countries of the projects. The documents typified the countries as whole entities and not ones with great linguistic and ethnic diversity. These statements of belief and/or commitment did not explicate what the institutions meant by *culture*; the meanings attached in the documents reflect those 'essentialist' understandings typified in the country of Project 1 as *traditional* and *hierarchical*. The meanings given to culture in these initial stages of the projects impacted on the implementation and running of an education project. They laid the foundation for inequality, setting up dominant/subordinate relations in all forms of capital. From the outset they paid lip service to other stated goals such as bilateral cooperation, collaboration, negotiation and partnership.

Project habitus

The data led me to investigate things that we might think of as 'culture' in terms of the notion of habitus. One is not necessarily aware of one's habitus, a point Bourdieu makes: in a familiar and comfortable context or one that someone has been trained for, one can feel 'meant to be there' until there is some sort of rupture in one's experience of social life. For many of the project participants an awareness of habitus came through an external experience; for example, for Yvonne, an Australian academic, the experience of teaching in an unfamiliar context allowed her to become more aware of her habitus as a teacher. She recognised that she held beliefs and values that were shaped by her experience and led to assumptions about how teaching is carried out. I personally have experienced this and have become much more aware of my educational habitus in relation to that of my students.

In my experience there are a range of learning habitus(es), which one gradually becomes more aware of. As an Australian state school and university educated person I immediately recognise an educational habitus similar to mine, whereas there are other educational habitus(es) that I am not so likely to immediately recognise. In recognising a familiar educational habitus we are able to engage in processes which are mutually understood and seem 'natural' to the educational context. The habitus of those agents situated near to each other in a field may be more similar, which means that what they see in the world, and what they think is important, is possibly more similar. This conceptual framework is complex and extremely delicate and requires teachers to adopt a reflexive stance in pedagogical work to try to make the issue of habitus more visible. This type of thinking is particularly relevant to educational contexts that are unfamiliar to us; the differences may not be what we perceive them to be. Habitus can transform, that is, agents are affected by the field and other conscious and unconscious processes. In the extract below Yvonne (P1AU1) described the transformation and recognition of her habitus:

> You know, once I got aware of the big picture and all the complexities and the big politics and the petty politics, did it actually change the way I operated? I think it probably did, I might have still been delivering the same kind of methodology, but there was more acknowledgment and recognition of me being an insider or an outsider.

In the spirit of Bourdieu (1986) I describe the work of the IELEP as a game. The game is played differently and more or less successfully by different players. There is diversity in the opinions of the groups; not all the expatriate project stakeholders felt the same way and not all host stakeholders spoke similarly about understandings of culture, as will be demonstrated later in this chapter. Lee (P1/2AU2) has, in earlier chapters, expressed a positive view of the professional development, relationships and cultural learning in the Project 1 field. He talked of the positive learning for the Australian university staff and felt that the experience of the local teachers was equally positive.

I think the Australian teachers who went over, their relationship with the country's teachers was truly fantastic. And they're enduring relationships. They're valued very much on both sides. It was for a number of university staff, one of the best professional experiences they'd ever had. And I think I can judge fairly well . . . from the host country's people comments about what they valued too. About our attempts to understand their culture, and to bring out the best in both cultures, so at that level, those stakeholders, at the grassroots level, it was great. It was the next level up, the management level, that it all went wrong, and that of course had direct implications on what we could do at the grassroots level.

His description of the delineations in the field is in sharp contrast to interviewees earlier in this chapter who view culture as a problem. He saw that the relationships between the Australian university staff and the course participants were strong and positive. He believed that the Australians academics were interested in the host country's culture and helped develop the positive relationships. He talked about the project management in a completely different, more negative, way; at this level 'it all went wrong.' He referred later in the interview to the management more explicitly and points to particular problems within the Australian project management team. The positive professional experience he spoke of here, that is, the relationship between the host-country teachers and the expatriate staff, was echoed by many of the other interviewees from both projects. Many of the expatriate staff commented on the fruitful learning experience of working closely with the host-country teachers. This experience was more limited by the nature of the project structure in Project 2.

Constructions of 'Culture' in Project Work

The theme of 'culture' emerged strongly as a way of defining agents' behaviour, knowledge and social norms. There was implicit reference to the notion of habitus in the sense that some agents were acculturated in the dispositions that were 'required' of project work while others are not. There is of course variance in the way that the notions are spoken of within the practices of project work and difference in how the describing of culture is predicated on strategies of domination and subordination.

In the interview data 'culture' is sometimes spoken about as though only those different from the dominated group (marked), that is, those who hold lesser amounts of the significant capital in the project, have this 'burden of culture'. It seems that there is an assumption by some of the participants that the project staff who occupy the dominant positions behave in a completely normal (unmarked) way and their work and other practices do not have to be investigated.

Australian participants from both projects embodied this sense of being 'normal' (unmarked) and assumed that other expatriate project advisers shared their view of what was a normal way to behave in project life. The interviewees' comments revealed how decisively the unmarked views of culture delineate the field. Comments from the Australian participants placed the host-country participants in subordinate positions: the host-country people 'do or don't do' things in the way that they think they should be done. For example, in Project 1, one participant described how people 'don't share information', and the reason she thought the host-country participants 'keep information to themselves' was because 'information is power.' She said that this behaviour was a 'thing of the system . . . I think that's a cultural or political thing.' When the Australian participants made these types of comments, they substantiated their views by claiming the authority to describe the real situation and that other project staff like themselves had the same opinion, for example, 'I certainly believe it to be real. It's the opinion of a lot of people on a lot of other projects.'

What was surprising was the extent to which the participants replicated the type of cultural stereotyping of Asian students and teachers described by Kumaravadivelu (2003a, 2008) in his studies of TESOL settings. Kumaravadivelu describes three enduring cultural stereotypes that are attributed to students from Asia: (1) are obedient to authority; (2) lack critical thinking; and (3) do not participate in classroom interaction. Phan Le Ha (2004) in her study of ELT and identity found similar stereotypes existed in the field. In Project 1 some of the expatriate staff described the host-country staff as 'linear thinkers'. The expatriates supported their views by accounts of workshops and teacher training sessions where the host-country participants responded to the project materials. The discussions at the workshops and sessions were conducted in English; the host-country participants were clearly at some disadvantage but this did not temper the Australian participants' views. One example was a workshop where the participants were discussing the writing of a course book and looking at the organisation of the document; the participants apparently focused on the structure of the book and the sequence of activities and so on. According to the Australian participants, this focus on structure and numbering of activities was a demonstration of linear thinking.

Kumaravadivelu (2003a, 2008) discusses how the level of participation in second language (L2) education settings is attributed to many other factors apart from culture: clearly level of language proficiency but also the particular context, the way the material is presented, participants' interest in the topic or the tolerance of risk-taking. While limited Kumaravadivelu points to research conducted with (so-called) native English speakers in L2 settings that shows students find speaking in discussion activities challenging and avoid these activities, feeling anxious and frustrated by their lack of proficiency in L2 which stops them participating fully in classroom and other situations.

An intriguing aspect of the Project 1 workshop interview samples described above is that the project participants did not discuss the context within which these events occurred; the workshop participants, and in fact all host-country participants in both projects, were teachers and learners of English with varying levels of proficiency in English. The project host-country teacher trainers used English in the workshops to discuss aspects of curriculum development and teaching methodology. A number of the workshop participants had limited linguistic resources to discuss the complexity of new teaching resources. This point becomes particularly pertinent as further comments about this workshop described the host-country participants as focusing on the size of the book, that 'it's too big,' and that 'they stayed on the surface.' An Australian participant dismissed the idea that it may have been that the participants were reluctant for whatever reason to give any other comments but went on to say that it's 'how people see things which in our sort of cultural perspective (Australian, unmarked) is seen as at a very surface level. People here do not have any analytical skill, it's the cultural perspective of the country.' A cultural stereotype which stubbornly endures is that Asian students and teachers lack critical thinking skills and this is somehow tied to their cultural beliefs (Kumaravadivelu, 2003a, 2008). No validity was given to the host-country participants' comments about the size of the book. Interestingly, this was a key issue in Project 2. The Australian team in Japan also believed that the host-country participants were only able to focus on surface issues. In defending the host-country teachers' views, Murray (P2AM1) explained why the size of the materials was of major concern in the development of the teaching materials in Project 2. He emphasised that the transportability of the course materials was important. The teachers often travelled great distances between work and home by public transport and were not able to carry around hefty documents in their daily travel. However, members of the Australian team trivialised the host-country teachers' comments and interpreted the comments about the organisation and size of the materials in a way that added depth to their argument that the local teachers and teacher educators did not go beyond the surface level of curriculum development.

Reflecting cultural stereotypes was one way that the notion of culture may be constructed. Some Australian staff were keen to get across the importance of the 'national characteristics' of the host-country staff; using expressions such as 'it's how people see things' and 'it's the cultural per-spective of the country' intimates that these characteristics were fixed and shared by all fellow country people, that is, there was no possibility that national or cultural identity or habitus will change or transform or, as Hall (1990) writes, that culture is constantly 'becoming'.

Expatriate Australians expressed the opinion that their host-country co-workers did not really know anything: that the teachers were of a very low educational standard, had very poor English skills, were proba-bly forced into retraining to be EL teachers and were 'people who didn't understand their own system at all'. This stereotyping of the host-country teachers in Project 1 was not isolated to this project, the Australian team or particular individuals. A description of someone as a 'linear thinker' is a way of placing that person in a subordinate position. I believe that from the Australian team and donors' perspectives, the host-country teachers were 'deficit'. The host-country teachers are spoken of as 'only capable of handling small bits of information at a time', 'needing very concrete examples' and repeatedly as not having any 'interpretive' or 'investiga-tive powers'. While this expresses perhaps the notion of 'an essentialist culture', in these particular instances it is commensurate with a conven-tional notion of culture as described by Putnis (1993: 39). This description draws on the notion of 'personality traits' that gives rise to the idea of 'personality types', that is, categories of people with similar patterns of personality traits. The categories become 'cultural types' via the idea that 'culture' moulds personality. This leads by extension to the idea of cul-tures having a 'personality'. This particular variation on the theme of the monolithic, essentialist view of culture is found in many texts on the 'role of culture' and 'intercultural communication' (Asante & Gudykunst, 1989; Dodd, 1987; Putnis, 1993).

This interpretation may seem harsh in the light of the partial nature of this study, but the sentiments expressed are powerful directives in the ways that the teaching and learning relationships are constructed within the projects. The host-country teachers, constructed as 'linear thinkers' as implicitly opposed to the creative, analytical thinking expatriate staff, were subsequently put in a subordinate position in the field. The host-country teachers were at best the 'counterparts', not the experts, and the notion of culture transposed to a personality type allowed the conservation of the power relations in the field. The comments from the expatriate advisers and other Australian staff revealed that in their minds the host-country staff's work and social practices, referred to as 'cultural traits', are enduring, undifferentiated and have essential features. This view of culture and habitus, the acquired dispositions that interact with the objective structures of the field, is extended to a large category of people by some interviewees. The categories of 'Asian' and 'European' were frequently called on and attributed the various characteristics that reflect widely held and perhaps idealised stereotypes.

Constructions of culture in teaching and learning components

Constructions of the notion of the host-country 'culture' emerged repeatedly in the writing of curriculum and teacher education materials. A depiction of the teaching and learning processes emerged which clearly delineated the project field. Mel, an Australian academic with Project 1, discussed a recent teacher training session where she worked with two counterparts who were lecturers with the local university and had been seconded to work on the project. She commented on the way that the counterparts ran the workshop and was particularly surprised at the seeming 'reliance on . . . rote learning techniques [and] listing sequentially the teaching strategies in the textbook'. She talked about the counterparts' approach as being 'superficial' and she spoke about it as being perhaps 'very Asian' and if not a general Asian characteristic then it was certainly 'in the style of this country's people'.

In the above comments Mel introduced a large category of peoples by using the term 'Asian' and attributed a number of characteristics to the term: a 'reliance on rote learning', attention to 'superficial things'. The mention of the larger category of 'Asian' pointed to a popular conceptualisation of the 'Asian' learner in the ELT field and the stereotypical characteristics that accompany this concept. This is yet again another example of the type of cultural stereotyping present in Kumaravadivelu's study, where he found that ELT teachers commonly draw on popular categories of people, for example, 'Europeans' and 'Asians', to substantiate an opinion and position held by a student or teacher in the field.

The differentiation enacted here, between the local staff's/participants' and the expatriates' 'cultures', which really speaks of knowledge, information, skills, resources and other material objects, is a feature of both projects. The project's goals were built upon the differences between the worlds of the donor/provider and the recipient. The difference was written in terms of the stakes (or capital) in the field as well as the even more abstract notions of social and historical traditions. The donor/provider, in differentiating between the worlds, was able to position itself more favourably, and this is particularly so in the area of teaching and learning skills.

In a Bourdieuian sense the act of talking about and enacting social relations and educational processes is predicated on symbolic violence. From this standpoint symbolic violence may seem to be an inevitable part of the educational process and underlies the relations in the field of education. However, in situations like the above where certain learning and teaching processes are so explicitly delegitimised, the act of symbolic violence must be addressed.

The way in which the notion of culture is used to separate and diminish certain practices within the project echoes Raymond Williams' (1983) caution about the potential symbolic violence in the use of the term 'culture' itself. By this, Williams means the extraordinary power of the word to define one's humanity at the expense of another's. The act of defining a culture in a certain way, as not as human as another, is an act of violence: 'cultural definitions are instruments of the political power of identity exclusion' (Bhabha, 1994). Certain participants were more than willing to claim that the successful way of working in a project is to be 'analytical, and a complex and lateral thinker' which, in their opinions, characterised the Australian project worker. The act of defining what behaviour is acceptable in project work puts these stakeholders in a dominant position in the field and allows them to maintain control over how project work is carried out. The habitus that these project advisors bring to the field is one that is at ease with the practices of the project.

It is interesting to note that not all project participants spoke about differences; Son (P1LM1), an MOE official, viewed Australians and people from her country as quite similar and suggested that the way for a collaborative effort to be developed was for the Australian team to understand more about her ministry's approach to project work and teacher training. While she identified some differences in the approaches to project work, she emphasised the need to work on the basis of a shared understanding. She also made an interesting point in claiming that the 'Australian temperament and her country's were not so different' but the difference was in the way that institutions such as her country's ministry and the relevant Australian institutions functioned. Such areas as 'initiatives about project planning, implementation' were carried out in different ways. She requested that the project management team should work more cooperatively and understand the procedure in her country.

Cultural practices: Teaching and learning

The projects' practices in teacher education and the subsequent teaching of English as a foreign language (EFL) provided an excellent opportunity to examine the notions of culture and habitus in practice and how these impacted on struggles around legitimacy, domination and subordination. The classroom is a site which yields contradictory and contested notions of culture. The ELT field is notorious for the way it has reduced notions of 'culture' to the observable behaviour of the students and teachers (Pennycook, 2000). Of particular interest here are the views of 'cultural difference' or rather, differentiation in the university environment and the TESOL context.

In this book the classroom (as analogous to the project) is not separate from the outside world; the relationship is two-way in the sense that what happens in the classroom is a reflection of social relations outside but also that what happens inside the classroom affects social life in the outside world (Auerbach *et al.*, 1996; Pennycook, 2000: 92). Yvonne (P1AU1) from Project 1 drew my attention to the interconnection between the classroom and the outside world:

> I initially was very ignorant of the politics of aid and what it meant for all the levels on both sides. I was apolitical in that sense. But . . . slowly I realised that what went on in the classroom somehow or other had to be, was being impacted by other levels and so I did learn through engagement in those conversations . . . [with project participants]

However, she felt unable to discuss the politics of aid with her students:

> we never engaged in dialogue with the students, like I would here [in Australia], about the politics of what we were doing.

The cultural politics of the projects lead to questions of struggles over difference; the projects in their very inception identify and reify a binary opposition in cultural difference but the relations in the field are much more complex than the donor and recipient cultures. This struggle among the divergent groups in the project is about whose version of reality gains legitimacy. (Pennycook, 2000)

The classroom, with its permeable boundaries through which forms of social relations pass back and forth and influence social life both within and outside its walls, is a far cry from the notion of Holliday's (1999) small 'culture', where there is cohesiveness among the 'inside' group members and no explicit relationship to the large national or international cultures outside of the classroom. The regularities of social life are not formed within the vacuum of the classroom but rather they are informed and shaped by the influences of the social, material and historical conditions within both the national and the international context.

The students (in the projects they are the teachers of English) were not recognised for the different roles they took up and activities they carried out in the world outside the classroom. This was a complex situation as represented by both the Australian and the host-country participants; all of the participants were divided by many things that were not necessarily appreciated by the Australian project team. It may not have been in the course participants' interests to discuss the broader politics of the education system and ministry policies.

There was, however, evidence of the enduring notions of difference in the data. Tong (P1LU3) from Project 1 commented on the behaviour of students from the host country: 'This country's student behaviour is quite different from the European way . . .' She had earlier spoken about the teaching approach used in the EFL classes: she felt that there were not great differences in methodology, theoretically speaking, between her country's approach to teaching English and the approach advocated in the Australian course. The differences lay in more material, social and economic areas; these differences manifested themselves in teacher–student behaviour, physical aspects of the classroom and economic conditions of teaching. In the following quotation she talked about the relationship between the students' behaviour and the teachers' methodology:

> in class the student tends to answer the questions the teacher asks. So, we have to ask them many questions until they raise their hand to answer. But the situation's different in your country. In Australia, the students are very brave to ask questions and they probably initiate the issues in class, raise [their hands] if in class discussion. But in our situation everything has to be raised by the teachers. So, even though we use the student centred [approach], but everything should be initiated by teachers first.

In describing this aspect of the classroom, the interviewee, similar to the extract from Mel, drew on common stereotypes of large categories of people. For example, she described Australian students as 'brave' if they asked questions or initiated a discussion. The interviewees from both host countries spoke of the valued role of the teachers, one where the teacher was the source of great knowledge and was held in very high esteem:

'They all respect the teachers. That means they find that the teachers know everything' (Tong P1LU3).

The host-country interviewees from Project 1 offered many descriptions of student–teacher behaviour which exemplified one way that they thought of cultural differences in the classroom. Weng below (P1LM2) talked about the ways students behave in classes run by Australian lecturers. In these classes the students are depicted as behaving in a 'more independent way'. The 'foreign teacher' enabled the students to 'feel freer' than they do with the teachers from the host country; this included engaging in discussions and 'critical thinking'. Weng and Min (P1LM3) both made interesting comments in relation to the difference in behaviour when students are with either the Australian teacher or the host-country teacher: with the latter the students 'behave nicely' and the 'teachers mostly talk'.

These descriptions appear to again draw on Kumaravadivelu's (2003a, 2008) framework of the very standard stereotypes of 'south-east Asian' students or teachers and 'western' students or teachers, that the foreign lecturer is a 'critical thinker' and allows the students to feel 'freer' in the classroom processes. Weng went on to imply that with their own teachers from the host country the students do not feel as 'free' to offer their own opinions or analysis. She then called on her 'culture' as a reason for doing this, that they may offend the teacher by acting in this 'foreign' way. Weng did not specify in this extract what she means by foreign; I believe that she meant the broad category: 'western', native English-speaking. She also referred to the 'nice' behaviour of students, that is, that students did not speak and the teachers did all the talking. Her comments were interesting in that a common stereotype of 'Asian' students that proliferates in cross-cultural, intercultural literature is that these students are passive in their own and 'western' contexts. Weng contested this prevailing idea and countered that students adopted the perceived 'western' approaches to education. Weng and Min had initially presented an idealised picture of 'western' education, but further on in the next response Min felt that her country's approach to education did have something to offer the Australian teachers: 'so sometimes, the Australian teacher should not let them feel free all the time. In some ways you can learn from our side.' In this comment she perceived that there was something to be learnt from her country's teaching and learning processes; this was a positive but vague comment and in this extract I can only assume what she referred to.

I do not intend to argue about what is 'true' or 'untrue' in these stereotypes but rather to investigate how they affected the relations in this project field and the value of this analysis to the IELEP field in general. The qualities attributed to the different stereotypes are not neutral markers; they work to place the host-country teachers and students in a subordinate position in the field. The host-country teachers are 'fish out of water' in the ELT field; their teaching practices need to be replaced however successful, relevant and useful they are to the host-country students. The dominant players deny the legitimacy of the teachers.

The description of homogenous groups of students and teachers and classroom behaviour in the host countries was challenged by my experience of observing classrooms in Weng and Min's country (Project 1) and in Japan, where Project 2 was located. The behaviour of the students certainly differed to that of students in Australian schools in ways that were underscored by the particular organisational features of the schools but in no sense could I characterise it, in either country, as homogenous. Students from the host country of Project 1 differed from region to region, from city to country, according to the social and economic class and in relation to the way the teachers took up their role in class and the type of lesson they were engaged in. My interactions with and observations of students belied the notion of a 'norm'; the students interacted with teachers in very different ways and teachers often assumed a collegial role with students, particularly when encouraging them to perform in English in interactive activities. What I noticed was the differences between schools within the major cities and the different types of relationships that students seemed to have with teachers. In some schools the teachers were able to carry out informal interactions with students and the students were more than willing to participate actively in the class. The students were far from passive. In one English class (fourth grade of secondary school) I observed the teacher set up a discussion and then debate about the comparative value of men and women's work (this was part of a larger lesson on using English to describe routines). The students were lively and interjected and gave support or otherwise to the different speakers. The teacher and students joked and teased each other. This was not the way this country's classes would usually be represented. In another school which was an academically selective school the lessons I observed were more formal and followed a structural approach to the teaching of English.

The students and teachers in Project 2 offered a similar diversity. Reports from the team which visited a number of schools in the host country noted the diversity of the educational contexts and the fact that it was impossible to typify a 'culture of teaching and learning in the country'. One report described a visit to a school which was located in a

provincial town a few hours away from the capital city of the highly industrialised country. The school was regarded as 'low status' and attracted
students who did not have high academic expectations and were more
likely to leave school to go straight into the workforce or attend a technical institution than to go to university. The EL teachers were highly
committed and were keen to engage students in the lessons. The report
described one lesson in depth; the students were around 14 years old and
English was a compulsory subject. When the class started the single desks
and chairs were in rows, a typical classroom organisation for this school;
almost immediately on entering the classroom the students moved the
desks to form what seemed to be friendship groupings. The boys and
girls then brought out their 'tools' for the lesson, make-up bags complete with desktop mirrors, mobile phones and other electronic gadgets.
The teacher had planned an interactive lesson and proceeded to teach,
and the students, in a non-hostile way, proceeded to 'do their own thing'.
Some students down the front listened, interacted and participated in the
communicative activities with the teacher while other students occupied
themselves with other activities. This meant for one student, going over to
the window and having an extended conversation with a friend outside.
It also meant an intensive grooming/beauty treatment time for others:
both boys and girls took up tweezers and spent quite a long time plucking
their eyebrows!

How would one describe this behaviour? Passive, teacher-centred, the
prevailing stereotypes of students and classroom organisation in this
country hardly fit! I give this example in depth to illustrate an underlying premise of this chapter, namely, that it is a particular context with a
particular group of students that can not be characterised by the fact that
they are Korean, Japanese, Chinese or Taiwanese. The reports offered similarly rich stories of other schools and classes that were visited during this
information-gathering tour where the schools, students and teachers varied considerably. In an academically-focused school, where students had
to compete via an examination for entry into the school, the class scenario
was completely different. The teacher and students focused diligently on
the text-based lesson.

Sal (P2LT3) from Project 2, a teacher, discussed the similarity between
teachers in his country and Australia. He had taught in Australia and felt
that 'the conditions of teaching his language in Australia and English in
his country are almost the same.' He continued to talk about the similarity in the processes of the lessons differentiating between the teaching
of the languages in terms of purpose. Sal expressed the opinion that the
teaching of Japanese in Australia is for use in 'the real world'; students

are taught the language in the context of where it will be used, for example, in the tourism industry, export industry and potentially for work in his country. He saw the teaching of English much more as a gate-keeping exercise in his country: students had to pass an English examination for entry into university and this was the motivation for most students studying English. Even though English was a compulsory subject he felt that the majority of students did not see any extrinsic benefits (other than access to university) in studying English.

Sal (P2LT3) taught in an 'alternative' government school, an innovative project developed by a municipal council in the capital city. The school was for students who for one reason or another could not stay in the mainstream schools. The school had a very flexible attitude in the organisation of teaching and learning and students were able to be 'creative' with the school uniform. Sal discussed the ways teachers in his school embraced learning about different approaches to teaching and then described how the teachers were constrained by structural factors in the education system, for example, the university entrance exams. As discussed previously, the exams, at this time, almost exclusively tested reading and writing skills and therefore influenced the way teachers taught in senior secondary school. Ministry officials interviewed for this study did express some concern about how the project courses will deal with the demands of the university entrance exam. These same officials were part of a significant push within the MOE to change both the university entrance exams and the English language curriculum, that is, to add a speaking and listening component to the exam and consequently broaden the curriculum to include more equal teaching of the four skills.

Knowledge of the local context

IELEPs and other international education activities are carried out in what is often referred to as a 'local context'. It is with great interest that I turn to this sub-theme in the data; it was spoken about in different ways by different participants. The interviewees from the projects' host countries spoke about contextual knowledge in terms of the specific pedagogic practices and material/social /historical conditions of the local teachers. They did not identify knowledge of essential features of the 'culture', for example, what was polite in their particular country as comprising knowledge of the local context. Participants from Australian universities did look more towards essentialist ways of doing things as examples of 'cultural difference'.

By contrast, many of the host-country interviewees gave their views on what Australian project staff needed to know about their country's education system, language and culture to make projects successful:

> my country's education, maybe before designing the program some- one should survey first what the real situation is . . . because the people that are going to train . . . from that situation. They can see the real situation of those people before designing the course. (Weng P1LM2)

Yvonne (P1AU1) spoke of the relevance and importance of knowledge of the local context:

> the knowledge of the social context, when we throw that word around, that question just in sharp relief makes me appreciate that in Australia . . . I know what's going on at every level and therefore that knowledge puts me in a more powerful position in a sense, but it also puts me in a position where I can more sensitively operate in it. In Laos . . . I couldn't read the culture and therefore . . . even what I was doing at the classroom level I'm sure it wasn't as relevant or localised and all those things that you talk about, even at the methodology level . . .

What comprised knowledge of the local context was a point of tension and struggle in the IELEP field in this study. Comments made by some Australian staff did not recognise the type of struggle experienced by Yvonne in coming to grips with her lack of knowledge of the Lao con- text. The majority of the dominant players assumed that their knowledge gained in Australia was sufficient to operate in this new context.

The 'local context' in both projects was not a straightforward entity; there are great differences in the educational environment, resources and provision between city and country (provincial) schools, and there are also differences between the perceived status of different schools. The human resource area was also not easily contextualised as the teachers have varying degrees of experience, educational background and English language proficiency. The importance of understanding the many facets of the ELT landscape in each country was urged by a range of host-country interviewees from both projects.

Son (P1LM1) reiterated that there needed to be more talk between both sides about project management. Her comment is important as much for what it does not say as for what it does say. Son, a ministry official, was asking that the expatriate team members understand the organisa- tional systems and the work practices, that is, the 'institutional practices' (Fairclough, 1989, 1995) in her country.

> They should understand our need and ... so the team leader should
> understand the MOE policy and understand our need and try to
> understand the way of working here for the success of the project.

Talking about what the team 'should' know implied that the team did not
have this information and that learning about the relevant procedures in
the host country was a precursor to an effective project. Tan (P2LM1) from
Project 2 was keen that the Australian project team find out the specific
professional development needs of the host-country teachers. To do this
the Australian universities should assess the abilities of these teachers:

> so the universities should know the ability, especially the communica-
> tive, the communication abilities, of the host-country teachers. But
> also not only the communicative abilities but also the writing and
> reading abilities of the teachers.

Shor (P2LU2), a university professor and a key member of the MOE
project committee, discussed how important it is for the content to
be based on the host country's English language textbooks and not on
Australian materials:

> one of the important things for them is to use the text book itself. Not
> your own [Australian] I mean, their [Japanese] own text books. As you
> know here in Japan in both senior and junior high schools, the text
> books authorised by the Minister of Education, are introduced and
> the teachers have to use those text books and if ... all the text books
> you give them are completely different ... from those which they are
> accustomed to use, they cannot adapt what they have learned in their
> project to their real situation, I mean in their own schools [Japanese].
> So ... approximately I think, one third of the text books for the situa-
> tion should be adjusted to the real situation here, including ... using
> their [Japanese teachers'] own text books. In that case, maybe you will
> produce or you will make the special workbooks which are adjusted
> to their own text books. This kind of thing has not yet been done in
> any of the English-speaking universities.

It is necessary to acknowledge and investigate the project implementers'
resistance to using the host-country materials and context. As reiterated
throughout this story, the explicit goals of both projects were to change
existing behaviour in the ELT field. The objectives of both projects were
to develop new courses or new materials and to train teachers and/or
teacher trainers. The objectives of Project 2 (P2D1: 3) stated that the materials developed for the courses were focused on the context and needs of

the particular teachers. Chris (P2AU3) from Project 2 below contested that this occurred, claiming that it was often 'just adapting very little...' She also added that the materials were based on adult ELT and did not really address teaching school children. However, she went on to say,

> On the other hand, I think for the teachers themselves, often they want to get out of their context a little bit...I think there's some appeal. Why would they do this course rather than a course that's with a university in Japan, because it does seem as though it's going to broaden their understandings, a little bit more. So I think it's good to provide some international context, maybe a little bit of comparison, letting them see what's happening in language teaching in other countries in schools, but don't know if it really addressed either issue very well.

The interview data with the expatriate staff from both projects revealed interesting macro depictions of the local context in which ELT takes place. These descriptions are time-honoured ways of thinking about teaching and learning practices in south-east and east Asia and they resonate strongly with Kumaravadivelu's (2003a, 2008) categories of cultural stereotyping mentioned earlier in this chapter. While there are material bases to some of the assumed realities about these practices, the speaking of such assumptions is another way of differentiating between Australia and the 'other'. The view of the dominant players in the data and one that informed the design and development of the teacher training materials was that there were specific teaching and learning practices in each country and these were somehow of lesser value than Australian ones. Comments about the teaching of English language, such as those below, were found throughout the interviews with Australian stakeholders: classes are large; students are passive; students are used to learning in teacher-centred classrooms; there is a reliance on rote learning and memorisation; students are well-behaved; teachers have a revered role in society; the lessons reflect the fundamental philosophies of the society.

As mentioned above, there are instances and perhaps regularities in the field where there are large classes and teachers do use a teacher-centred approach to teaching English in the host countries, but the assumptions play a more significant role than objectively describing a context. A short comment such as 'students are passive' delivers a powerful statement about the teaching context and belies the reality of the necessary diversity of the local context. This stereotyping of education in any given context, regardless of national groups, has been unmasked time and time again (Kubota, 1998, 1999, 2001a; Kumaravadivelu, 2003a, 2008; Penny-cook, 1998, 1999, 2000), yet the classic stereotyping of the behaviour of students and teachers continues to hold academic credibility. The strength and endurance of the aforementioned cultural stereotyping are one of the key power lines which criss-cross and delineate the IELEP field. Those players whose dispositions and behaviours are marked are placed in a subordinate position.

The curriculum writers (and many team members) on Project 2 had very little experience of the host country's education system and the project manager was keen for the writers and other members of the team to visit schools in this country to assist in the development of high-quality course materials. The gathering of some ethnographic data to inform the project did occur some time after the project started. A small group of academics, including one of the curriculum writers, visited a number of the country's high schools to observe English language classrooms. As described earlier in this chapter, reports from this visit comment on the extraordinary diversity of teaching contexts, behaviour of students and teachers and content of lessons in the Project 2 country. A number of comments suggested that the team did not anticipate the diversity and were astounded by the differences and similarities to the Australian context. The differences between the expectations of the Australian team and the observed classrooms again reflect the depth and strength of the cultural stereotypes of Asian students discussed in Kumaravadivelu's (2003a, 2008) studies. The Japanese classrooms varied as significantly as classrooms do in Australia (and elsewhere in the world) and reflected the social and material conditions of the schools and students. Some of the Australian visitors recounted how the visit, the discussions with students, teachers, teacher educators and ministry officials had a dramatic effect on the team, revealing an intricacy of the context that had not been apparent to the team members prior to the visit.

The team arrived back to Australia inspired by the field work and by the challenges of creating course materials which combine the best of lan-guage teaching materials in Australia and meeting the needs of Japanese teachers. The course development would need further funding to give the writers more time to develop materials with new input. The response to this challenge was at best disappointing and at worst demonstrated the primacy of struggle to accumulate economic capital in the IELEP field. In respect to the latter, the faculty was reluctant to provide more funds for any further development highlighting the struggle between the accumu-lation of economic and cultural capital. The curriculum writing proved to be problematic, and the writers experienced difficulty in shifting from models provided by the commonly used Australian ESL type courses. The MOE representatives and other host-country members of the project team expected to see a curriculum that responded to the Japanese teachers' needs.

There seems to be a number of things happening here. One was that the visit to the host country and brief encounter with the students and teachers and the physical sites of language teaching sparked interest in producing some exciting new materials and ones that would show some expertise in international language education. The response from the curriculum writers was mixed; although one of the writers was inspired by the visit, it was difficult for this writer to generate enthusiasm for further exploration of how the materials might better meet the needs of the students and teachers. The project's development was constrained by funding and institutional restrictions and this had an impact on the way the project could extend itself. So there was this split in terms of the way 'culture' is thought and talked about in international projects. There was an imperative to be seen to work with the specificities of the project's context and to encourage the project teams to respond to this context but also to work within the institutional constraints and to maintain a dominant position in the field.

The host-country interviewees and a majority of the Australian interviewees from both projects identified the lack of local knowledge as the most significant threat to the 'success' of an IELEP. Yet this aspect of pre-project preparation was seriously neglected. Chris (P2AU3) from Project 2 expressed surprise about the project's curriculum writers' lack of knowledge of the local context and the little importance they attached to gaining this knowledge:

> you would expect that the writers were well versed in the host country's situation, or they'd been to schools or they knew about the education system. They did have some knowledge of it, but it was fairly limited I think. And there were attempts made to redress that by having trips to Japan. But it was a little bit ad hoc, I think and involved only one of the writers. Information was dispersed but, I think the writers had their own agenda in a certain way, I think perhaps they weren't tailoring it as much to the host country's context as they could have.

Chris has extensive knowledge of the host country, including bilingual skills, but she commented that this was not utilised nor seen as a resource by the project management. She was surprised at how she was positioned in the project: she talked about how she expected to take a more integral role in the conceptualisation of how the project would present itself and was taken aback by her marginalisation within the team. Other Australian academics also expressed their surprise at the way she was sidelined by the project management; for example, Carla was quite candid about the way Chris was treated and saw her marginalisation as a deliberate strategy to keep her institution (the private language teaching organisation) in a subordinate position.

This view offered an insight into motives for decision making and revealed the project management's multiple interests at play. Chris's contribution to the development of the project was substantial but she could have been more centrally involved. She described her connections with commercial and educational organisations in the host country as well as collegial relations with some colleagues in one of the partner universities. She also had significant involvement with a university post-graduate programme, a teacher training course for native speakers of Japanese. One analysis could place her in a strong position in terms of social and cultural capital: she had a high-level post-graduate qualification from one of the best universities in the host country, her bilingual skills were highly regarded in Australia and she had strong connections with the university. However, the important determiners in the field were the different roles assigned to the academic institutions and the social capital accumulated by the academic connections; participants like Chris were really just from the wrong side of the academic tracks.

The lack of knowledge of the host-country context was given a more personal view by Yvonne (P1AU1), an Australian university lecturer from Project 1. She candidly discussed what she saw as her lack of knowledge about all aspects of the work of the project, from the more global aspects to the pedagogical practices. I quote Yvonne at length as I believe she allowed me to engage with some of the ways that project work was organised in terms of knowledge of the host-country context. The projects, in quite significant ways, were a realisation of the university's critical development themes of internationalisation and fortunately this individual staff member experienced internationalisation as a two-way process. But in general, the view from the university as represented in the data was that it had the authority to export its product unconditionally into the host-country context. In her comments about the organisation and work practices of the project she felt that she started work in an area that she knew nothing about.

> I was invited to do it, and I said, no, I can't do this work, I've got no experience. I only know how to teach literacy to natives speakers. And

my other colleagues said, of course you can. So I went off naively and now, I know that I was right . . . , I didn't know how to do it.

Yvonne (P1AU1) does hold a post-graduate qualification in TESOL and did lecture on MA TESOL/Masters in Applied Linguistics type programmes in Australia. I reminded her of that and asked why she felt unqualified to teach in the project.

> Yes. But you know, I'd never worked in that country or the region, and I think that makes all the difference too. So, you know, I was a teacher, I went there with my bundle of goodies about what constitutes effective ELT. I shudder to think of what even in the first couple of years, what I did give the students, but I suppose over the years, and what makes it successful, I think one factor is time and immersion in the context.

In Project 1 she was a lecturer in ELT teacher education; she conducted lectures for the host-country teachers on classroom practices, that is, the theory and practice of ELT. She had taught on a short post-graduate course in the host country 1 year prior to the commencement of Project 1. Her work with the short course dovetailed into the large aid project. Below she talked about how when she started her teaching in this particular country, she felt the need for knowledge about the Lao context:

> I became aware of the teachers' local needs because I had actually gone out into their context. I mean, when I think about not ever even having darkened the door of a classroom . . . And there was no provision for us to do that. So, we went in with a whole set of assumptions that we could deliver this, you know, from one context or another. I tried to transfer the art of language teaching as I knew it into a context with which I was totally unfamiliar.

Yvonne spoke of many issues which are critically relevant to the work of IELEPs. She also talked of the immense learning potential inherent in the practices of the project. In her earlier extracts she described herself as completely uninitiated into IELEP work; her academic habitus is acculturated to working with Australian teachers (native speakers of English) engaged in post-graduate language and literacy education. Yvonne was particularly critical of the structure of the programme, taking courses used in Australia to a new context which she knew nothing about.

Mara (P1AP2) from Project 1, an Australian teacher with the project, thought that knowledge of the host-country context is highly significant. She was bilingual and had lived in the region for many years. These skills allowed her to connect with the host-country participants in different ways. She conducted introductory sessions and parts of other sessions in the participants' first language and thought that 'giving people a chance to talk about what their situations are like is really important.' In these sessions the participants spoke about their social and work situations; because the sessions were conducted in the host-country language, the linguistic capital was more evenly distributed during these times. Mara thought that this type of discussion was beneficial because it allowed the participants to establish links with each other: 'sometimes students sit in class and they think this has nothing to do with me because I'm not like these people around me. I'm not like the people who seem to be at the top of the class . . . .'

Mara (P1AP2) thought that giving space for the students to talk about their situation and ideas also gave them the freedom to accept new ideas, particularly for those students from the more remote regions:

> So, I think in the provinces people have a much harder time taking on new ideas sometimes and that is one of the reasons that getting a chance to say something, getting a chance to think people are listening to them is – and appreciating the differences helps them to move towards making a change themselves.

In this extract she also demonstrated how projects such as these can encourage many forms of learning. The students referred to in the above quotation, while situated within a formal learning setting, were engaged in informal learning processes where new understandings emerge from conversations that may seem peripheral to the main purpose of the event.

Critiques of the project model (Holliday, 1992, 1994, 1995, 1999, 2005; Morris, 1991, 1996; Pottier, 1993; Swales, 1980) document the negative ways in which expatriate project advisors evaluate the work of host-country project participants/stakeholders. Alongside this, they question the ability of the expatriate project advisors to work in ways that they consider successful. Morris (1991), in his severe critique of a range of aid project work in Yemen, comments that expatriate aid workers were largely 'unequipped to cope with the discrepancy between image and reality'. The result was that 'When they fail to achieve the goals set themselves they may become consumed by guilt, attempt to disguise their enforced idleness by a charade of hard work, immerse themselves manically in diversionary activities, and hoard information in order to inflate their own importance' (Morris, 1991: 4). Other authors (Holliday, 1992, 1994, 1995,

1999, 2005; Swales, 1980) also identify this strategy of expatriate advisors immersing themselves in 'busy work' as a strategy of maintaining a dominant position in the field.

The above approach to working in an international context has led to the overwhelming sense of the failure of international projects to fulfill their goals. Yvonne (P1AU1) addresses this dis-ease with working in an unfamiliar context and shows how, through a long-term involvement, she was able to more fully engage with the new context and the students. She explains that at first she did not recognise the issue at all: 'I didn't appreciate that that was even a problem.' She discussed the difficulties she had in working in the host-country context and especially how hard it was to 'get into another context when you're an occasional visitor. You can't do it.' She found that with more trips and longer periods of time with the project, she was able to interact more with the teachers and here she says that she was able to 'recognise their culture'. She made a crucial point; she listened as the Lao teachers talked to her about their work 'and there was real dialogue.'

The project field is delineated by the notion of culture, in particular through the ostensibly primary goal of teacher education. As mentioned in the introduction, the projects are predicated on misrecognised differences and inequalities between the teaching of English in the host countries and teaching of English in Australia. The host countries' teaching and learning processes were depicted in ways that suggested they were inferior to the Australian approaches and the host-country teachers were seen to be inadequately trained. I suggest that the absence of discussing the field of teaching and learning in a way which may identify similarities between Australia and the host countries' teaching and learning contexts (homologies in the field) is in the interest of maintaining a particular power relationship. The manufactured or perceived inequalities between the learner (teacher and school student) and the target language (drawing on Pennycook, 2000) give the Australian project a marketable product in the host countries.

A key question for work in IELEPs is through what processes would these views of 'culture' change? Australian universities are wedded to the strategic aims of internationalisation, yet the hegemonic views of 'culture' which prevail in the university-led projects are in stark contrast to the ways that the host-country interviewees perceived the process of collaborative project work. A related issue is the relevance of knowledge of the local context.

I have illustrated throughout this chapter that the lack of knowledge on the provider's/donor's part about the social, historical and material conditions of the context in which the project will run is a powerful theme in the data. The Australian project management teams did not value the accumulation of this knowledge and consequently delivered projects that did not reflect the priorities of the local host-country participants. The challenge that faces those of us who work in the international language education field is that of how we foreground the importance of this knowledge of local context.

Chapter 7
The IELEP: An Illegitimate Field

The picture that has emerged of the IELEP is one of a messy venture doomed for failure. Struggle delineates the field. The dominant players, the donors and Australian universities hold the validated, most valued capital in the field. Symbolic violence underlies the projects' delivery of ELT and EL teacher education. Host-country teachers and ministry officials' skills, knowledge and interests are invalidated and stigmatised. The IELEP is premised on a denial of rights. Bilingual host-country teachers are denied the opportunity to accumulate linguistic capital; these teachers and their students are denied the right to bilingual education. The IELEP works in opposition to the advice of current evidence from the language teaching field, where languages are best learned when taught additively (Phillipson, 2001; Skutnabb-Kangas, 2000) complementing the existing national languages. The premise of the IELEP is that English is best.

The IELEP field is revealed as a terrain of conflicting and contested practices: the practices within Australian universities, aid and development projects, investment projects and the teaching and learning of English as a foreign language are sites of ongoing struggle. There are clearly deep problems with the project approach; these problems are summarised as relating to who owns and controls the project, the short time-frame given for project implementation, development and completion, a mismatch between the goals of the project and the needs of the host country, communication issues and the expected heavy workload (especially for host-country project participants). Related literature speaks of the failure of projects. An underlying premise in this book is that maybe projects do not really succeed (as per their documented goals) because no one has a stake in that success; their benefits are all elsewhere. The stories in this book show that all the players do have a stake in the project; there are no disinterested players but a complication is that success means different things to different players and benefits are accrued differently.

185

Bourdieu and the Story of the IELEP Field

Bourdieu's conceptualisations of power, struggles and analysis of the multiple ways that the dominant players maintain their position are key to unravelling the dynamics of the IELEP. My aim was to arrive at a deep understanding of how this particular 'game' of EL teacher education is played. My personal experience of work in this area showed that this 'complicated and messy' (Crehan & Von Oppen, 1988) field is shaped by layers of opaque tributes to particular government and donor policies and slight attention to the goals and activities of the projects. And while current literature and reports about IELEP work give some critical insight into the machinations of the field, the available analysis does not delve deeply enough into the invisiblised power struggles. Bourdieu's thinking tools are highly appropriate for a number of reasons: the relational tools of field, capital and habitus resonate with my own sense of the ways in which power, resources and the agents' position in society act in relation to each other; his research areas include universities, language and the ways in which individuals or organisations occupy different positions of power within and across institutions.

The question of legitimacy is a strong theme in this story. Questions such as what is legitimate project work? what is a legitimate language? or an effective teaching approach? dominate the field. Related questions of who makes this decision and how are critical. The project, in Bourdieu's terms, is a site of struggle where particular players, according to the capital (cultural, linguistic, social and economic) they accumulate and the habitus they bring to the project field, employ strategies to dominate and legitimate certain ways of behaving in the project. These players are most usually the representatives of the funding organisation or tertiary institution providing the services.

An additional point of interest is that there is homology between aid-funded and fee-based projects. The donor's and/or provider's ways of working in projects and their approach to teaching are glorified. They are positioned as superior to the existing systems in the recipient countries; these dominant practices are not only superior but significantly different from the stigmatised practices in the host countries. There is also an underlying assumption that there will be resistance to this new approach or methodology. These types of assumptions underpin the way in which the Australian universities are able to rationalise their approaches and take up the 'legitimate' position in the field.

A critical question for the IELEP is how can the recipient countries claim their practices as legitimate and then in subsequent negotiations work towards genuine collaboration. A related question is how can a change in Australian academic discourse effect a change in the relations in the field: in developing new educational practices in internationalisation, the contextualisation of the educational innovations is consistently thwarted by the individualisation and atomisation of academic work (Stirrat, 2000). So, whereas on an individual level the stories of development and inequity in the international economy (in relation to aid-funded educational work) and the position of English as a desired foreign language are legitimate areas of study for the academic, this legitimation does not usually take place at an institutional level. Foregrounding human and linguistics rights in IELEP or other international work is often regarded as an individual stance towards these practices rather than offering a way to seriously effect fundamental change to hegemonic knowledge and history (Talpade Mohanty, 1994: 54). The Australian university field is left relatively unchanged by its experiences of international work; the political significance of new types of knowledge and new types of practices are incapacitated through their entry into a pre-established field. An obvious example is the one-way process of internationalisation, where the process is represented by enrolment of fee-paying international students into an Australian university, but this does not impact the university's curriculum or academic practices. So in reality internationalisation is the commodification of Australian education and the university's core values and practices remain untouched.

Bourdieu's approach illuminated the dimensions and dynamics of the field; for example, I was able to explore questions such as what accumulates capital in the particular project contexts? And I was able to tell the history of this aspect of the field and to look at the whole issue of winning project tenders, the type of textual practices involved and what areas of expertise are important to the grand interests of funding agencies.

The story is set within current Australian university internationalisation endeavours (though as illustrated throughout, it is a story relevant to the ventures of other NABA (North American, British and Australian) countries); the IELEP exploits the international demand for English and maintains a dominant myth, ELT is best provided by so-called English-speaking countries. This story draws on Bourdieu to illustrate that 'everything is not as it seems' and indeed aspects of project work such as those listed in the above paragraphs are contested constructs. The 'beneficiary' of university-led international language education projects cannot be viewed as a single entity. The projects required a great investment of time and money all purportedly aimed towards increasing English language proficiency; but really who benefits? Bourdieu's work is centrally concerned with the unequal distribution of power, resources and rights. The IELEP field is able to endure in spite of its denial of linguistic, educational and economic rights to the acclaimed beneficiaries. The stories in this book exposed how the aid agencies, universities and corporate bodies continue to establish IELEP ventures in the face of the overwhelming evidence of the projects' failure to meet the needs of the recipients. As the stories in this book unfold, it is clear that the ELT project field is reproduced because it continues to meet the varied interests of the dominant players.

Boudieu's analysis shows that the promulgation of the rhetoric of the binary relationship between the donor and the recipient dominates the field. This rhetoric serves to mask the gain or profit that the donor or the funder receives from the project and maintains the recipient in the subordinate position. It can also lead to the project meeting only the narrowest of its objectives, namely, that of the major financial investor. It is difficult to isolate an ultimate beneficiary and the identification of the beneficiary is dependent upon the interests of the particular stakeholder and their interests may be conflicting and competing. The benefits accrued through the project work may bear no relationship to what or who the beneficiaries are assumed to be in the project goals. In this sense the majority of stakeholders in this framework are beneficiaries of some sort. Clearly different interests are served by different language projects.

The IELEP field is an interface between the academic world (public good) and business world (profit) and it is an uneasy process to bring these worlds together. Another complication in the field is that tensions also exist among university participants collaborating within consortiums. In light of the more interpersonal accounts of project work in which the educational providers may be left feeling frustrated, the project participants, specifically the students, may feel disenfranchised (Marginson, 1997b). Why does this situation exist? I contend it is because of the lack of visibility about who is and who is not benefiting from the project.

The interests of the stakeholders are intrinsically linked to the notions and assessment of success and failure. The meaning of success in relation to a 'successful' project is determined by whose interests are being met by particular activities within the project. The success of the individual stakeholders within the project is not necessarily related to the success of the project. The project cycle involves academics like myself, selling my services to multinational capital and aid agencies (an imperative now in Australian university business). The next step is that the university 'team' establishes its relationships with project management companies and works out the scheduling and funding cycles which best fit with the institutional demands. The Australian institutions may then take the step of establishing a relationship with a host-country 'partner' and present the design of the project. The project management company is essentially responsible for designing the criteria for how the project will succeed or fail. This model of project implementation is far more reminiscent of relations under imperial rule of the colonies than anything remotely collaborative.

One of the critical features of the project field as I see it is the role of project management companies and their relative unaccountability in their use of public money. This is relevant to both the aid and development context and fee-based projects as both draw on public money, the former through direct aid funding and the latter through the use of university funds to establish the projects. The literature on projects, both aid-funded and fee-based, reflects an area of work that is virtually unregulated, and the field abounds with stories of projects that do not seem to complete their tasks. According to the stories in this book, the expensive expatriate consultants and/or faculty managers are not accountable in terms of the goals of the project, let alone being involved with a process that is culturally and socially relevant.

A central proposition of this book is that if IELEP work is going to be truly bilateral it must engage with the needs of all participants, develop participants' 'feel for the game' and make explicit the range of strategies available to 'play the game' of international project education. Additionally, project planners must heed the advice that comes from previous stories of failed projects and act on ethnographic information about the social and material conditions of the host countries.

The 'English Only' IELEP

Language and discourse are sites of struggle and these struggles are interrelated. A powerful discourse in IELEPs is about the legitimacy of the so-called 'native speaker'. This discourse in the first instance positions the speaker of English as the norm, the unmarked, and the speakers of the host-country languages as holding the 'problem', the marked. This is thematised by the way that host-country students and teachers are invalidated or delegitimated as language experts. Objectives of both projects glorified English, stigmatised the host-country language and rationalised the approach of providing ways to improve students' and teachers' proficiency in English language and to introduce more western-based teaching approaches. Also, on a project management level, all members of the projects' committees were destined to negotiate all aspects of the project's work and life in English regardless of those committee members' experience and proficiency in English or their other areas of language expertise.

Another powerful discourse underpinning much of the discussion of English language and teaching and learning is that 'the better teacher is a native speaker of English' (see Chapter 3). This reflects one of Phillipson's (1992b) key myths of ELT, that 'the native speaking teacher of English is better.' This myth has great currency in Project 1; the host-country teachers believed that course participants in Laos would not 'trust' an EL teacher education course run by host-county teacher educators. The myth is supported by comments such as 'the host-country participants would more clearly know who the teacher is if it is a native speaker of English and that because they are learning a foreign language would gain more than the "50 per cent" that they get from a host-country teacher educator.' Other comments negated the host-country participants' concern about the level of skill that the expatriates brought to the course; participants would not be concerned 'if the native speaker was a good teacher or not'. In this story the Australian lecturers held the cultural and linguistic capital; the myth of their skill and knowledge is difficult to dispel. It is a myth supported by subtle changes in the courses to further embed the imported methodology and delegitimise the host-country teachers. A clear example of the way the project's goals were rationalised was when the Australian team introduced a teaching practicum component into the TESOL course after the first year. The intention of the practicum was to give teachers an opportunity to team teach with a peer, to get peer feedback and feedback from a course lecturer. The host-country participants were initially impressed that the programme was changed to give the teachers more opportunities to practise the approaches taught by the lecturers. However, there was an undercurrent of concern; they were already qualified teachers and the course did not address their classroom realities so how can they be assessed in this situation?

The Australian staff replicated the type of teacher training programmes that are currently delivered by Australian universities; the introduction of the practicum could be viewed as an addition that allowed the Australian staff to feel more comfortable with their work in an unfamiliar context. This was certainly not an innovation for this context; this type of assessment did not take the particularity of the context into account, nor did it encourage any teacher-generated theory of practice (Kumaravadivelu, 2003a). This was a dire situation: the teachers' qualifications were invalidated within their own country. The Lao teachers did query the practicum arrangements, but they did not have the authority to make any changes. Project 2 required the students (qualified teachers) to do a similar practicum subject and the responses of the Japanese teachers (see Chapter 5) evidenced great concern that their teaching qualifications and status were not recognised or validated by the Australian project. In introducing a practicum for already trained teachers, the Australian teacher educators were delegitimating, or invalidating, the teaching qualifications and skills of the host-country teachers.

Knowledge of the host-country context and practices was sorely lacking prior to the establishment of the IELEPs. While this may seem unbelievable, and many of the participants saw it as a major factor in limiting the projects' work, it is a regularity of the field. Literature about IELEPs consistently addresses the lack of ethnographic research and knowledge of the context of the proposed project. Because of this lack of knowledge, project designers fall back on commonly held ideas or normative ideals of particular cultures and practices. Constructs of culture were central themes in the design and implementation of the projects; the way this concept was used and understood influences the positioning of agents in the field. 'Culture' is an unsatisfactory term; yet, as shown in Chapter 6, this notion was widespread in many areas and levels of ELT education in both the international and the Australian context. The participants' stories revealed a field delineated by the essentialist understandings of national groupings and the way in which one knows a 'culture'.

A paradox emerged in the data: the international language education projects were developed and established on the premise of responding to the specific needs of their particular cultural context. The universities sold themselves through their knowledge of the local cultural context. But the Australian staff were not necessarily chosen for their knowledge of familiarity with the host countries or encouraged to develop knowledge about the specific contexts. In fact, in most cases ethnographic advice was ignored by project management.

The projects documents and the practices that emerged give scant attention to the national language(s) of the project sites. The projects exerted symbolic violence in the way they positioned the host-country languages; they dispensed with current thinking about language learning and teaching which foregrounds the importance of learners' first language. Additionally, much of the critical literature on project design and implementation raises the point about the way that language is used as a tool to dominate project-planning processes. The stories gave voice to the ways English was used in the running of project business and how this worked to invalidate the host-country participants from full involvement in the management of project work.

The book demonstrates that English is positioned as a highly valued resource; it dominates the accumulated linguistic capital. Bourdieu's analytical framework is extremely useful in distinguishing between how the different interviewees saw the value of English. For example, on the one hand, English was seen to provide a way out of 'desperate situations' for the host-country students and teachers; other Project 1 host-country participants concurred with this view. The host-country interviewees from Project 2 had a slightly different take on the importance of English. From their perspective learning English was viewed as pragmatic; it was what school students needed for their entrance into university. But a number of the Project 2 participants felt that for some students it was a waste of time as they were not intending to go to university and they would not use English in their daily lives. The Australian representatives of the government agencies in both projects did not represent English as a skill that would lift people out of their economic realities but rather as a 'reality' of international relations. The Australian university participants had a professional commitment to the teaching of English. These latter participants expressed a range of opinions about the work of IELEPs; a number of them critiqued aspects of the programmes in terms of the dominant and subordinate roles in the project, the role of the first language and positioning of the bilingual teacher and the distribution of resources and agreed with writers such as Bruthiaux (2002), Graddol (1997, 2006), Phan Le Ha (2008), Phillipson (1992b) and Skutnabb-Kangas (2005), who question the benefits of the spread of English.

The above array of views of the role of English, ELT and linguistic rights paint a dismal, fractured picture of ELT in IELEPs. This picture questions the legitimacy of the project model in the international ELT field; the model I believe has too much ideological baggage to be of much use, and the project model as previously explained comes from the agricultural and technical sectors. The problematic aspects of the model for the education sector are as follows:

- The projects are planned on a short cycle and by definition have an end date.
- They are unique and one-off and these features and the underlying pressure on a project are that the design and implementation team must get it right the first time. An impact of the short cycle and finite resources is that the project team may 'reinvent the wheel'. The donor or provider institutions do not often allow time to investigate what innovations or initiatives have been previously undertaken.

This links with Hall's (1997) and Smith's (1997) points about project work having 'no institutional memory'.

- The project teams lack continuity. Participants raised this issue in relation to two features of the projects: one was the 'visiting' academics, the lecturers were not in-country for long periods of time and the same lecturers did not necessarily return; and the second was the changes in the 'counterpart' personnel (this was specifically for Project 1).
- The project designs tend to be too rigid. Participants pointed to how the guidelines were not well thought out but there seemed little opportunity for the recipients to effect change. This issue is supported in project literature; in general, the projects in this story developed in the way they were originally designed even if the social context was changing rapidly.
- The question 'What happens after the project?' was frequently raised. The projects' cycle dictates that as soon as the core work of the project is finished, the expatriated staff, the project management and the respective institutions leave. What about sustainability?

If international ELT initiatives continue to be undertaken by Australian educational institutions (or other NABA agents), it is imperative to rethink how best to work in a collaborative and productive way. The stories in this book have shown the necessity to reiterate the demand for the development of a critical pedagogy of ELT that takes on board the ideological knowledge about English as a language of power and oppression as well as a language that is currently functioning as a means of international communication (Kubota, 1998). The development of a critical pedagogy has strong foundations; Kumaravadivelu, in his books on postmethod pedagogy (2003b) and cultural globalisation (2008), provides a framework and approach that embraces the particularities of the context and the needs of the participants. Critical ELT pedagogy involves a genuine engagement in collaborative ethnographic studies. Kumaravadivelu's framework includes a dimension of social and individual action (2003a); in his later work (2008) he puts forward a grounded and inclusive approach to language education within a global context. His understanding of the global context is usefully applied to the work in the international ELT field as it recognises inequities in power, language rights and the cultural interface between host country and donor/providers. Critical ELT pedagogy is built on the premise of linguistic rights: the right for learners to maintain and develop their first language, the right of access to additive bilingual education (Phillipson, 2008; Skutnabb-Kangas, 2008) and the right to freely use their own language. International ELT education will need to embed a rights framework within their programmes to ensure that benefits are distributed equally in the field. The word 'counterpart' would disappear from the international education field and be replaced with a term suitable to signal host-country expertise. A critical ELT pedagogy would also evenly distribute the positions of language expert and technical adviser within the field; Rampton's (1990) challenges to the traditional delineations of native and non-native speaker of English provide a basis for establishing collaborative relationships in the language teaching field. His naming of language expertise, inheritance and affiliation advocate a rights framework and legitimate and validate the skills and knowledge of all participants.

The Legitimate ELT Field: A Possibility or Dream?

Australian universities need to understand how future work in international language education can to be carried out in ways that encourage collaborative, cooperative and productive understandings to develop among the stakeholders. The current global trend is that universities continue to seek revenue from international activities. What kind of global strategies should Australian universities pursue in onshore international education, offshore international education, in franchising and twinning relationships with universities in other countries and in staff and student exchanges (Marginson, 2002b)? Marginson poses questions that help universities to become more aware of the skills and knowledge they need to successfully engage with international work. Specifically the research should investigate the type of practices needed to conduct more effective relationships and challenge the usual patterns of domination and subordination in the field:

- How can universities focus and intensify their involvement in international project work in the light of their available human, material and financial resources and the real difficulties of productively engaging with a broad range of countries and contexts?
- How can universities engage with local and international communities in a way that represents the collaboration and cooperation that internationalisation implies?
- A view that underlies this book is that there is an inequity in the distribution of the world's resources. How can the universities be 'good' international citizens? How can the universities work to mitigate against negative effects of globalisation (e.g. the growing

divide between the rich and poor, inequitable trade relations and the injustices of war)? A partial answer to this is to find ways of designing projects and conducting feasibility studies that involve host-country participants as equal partners. It also means giving voice to the groups or organisations designated to be 'the ultimate beneficiaries'.

This book critically engages with the IELEP field; by gathering the participants' stories about project work my own understandings of the way the projects work have deepened and will hopefully change the way I work or rather my academic habitus in the context of international language education work. I better understand how different interests are met; for example, at one level the projects are purely an exercise in maintaining inequitable international economic and/or social relations. At other times I can acknowledge the enormity of what I have learned from my host-country colleagues in terms of growing to understand different organisational structures and the values and benefits inherent in different ways of doing things. At yet other times I realise the way the interpersonal relationships I have developed have impacted and changed my life. My educational habitus has shifted and my own sense of identity and values has been 'internationalised'. This shift identifies the positive aspects of working in this challenging field; participants acknowledge freely some of these aspects and as expected many of the examples are around the interpersonal relationships. I grew to understand more about arguments such as those put forward by Abdul-Raheem (2000), where he fears that the 'developing' world will be kept in a permanent state of crisis to provide lucrative jobs for aid workers from the 'developed' world. This is clearly a dangerous dynamic of the IELEP field and must be contested; if Australian academics are to become 'good' international citizens, the resources in the field must be redistributed.

Appendix

Description of Participants

Project 1 (P1) Participants

Son (P1LM1) – late 40s, native Lao speaker, fluent in a European language, studying English, trained teacher and worked in management level in teacher training section in the Ministry of Education (MOE).

Weng (P1LM2) – mid-30s, native Lao speaker, fluent in English, was English teacher, completed post-graduate study in Australia, worked with the MOE in teacher training and worked with P1 in various capacities.

Min (P1LM3) – early 30s, native Lao speaker, intermediate fluency in English and worked in project administration with the MOE.

Trong (P1LM4) – early 50s, native Lao speaker, fluent in English, speaks a number of European languages, management position in the MOE, trained teacher, experience in working with foreign projects and has post-graduate qualifications from an Australian university.

Thanh (P1LM5) – late 40s, native Lao speaker, advanced proficiency in English. A secondary school teacher and then teacher trainer of English with the MOE. Has had a long history of working with international projects.

Vong (P1LU1) – late 40s, native Lao speaker, fluent in English, in management level in a university faculty, trained teacher, long history in ELT and involvement in foreign projects, has post-graduate qualifications from Australia and is currently undertaking PhD studies.

Song (P1LU2) – late 30s, native Lao speaker, high-level fluency in English, trained teacher, university lecturer in EL, worked with P1 as a counterpart over several years and has post-graduate qualifications from Australia.

Tong (P1LU3) – mid-40s, native Lao speaker, fluent in English, trained teacher, university lecturer in EL, worked with a number of foreign projects and worked with P1 in various capacities, has studied in the USA, has post-graduate qualifications from Australia and is currently undertaking PhD studies.

Sol (P1LU4) – early 40s, native Lao speaker, fluent in English, trained teacher, university lecturer in EL, worked with a number of foreign projects and worked with P1 in various capacities and has post-graduate qualifications from Australia.

Con (P1AM1) – early 50s, native English speaker, Australian government aid agency official, trained teacher, spent a short time living in country of P1, did not speak the language, had some knowledge of a European language and had a long history of work in the aid and development sector.

Mel (P1AP1) – early 40s, native English speaker (monolingual), a project team member, trained teacher, had worked in the Australian ELT sector for many years, had no experience with country of P1 prior to going there, had worked for a short time with an aid-funded ELT project in a neighbouring country and has an MA TESOL (course work) completed in Australia.

Mara (P1AP2) – late 30s, native English speaker, trained teacher, had worked in the ELT sector of Laos for many years, fluent Lao speaker, has worked mainly in the aid-funded sector in this country, spent many years working in a neighbouring country – is also fluent in Thai, is currently undertaking M.Ed. studies in educational management distance study from Australia and has a diploma level qualification in TESOL.

Project 2 (P2) Participants

Tan (P2LM1) – mid-40s, native Japanese speaker, fluent in English, trained teacher, studied in North America, currently working a teacher's education centre and involved in the development of P2.

Sen (P2LM2) – late 40s, native Japanese speaker, fluent in English, trained teacher, management level of a teacher education centre and a member of the committee for P2.

Lin (P2LT1) – late 20s, native Japanese speaker, fluent in English, trained teacher, works in a high school, has not studied in another country and member of the group who trialled the project materials.

Mak (P2LT2) – late 40s, native Japanese speaker, fluent in English, trained teacher, works in a high school which has a culturally diverse population, involved in the national EL teachers' professional organisation and member of the MOE committee for P2.

Sal (P2LT3) – early 40s, native Japanese speaker, fluent in English, trained teacher, had worked in Australia as an exchange teacher, works in an alternative high school and involved with the development of the project.

Lan (P2LT4) – early 30s, native Japanese speaker, fluent in English, trained teacher, has worked and studied in North America and a member of the group of teachers who trialled the materials.

Ken (P2LU1) – early 50s, native Japanese speaker, fluent in English, trained teacher, university professor, a member of the MOE committee for Project 2 and is currently undertaking post-graduate studies.

Shor (P2LU2) – early 50s, native Japanese speaker, fluent in English, trained teacher, university professor, a member of the MOE committee for Project 2 and is a highly regarded author of numerous ELT texts.

Murray (P2AM1) – mid-40s, native English speaker, fluent Japanese speaker, the Director of the Australian government agency (AGA) in Japan and had spent several years in country of P2. He manages many projects in his role as director.

Australian University-Based (AU) Participants

Yvonne (P1AU1) – early 50s, native English speaker, university lecturer, had no experience with overseas work or international students before working on the project, had not travelled to this part of the world before, masters in literacy education and a GD in TESOL completed in Australia, spoke only English and had no experience of studying a foreign language.

Lee (P1/2AU2) – late 40s, native English speaker, university lecturer, has extensive experience of living in and working with adults and children in South East Asia, speaks a number of foreign languages including the language of P1 country, has higher degrees completed in Australia and has worked extensively in South East Asia.

Chris (P2AU3) – late 40s, native English speaker, fluent speaker of Japanese, lecturer and manager in a private language college, has lived and worked in P2 country in the education sector and has a masters qualification from P2 country which she completed in the language of the country. Since living in Australia she has worked with teachers and other professionals from P2 country in either joint teacher training programmes or language training. Has visited the P2 country many times on behalf of one of the main consortium members to do work with business partners and course promotion.

Carla (P1/2AU4) – early 40s, native English speaker and has studied a number of languages. Has worked in South East and East Asia, has worked with international students at university level for many years and has higher degrees completed in Australia.

References

Abdul-Raheem, T. (2000) Impact of angels. *New Internationalist* 326, 20–21.

Accounting for Development (2000) *Conference Proceedings*, Australian Mekong Resource Centre, University of Sydney.

Achren, L. (2007) Whose development? A cultural analysis of an AusAID English Language Project in the Lao People's Democratic Republic, PhD thesis, Victoria University.

Achren, L. and Keolivay, B. (1998) Communicative language teaching and cultural difference. In A. Abdullah *et al.* (eds) *Language in Development: Access, Empowerment and Opportunity. Proceedings of the Third International Conference on Language in Development, Langkowi, Malaysia, July 1997.* Kuala Lumpur: National Institute of Public Administration (INTAN).

ADB (2000) *Lao People's Democratic Republic: Education Sector Development Plan Report.* Manila: Asian Development Bank.

Appleby, R. (2002) English and East Timor. In J. Lo Bianco (ed.) *Voices from Phnom Penh Development and Language: Global Influences and Local Effects* (pp. 23–36). Language Australia, NLLIA.

Appleby, R., Copley, K., Sithirajvongso, S. and Pennycook, A. (2002) Language in development constrained: Three contexts. *TESOL Quarterly* 36 (3), 323–346.

Arnold, E. and Sarhan, G. (1994) Ten tips for making ELT counterparting work. *ELT Journal* 48 (1), 13–21.

Arnst, R. (1997) International development versus the participation of indigenous peoples. In D. McCaskill and K. Kampe (eds) *Development or Domestication? Indigenous Peoples of South East Asia* (pp. 45–61). Chiang Mai: Silkworm Books.

Asante, M.F. and Gudykunst, W.B. (1989) *Handbook of International and Intercultural Communication.* Newbury Park: Sage.

Auerbach, E., Barahona, B., Midy, J., Vaquerano, F., Zambrano, A. and Arnaud, J. (1996) *Adult ESL/Literacy from the Community to the Community: A Guidebook for Participatory Literacy Training.* New York: Lawrence Erlbaum Associates.

Australian Government (2006) *Australian Aid: Promoting Growth and Stability – White Paper on the Australian Government's Aid Programme.* AusAID: Canberra.

AusAID (2001) *Strategic Plan: Improving Effectiveness in a Changing Environment.* Australian Government.

Bax, S. (2003) The end of CLT: A context approach to language teaching. *ELT Journal* 57 (3), 278–287.

Bhabha, H. (1994) *The Location of Culture.* New York: Routledge.

Bolitho, R. and Medgyes, P. (2000) Talking shop: From aid to partnership. *ELT Journal* 54 (4), 379–388.

Bourdieu, P. (1984) *Distinction: A Social Critique of the Judgement of Taste* (R. Nice, trans.). Cambridge: Harvard University Press.

Bourdieu, P. (1988) *Homo Academicus*. Cambridge: Polity Press.

Bourdieu, P. (1986) Forms of capital. In J. Richardson (ed.) *Handbook of Theory and Research for the Sociology of Education* (pp. 241–258). New York: Greenwood.

Bourdieu, P. (1990a) *In Other Words* (M. Adamson, trans.). Oxford: Polity Press.

Bourdieu, P. (1990b) *The Logic of Practice* (R. Nice, trans.). Oxford: Polity Press.

Bourdieu, P. (1991) *Language and Symbolic Power*. Cambridge: Polity Press.

Bourdieu, P. (1992) Thinking about limits. *Theory, Culture and Society* 9, 37–49.

Bourdieu, P. (1993) *Sociology in Question* (R. Nice, trans.). Oxford: Polity Press.

Bourdieu, P. (1998) *Practical Reason*. London: Polity Press.

Bourdieu, P. (1999) *The Weight of the World*. Cambridge: Polity Press.

Bourdieu, P. (2000) *Pascalian Meditations*. Cambridge: Polity Press.

Bourdieu, P. and Eagleton, T. (1992) Doxa and common life. *New Left Review* 199, 111–121.

Bourdieu, P. and Passeron, J.C. (1977) *Reproduction in Education, Society and Culture*. London: Sage Publications.

Bourdieu, P. and Wacquant, L. (1992) *An Invitation to Reflexive Sociology*. Chicago: University of Chicago Press.

Braine, G. (1999) *Non-Native Educators in English Language Teaching*. Mahwah, NJ: Lawrence Erlbaum.

Brown, I. (2001) This is my story. *New Internationalist* 334 (May), 33–35.

Brown, R. (2000) Cultural continuity and ELT teacher training. *ELT Journal* 54 (3), 227–235.

Bruthiaux, P. (2002) Hold your courses: Language education, language choice, and economic development. *TESOL Quarterly* 36 (2), Autumn, 275–296.

Canagarajah, A.S. (1999) On EFL teachers, awareness, and agency. *ELT Journal* 53 (3), 207–214.

Canagarajah, S., (2005) Restructuring Local Knowledge, Reconfiguring Language Studies. In S. Canagarajah, (ed.) *Reclaiming the local in language policy and practice* (pp. 3–24) USA: Routledge.

Canagarajah, A.S. (2006) TESOL at forty: What are the issues? *TESOL Quarterly* 40 (1), 9–34.

Chiapello, E. and Fairclough, N. (2002) Understanding the new management ideology: A transdisciplinary contribution from critical discourse analysis and new sociology of capitalism. *Discourse and Society* 13 (2), 185–208.

Chowdhury, R. (2003) International TESOL training and EFL contexts: The cultural disillusionment factor. *Australian Journal of Education* 47 (3), 283–302.

Clayton, T. (2002) International languages in education in developing countries: Implications for Cambodia. In J. Lo Bianco (ed.) *Voices from Phnom Penh Development and Language: Global Influences and Local Effects* (pp. 87–102). Melbourne: Language Australia, NLLIA.

Coleman, H. (1992) Moving the goalposts: Project evaluation in practice. In J.C. Alderson and A. Berreta (eds) *Evaluating Second Language Education* (pp. 222–249). Cambridge: Cambridge University Press.

Coleman, H. (1995) Problematising stakeholders: Who are the holders and what are the stakes? In T. Crooks and G. Crewes (eds) *Language in Development Conference Papers* (pp. 45–62). Indonesia Australia Language Foundation.

Coleman, H. (2002) Evaluating development programs: Time to watch our language. In J. Lo Bianco (ed.) *Voices from Phnom Penh Development and Language: Global influences and Local Effects* (pp. 103–116). Melbourne: Language Australia, NLLIA.

Copley, K. (1997) The management of development: A case of talk and text. In *Language and Development: Access, Empowerment and Opportunity*, Conference Proceedings (pp. 79–94). Malaysia: INTAN.

Copley, K. and Widin, J. (2001) Talking up the project: Discursive manipulations in international language education projects. Unpublished paper presented at the *Discourse on Discourse Conference*, UTS.

Cornford, J. (1999), *Australian Aid, Development Advocacy and Governance in the Lao PDR*. Sydney: Australian Mekong Resource Centre.

Cornford, J. and Simon, M. (2001) *Breaking the Banks*. Fitzroy: Oxfam Community Aid Abroad.

Crewe, E. and Harrison, E. (1998) *Whose Development? An Ethnography of Aid*. London: Zed Books.

Crehan, K. and Von Oppen, A. (1988) Understandings of development: An arena of struggle. *Sociologia Ruralis* XXVIII (2/3), 113–145.

Crooks, T. and Crewes, G. (eds) (1995) *Language and Development*. Indonesia Australia Language Foundation.

Crystal, D. (1997) *English as a Global Language*. Cambridge: Cambridge University Press.

Cummins, J. and Hornberger, N.H. (eds) (2008) *Encyclopedia of Language and Education* (2nd edn) *Volume 5: Bilingual Education*. New York: Springer.

Davis, C. (1991) Vocational education project planning in developing countries: A critical theory paradigm. *Journal of Industrial Teacher Education* 28 (3), 35–45.

Delamont, S., Parry, O. and Atkinson, P. (1991) Critical mass and pedagogic continuity: Studies in academic habitus. *British Journal of Sociology of Education* 18 (4), 533–549.

Devos, A. (2003) Academic standards, internationalization and discursive constructions of the international student. *Higher Education Research and Development* 22 (2), 155–166.

Dilley, R. (1999) *The Problem of Context*. New York: Bergahn.

Dodd, C.H. (1987) *Dynamics of Intercultural Communication* (2nd edn). Dubuque: Wm. C. Brown.

Ellis, L. and Kelly, S. (1997) Cross cultural teachers education: Issues and values in the Lao context. In *Language and Development: Access, Empowerment and Opportunity*, Conference Proceedings (pp. 95–104), Malaysia: INTAN.

Escobar, A. (1985) Discourse and power in development: Michel Foucault and the relevance of his work to the third world. *Alternative* 10 (3), 377–400.

Evans, G. (2002) *A Short History of Laos: The Land in Between*. Crows Nest, NSW: Allen & Unwin.

Fairclough, N. (1989) *Language and Power*. London: Longman.

Fairclough, N. (1992) *Discourse and Social Change*. Cambridge: Polity Press.

Fairclough, N. (1995) *Critical Discourse Analysis*. London: Longman.

Fairclough, N. (2001) The discourse of new labour: Critical discourse analysis. In M. Wetherell, S. Taylor and S.J. Yates (eds) *Discourse as Data: A Guide for Analysis* (pp. 229–266). London: Sage Publications.

Forman, R. (1999) Monolingual and bilingual TESOL teaching: Differing positions of knowledge and empathy. Paper presented at RELC Seminar, *Language in the Global Context: Implications for the Language Classroom.*

Gee, J. (1996) *Social Linguistics and Literacies: Ideology in Discourses.* London: Taylor and Francis.

Gee, J. (1999) *An Introduction to Discourse Analysis.* London and New York: Routledge.

Gee, J. (2000) New people in new worlds: Networks, the new capitalism and schools. In B. Cope and M. Kalantzis (eds) *Multiliteracies: Literacy Learning and the Design of Social Futures* (pp. 43–68). London: Routledge.

Gordon, R.G. (2005) *Ethnologue: Languages of the World* (15th edn), Summer Institute of Languages.

Gorsuch, G.J. (1999) Monbusho approved textbooks in Japanese high school EFL classes: An aid or a hindrance to educational policy innovations? *The Language Teacher* 23 (10), 5–15.

Goulet, D. (1995) *Development Ethics: A Guide to Theory and Practice.* New York: Apex Press.

Graddol, D. (1997) *The Future of English.* London: British Council.

Graddol, D. (2006) *English Next.* London: British Council.

Grenfell, M. (1996) Bourdieu and initial teacher training. *British Educational Research Journal* 22 (3), 287–303.

Grenfell, M. (1998) Language and the classroom. In M. Grenfell and D. James (eds) *Bourdieu and Education: Acts of Practical Theory* (pp. 72–89). London: Falmer Press.

Grenfell, M. and Hardy, C. (2003) Field manoeuvres: Bourdieu and young British artists. *Space and Culture* 6 (1) (February), 19–34.

Grenfell, M. and James, D. (eds) (1998) *Bourdieu and Education: Acts of Practical Theory.* London: Falmer Press.

Griffin, K. (1991) Foreign aid after the Cold War. *Development and Change* 22, 645–685.

Grin, F. (2006) Economic considerations in language policy. In T. Ricento (ed.) *An Introduction to Language Policy: Theory and Method* (pp. 77–94). Malden and Oxford: Blackwell.

Gunning-Stevenson, H. (2001) *Accounting for Development: Australia and the Asian Development Bank in the Mekong Region.* AMRC, University of Sydney.

Habu, T. (2000) The irony of globalisation: The experience of Japanese women in British higher education. *Higher Education* 39, 43–66.

Hague Recommendations Regarding the Education Rights of National Minorities and Explanatory Note (1996) The Hague, The Netherlands: Organisation for Security and Cooperation in Europe.

Hall, D. (1997) Why projects fail. In B. Kenny and W. Savage (eds) *Language in Development: Teachers in a Changing World* (pp. 258–267). London: Longman.

Hall, J.K. and Eggington, W.G. (2000) *The Sociopolitics of English Language Teaching.* London: Multilingual Matters.

Hall, S. (1990) Cultural identity and diaspora. In J. Rutherford (ed.) *Identity, Community, Culture, Difference* (pp. 222–237). London: Lawrence and Wishart.

Halliday, M.A.K. (1978) *Language as Social Semiotic: The Social Interpretation of Language and Meaning.* London: Edward Arnold.

Harker, R., Mahar, C. and Wilkes, C. (1990) *An Introduction to the Work of Pierre Bourdieu*. London: Macmillan.

Hashimoto, K. (2000) 'Internationalisation' is 'Japanisation': Japan's foreign language education and national identity. *Journal of Intercultural Studies* 21 (1), 39–51.

Hird, B. (1995) How communicative can language teaching be in China? *Prospect* 10 (3), 21–27.

Holliday, A.R. (1992) Intercompetence: Sources of conflict between local and expatriate ELT personnel. *System* 20 (2), 234–243.

Holliday, A.R. (1994) *Appropriate Methodology and Social Context*. Cambridge: Cambridge University Press.

Holliday, A.R. (1995) Handing over the project: An exercise in restraint. *System* 23 (1), 57–68.

Holliday, A.R. (1996) Developing a sociological imagination: Expanding ethnography in international English education. *Applied Linguistics* 17 (2), 234–255.

Holliday, A.R. (1999) Small cultures. *Applied Linguistics* 20, 237–264.

Holliday, A.R. (2005) *The Struggle to Teach English as an International Language*. Oxford: Oxford University Press.

Holliday, A.R. (2006) Native-speakerism. *ELT Journal* 60 (4), 385–387.

Iredale, R. (1990) International agencies: Learning how to identify and meet needs. *International Journal of Educational Development* 10 (2/3), 163–168.

James, D. (1998) Higher education field-work: The interdependence of teaching, research and student experience. In M. Grenfell and D. James (eds) *Bourdieu and Education: Acts of Practical Theory* (pp. 104–121). London: Falmer Press.

Jenkins, J. (2006) Current perspectives on teaching World Englishes and English as a Lingua Franca. *TESOL Quarterly* 40 (1), 157–181.

Joseph, M. and Ramani, E. (1998) The ELT specialist and linguistic hegemony: A response to Tully and Mathew. *ELT Journal* 52 (3), July, 214–222.

Kachru, B.B. (1986) The power and politics of English. *World Englishes* 5 (2/3), 121–140.

Kachru, B.B. (1992) World Englishes: Approaches, issues and resources. *Language Teaching* 25, 1–14.

Kamhi-Stein, L.D (1999) Preparing non-native professionals in TESOL: Implications for teacher education programs. In G. Braine (ed.) *Non-Native Educators in English Language Teaching* (pp. 145–158). Mahwah, NJ: Lawrence Erlbaum.

Kaplan, R.B. (2000) The forward. In J.K. Hall and W.G. Eggington (eds) *The Sociopolitics of English Language Teaching* (pp. vii–xiv). Clevedon: Multilingual Matters.

Kenny, B. and Savage, W. (eds) (1997) *Language in Development: Teachers in a Changing World*. London: Longman.

Keolivay, B. (2005) *Teaching and Learning Language through Literature*. Unpublished PhD thesis, UTS Sydney Australia.

King, S. and Bessell-Brown, G. (1993) You can learn without understanding – Culture, teaching and learning in English language teaching programs, Lao PDR, in Conference Proceedings, *Cultural Diversity and Higher Education*. University of Technology, Sydney.

Krais, B. (1996) The academic disciplines: Social field and culture. *Comparative Social Research* 2, 93–111.

Kramsch, C. (2008) Pierre Bourdieu: A biographical memoir. In J. Albright and A. Luke (eds) *Pierre Bourdieu and Literacy Education*. London: Routledge.

Kubota, R. (1998) Ideologies of English in Japan. *World Englishes* 17 (3), 295–306.

Kubota, R. (1999) Japanese culture constructed by discourses: Implications for applied linguistics research and ELT. *TESOL Quarterly* 33 (1), 9–35.

Kubota, R. (2001a) Discursive construction of the images of U.S. classrooms. *TESOL Quarterly* 35 (1), Spring, 9–38.

Kumaravadivelu, B. (1994) The postmethod condition: (E)merging strategies. *TESOL Quarterly* 29, 27–48.

Kumaravadivelu, B. (2001) Towards a postmethod pedagogy. *TESOL Quarterly* 35 (4), 537–560.

Kumaravadivelu, B. (2003a) Problematising cultural stereotypes in TESOL. *TESOL Quarterly* 37 (4), 709–719.

Kumaravadivelu, B. (2003b) *Beyond Methods: Macrostrategies for Language Teaching*. New Haven: Yale University Press.

Kumaravadivelu, B. (2006) Dangerous Liaison: Globalisation, empire and TESOL. In J. Edge (ed.) *(Re) Locating TESOL in the Age of Empire* (pp. 1–26). London: Palgrave MacMillan. Mahwah, NJ: Lawrence Erlbaum, 2005.

Kumaravadivelu, B. (2008) *Cultural Globalisation and Language Education*. New Haven: Yale University Press.

Language in Development: Access, Empowerment, Opportunity (1997) *Third International Conference on Language in Development*. Langkowi, Malaysia: INTAN.

Little, I.M.D. and Mirrlees, J. (1974) *Project Appraisal and Planning for Developing Countries*, Brookfield: Gower.

Liu, D. (1998) Ethnocentrism in TESOL: Teacher education and the neglected needs of international TESOL students. *ELT Journal* 52 (1), 3–10.

Lo Bianco, J. (2002a) Destitution, wealth, and cultural contest: Language and development connections. In J. Lo Bianco (ed.) *Voices from Phnom Penh Development and Language: Global Influences and Local Effects* (pp. 3–22). Melbourne: Language Australia, NLLIA.

Lo Bianco, J. (ed.) (2002b) *Voices from Phnom Penh Development and Language: Global Influences and Local Effects*. Melbourne: Language Australia, NLLIA.

London, N.A. (1993) Why education projects in developing countries fail: A case study. *International Journal of Educational Development* 13 (3), 265–275.

MacArthur, J.D. (1993) *The Logical Framework – A Tool for the Management of Project Planning and Evaluation*. Development and Project Planning Centre, University of Bradford, New Series Discussion Paper No. 42.

Maffi, l. (2002) Endangered languages, endangered knowledge. *International Social Science Journal* 173, 385–395.

Magrath, J. (2001) This is our story. *New Internationalist* 334, 34–35.

Marginson, S. (1995) Markets in higher education: Australia. In J. Smyth (ed.) *Academic Work: The Changing Labour Process in Higher Education* (pp. 17–40). Buckingham: SRHE and Open University Press.

Marginson, S. (2000) Rethinking academic work in the global era. *Journal of Higher Education* 22 (1), 23–35.

Marginson, S. (2002a) Education in the global market: Lessons from Australia. *Academe* 88 (3), 37–41.

Marginson, S. (2002b) Nation-building universities in a global environment: The case of Australia. *Higher Education* 43, 409–428.

Marginson, S. (2002c) The phenomenal rise of international degrees down under. *Change* 34 (3), 34–43.

Marginson, S. (2004) National and global competition in higher education. *The Australian Educational Researcher* 31 (2), 1–29.

Marginson, S. (2008) Global field and global imagining: Bourdieu and worldwide higher education. *British Journal of Sociology of Education* 29 (3), 303–315.

Marginson, S. and Ramsden, P. (2000) Introduction. *Journal of Higher Education* 22 (1), 5–7.

Marginson, S. and Rhoades, G. (2002) Beyond national states, markets, and systems of higher education: A glonacal agency heuristic. *Higher Education* 43, 281–309.

Marsden, D. and Oakley, P. (1990) *Evaluating Social Development Projects*. Oxford: Oxfam.

Maton, K. (2008) Habitus. In M. Grenfell (ed.) *Pierre Bourdieu: Key Concepts*. Stocksfield: Acumen.

Matsuda, A. (2002) Symposium on World Englishes and teaching English as a foreign language. *World Englishes* 21 (3), 421–455.

Mbida-Essama, B. (2002) The return on investment from the donor's perspective. In J. Lo Bianco (ed.) *Voices from Phnom Penh Development and Language: Global Influences and Local Effects* (pp. 277–286). Melbourne: Language Australia, NLLIA.

McGinn, N. and Warwick, D. (1979) Educational planning as political process: Two case studies from Latin America. *Comparative Education Review* 23, 218–239.

McGovern, J. (1995) Changing paradigms: The project approach. In G. Crewes and A. Crooks, (eds) *Language and Development* (pp. 3–15). Indonesia Australia Language Foundation.

Medgyes, P. (1994) *The Non-Native Teacher*. Hong Kong: Macmillan.

Medgyes, P. (1996) Native or non native: Who's worth more? In T. Hedge and N. Whitney (eds) *Power, Pedagogy and Practice* (pp. 31–42). Oxford: Oxford University Press.

Medgyes, P. (1999) Language training: A neglected area in teacher education. In G. Braine (ed.) *Non-Native Educators in English Language Teaching* (pp. 177–196). Mahwah, NJ: Lawrence Erlbaum.

Medgyes, P. (2002) Book review – An Introduction to Foreign Language Learning and Teaching. *ELT Journal* 56 (3), 333–335.

Meiras, S. (2004) International education in Australian Universities: Understanding, dimensions and problems. *Journal of Higher Education Policy and Management* 26 (3), 371–380.

Mitsikopoulou, B. (2002) Book review – Resisting Linguistic Imperialism in English Teaching. *ELT Journal* 56 (3), 330–333.

Mohanty, Ajit K. (2000) Perpetuating inequality: The disadvantage of language, minority mother tongues and related issues. In A.K. Mohanty and M. Girishwar (eds) *Psychology of Poverty and Disadvantage* (pp. 104–117). New Delhi: Concept Publishing Company.

Morris, T. (1991) *The Despairing Developer: Diary of an Aid Worker in the Middle East*. London: Tauris.

Morris, T. (1996) Non-state actors in externally funded development projects in Vietnam – Considerations and approaches. *Intercultural Interaction and Development*, Conference Proceedings (pp. 155–160). Hanoi, Sydney: UTS.

Murni, D. and Susan, S. (1997) Consultants and counterparts. In B. Kenny and W. Savage (eds) *Language in Development: Teachers in a Changing World* (pp. 218–230). London: Longman.

Murphy, D. (1999) Patrons, clients and projects. *ELT Journal* 53 (3), 217–219.

Naidoo, R. (2003) Repositioning higher education as a global commodity: Opportunities and challenges for future sociology of education work. *British Journal of Sociology of Education* 24 (2), 249–259.

Nayar, P.B. (1997) ESL/EFL dichotomy today: Language politics or pragmatics? *TESOL Quarterly* 31 (1), 9–38.

Norton, B. (1997) Language, identity, and the ownership of English. *TESOL Quarterly* 31 (3), 409–429.

Nunan, D. (2002) English as a global language. *TESOL Quarterly* 36 (2), 605–606.

Oda, M. (1999) English only or English plus? The language(s) of EFL organisations. In G. Braine (ed.) *Non-Native Educators in English Language Teaching* (pp. 105–122). Mahwah, NJ: Lawrence Erlbaum.

Oda, M. (2000) Linguicism in action: Language and power in academic institutions. In R. Phillipson (ed.) *Rights to Language: Equity, Power and Education*. Mahwah, NJ: Lawrence Erlbaum.

Oda, M. (2008) NNEST in TESOL (NNEST) of the month blog, 1 November, http://nnest.asu.edu/blog/2008/11/masaki-oda.html. Accessed on 23 November 2009.

Okada, A. (1999) Secondary education reform and the concept of equality of opportunity in Japan. *Compare: A Journal of Comparative and International Education* 29 (2), 171–189.

Organisation for Economic Cooperation and Development (2005) *Education at a Glance*. Paris: OECD.

PAID (1981) *The Project Approach to Rural Development: An Internal Critical View*. Douala: PAID.

Pennycook, A. (1994) *The Cultural Politics of English as an International Language*. London: Longman.

Pennycook, A. (1995) English in the world/The world in English. In J.W. Tollefson (ed.) *Power and Inequality in Language Education* (pp. 34–58). Cambridge: Cambridge University Press.

Pennycook, A. (1996) Borrowing others' words: Text, ownership, memory, and plagiarism. *TESOL Quarterly* 30 (2), 201–230.

Pennycook, A. (1998) *English and the Discourses of Colonialism*. London: Routledge.

Pennycook, A. (1999) Introduction: Critical approaches to TESOL. *TESOL Quarterly* 33 (3), 329–349.

Pennycook, A. (2000) The social politics and the cultural politics of language classrooms. In J.K. Hall and W.G. Eggington (eds) *The Sociopolitics of English Language Teaching* (pp. 89–103). Clevedon: Multilingual Matters.

Pennycook, A. (2007) ELT and colonialism. In J. Cummins and C. Davison (eds) *The International Handbook of English Language Teaching* (pp. 13–24). New York: Springer.

Phan Le Ha (2004) University classrooms in Vietnam: Contesting the stereotypes. *ELT Journal* 58 (1), 50–57.

Phan Le Ha (2008) *Teaching English as an International Language: Identity, Resistance and Negotiation.* Clevedon: Multilingual Matters.

Phelan, L. and Hill, D. (1998), *To Whose Benefit? Australian Education Aid to Papua New Guinea.* Sydney: AID Watch.

Phillipson, R. (1992a) ELT: The native speaker's burden? *ELT Journal* 46 (1), January, 12–18.

Phillipson, R. (1992b) *Linguistic Imperialism.* Oxford: Oxford University Press.

Phillipson, R. (1994) English language spread policy. *International Journal of the Sociology of Language* 107, 7–24.

Phillipson, R. (1998) Global English. *The European English Messenger* 7 (2), 53–56.

Phillipson, R. (1999) Voice in global English: Unheard chords in crystal loud and clear. *Applied Linguistics* 20 (2), 265–276.

Phillipson, R. (2000) *Education Rights to Language: Equity, Power and Education.* New York: Lawrence Erlbaum Associates.

Phillipson, R. (2001) English for globalisation or for the world's people? *International Review of Education* 47 (3–4), 185–200.

Phillipson, R. (2002) Global English and local language policies. In Andy Kirkpatrick (ed.) *English in Asia: Communication, Identity, Power and Education* (pp. 7–28). Melbourne: Language Australia.

Phillipson, R. (2003) *English-Only Europe? Challenging Language Policy.* London: Routledge.

Phillipson, R. (2005) Linguistic imperialism. In K. Brown (ed.) *Encyclopedia of Language and Linguistics* (2nd edn, Vol. 10, pp. 44–47) (under 'Linguistic pragmatics', ms 4309). Oxford: Elsevier.

Phillipson, R. (2006) Language policy and linguistic imperialism. In T. Ricento (ed.) *An introduction to Language Policy. Theory and Method* (pp. 346–361). Oxford: Blackwell.

Phillipson, R. (2008) The linguistic imperialism of neoliberal empire. *Critical Inquiry in Language Studies* 5 (1), 1–43.

Phillipson, R. and Karmani, S. (2005) Linguistic imperialism 10 years on: An interview with Robert Phillipson. *ELT Journal* 59 (4), 244–249.

Phillipson, R. and Skutnabb-Kangas, T. (1996) English only worldwide or language ecology. *TESOL Quarterly* 30 (3), 429–451.

Poole, D. (2001) Moving towards professionalism: The strategic management of international education activities at Australian universities and their faculties of business. *Higher Education* 42, 395–435.

Porter, D. (1995) Scenes from childhood: The homesickness of development discourses. In J. Crush (ed.) *The Power of Development* (pp. 63–86). London: Routledge.

Porter, D., Allen, B. and Thompson, G. (1991) *Development in Practice: Paved with Good Intentions.* London: Routledge.

Pottier, J. (1993) The role of ethnography in project appraisal. In J. Pottier (ed.) *Practising Development* (pp. 13–34). London and New York: Routledge.

Prabu, N.S. (1990) There is no best method – Why? *TESOL Quarterly* 24 (2), 161–176.

Putnis, P. (1993) Cultural generalisations: Help or hindrance? In T. Boswood, R. Hoffman and P. Tung (eds) *Perspectives on English for Professional Communication* (pp. 37–53). City Polytechnic of Hong Kong.

Rajagopalan, K. (1999) Of EFL teachers, conscience and cowardice. *ELT Journal* 53 (3), 200–206.

Ramanathan, V. (2005) *The English-Vernacular Divide: Domination Postcolonial Language Politics and Practice.* Clevedon: Multilingual Matters.

Rampton, B. (1990) Displacing the 'native speaker': Expertise, affiliation, and inheritance. *ELT Journal* 44, 97–101.

Rhoades, G. (2002) Globally, nationally and locally patterned changes in higher education. *Higher Education* 43, 279–280.

Robbins, D. (1993) The practical importance of Bourdieu's analyses of higher education in studies. *Higher Education* 18 (2), 151–163.

Robbins, D. (1998) The need for an epistemological 'break'. In M. Grenfell and D. James (eds) *Bourdieu and Education: Acts of Practical Theory* (pp. 55–71). London: Falmer Press.

Romiszowski, A. (1989) Avoiding failure through better project planning and analysis: Case studies of avoidable failure in instructional systems design and development projects. *Education and Training Technology International Education Journal* 26 (2), May, 95–112.

Sachs, W. (1992) *The Development Dictionary.* New York: Zed Books.

Said, E. (1978) *Orientalism.* New York: Pantheon Books.

Sammels, M. (2006) *Australian Aid: Promoting Growth and Stability.* A White Paper on the Australian Government's Overseas Aid Program. Submitted by the Australian Reproductive Health Alliance.

Sharp, A. (1998) ELT project planning and sustainability. *ELT Journal* 52 (20), April, 140–145.

Shaw, S. (1997) The political nature of needs. In B. Kenny and W. Savage (eds) *Language in Development: Teachers in a Changing World* (pp. 231–240). London: Longman.

Sithirajavongsa, S. (2003) English in the Lao Context: A study of policy and practice in implementing the existing ELT curriculum at the National University of Laos. PhD thesis, UTS.

Skutnabb-Kangas, T. (1996) The globalisation of (educational) language rights. *International Review of Education* 47 (3–4), 201–219.

Skutnabb-Kangas, T. (1998) Human rights and language wrongs – A future for diversity? *Language Sciences* 20 (1), 5–27.

Skutnabb-Kangas, T. (1999) Linguistic human rights – Are you naïve or what? *TESOL Journal* 8 (3), Autumn, 6–12.

Skutnabb-Kangas, T. (2000) Linguistic human rights and teachers of English. In J.K. Hall and W.G. Eggington (eds) *The Sociopolitics of English Language* (pp. 22–45). Clevedon: Multilingual Matters.

Skutnabb-Kangas, T. (2001) Linguistic human rights in education for language maintenance. In L. Maffi (ed.) *On Biocultural Diversity. Linking Language, Knowledge and the Environment* (pp. 397–411). Washington, D.C.: The Smithsonian Institute Press.

Skutnabb-Kangas, T. (2005) Can a "linguistic human rights approach" "deliver"? Reflections on complementarities, tensions and misconceptions in attempts at multidisciplinarities. Plenary paper at the International conference on

Language, Education and Diversity, University of Waikato, Hamilton, Aotearoa/New Zealand, 26–29 November 2003. In S. May, M. Franken and R. Barnard (eds) *LED 2003: Refereed Conference Proceedings of the 1st International Conference on Language, Education and Diversity*. Hamilton: Wilf Malcolm Institute of Educational Research, University of Waikato. CD Rom.

Skutnabb-Kangas, T. (2008) Language education and (violations of) human rights. Keynote address presented at *Linguistic Human Rights Symposium*, www.linguistic-rights.org, accessed on 10 October 2008.

Skutnabb-Kangas, T. and Phillipson, R. (2001) Language ecology. In J. Verschueren, J-O. Östman, J. Blommaert and C. Bulcaen (eds) *Handbook of Pragmatics* (pp. 1–18). Amsterdam and Philadelphia: John Benjamins.

Smith, H. (1997) Donors and recipients. In B. Kenny and W. Savage (eds) *Language in Development: Teachers in a Changing World* (pp. 208–217). London: Longman.

Smith, H. (1998) Perceptions of success in the management of aid-funded English language teaching projects. PhD thesis, University of Reading, UK.

Stirrat, R.L. (2000) Cultures of consultancy. *Critique of Anthropology* 20 (1), March, 31–46.

Swales, J. (1980) The educational environment and its relevance to ESP programme design. In J. Swales (ed.) *Projects in Materials Design* (pp. 61–70). ELT Documents Special, London: British Council.

Swartz, D. (1997) *Culture and Power: The Sociology of Pierre Bourdieu*. Chicago and London: University of Chicago Press.

Talpade Mohanty, C. (1994) Survival is not an academic skill. In S. Kahn (ed.) *How People Get Power: Organising Oppressed Communities for Action*. NASW Press.

Tollefson, J.W. (ed.) (1995) *Power and Inequality in Language Education*. Cambridge: Cambridge University Press.

Tollefson, J.W. (2000) Policy and ideology in the spread of English. In J.K. Hall and W.G. Eggington (eds) *The Sociopolitics of English Language* (pp. 7–21). Clevedon: Multilingual Matters.

Wacquant, L. (1989) Towards a reflexive sociology. *Sociological Theory* 7, 26–63.

Way, N. (2002) Offshore, off course. *Business Review Weekly*, 12–18 September, 68–72.

Williams, R. (1983) *Keywords*. New York: Oxford University Press.

World Bank (1998) *Assessing Aid: What Works, What Doesn't and Why*. Oxford: Oxford University Press.

Index